T0326409

Coffee certification in East Africa

Coffee certification in East Africa

Impact on farms, families and cooperatives

edited by:
Ruerd Ruben
Paul Hoebink

Wageningen Academic
P u b l i s h e r s

EAN: 9789086862559
e-EAN: 9789086868056
ISBN: 978-90-8686-255-9
eISBN: 978-90-8686-805-6
DOI: 10.3920/978-90-8686-805-6

First published, 2015

© Wageningen Academic Publishers
The Netherlands, 2015

Preface

Certification of coffee producers is frequently advocated as a key strategy for reinforcing farmers' livelihoods and for strengthening smallholder integration into sustainable supply chain management. The credibility of these claims has been scarcely documented and field evidence on real welfare effects and changes in bargaining power is notable absent.

This collection of empirical field studies provides new and unique insights into the impact of coffee certification in East African countries, based on a thorough combination of extensive farm-household and cooperative survey data with in-depth interviews with male and female farmers, their families, village and community focus groups and cooperative authorities. All papers rely on a careful combination of quantitative and qualitative field data and thus represent a balanced mixed-methods approach that enables a better understanding of the dynamic effects and the long-term implications of coffee labelling.

This collection of article includes three types of studies. First, we present a set of three country studies on the effects of certification on farm-household welfare and cooperative organisation in Uganda, Kenya and Ethiopia. These studies are based on unique longitudinal survey data collected in 2009 and 2012 from a balanced sample of certified coffee farmers and a non-certified control group in order to be able to identify the net impact of certification. The field study in Ethiopia focuses particularly on the effects of multi-certification. Together, these studies represent a follow-up to our earlier study on 'The impact of Fair Trade' (edited by Ruerd Ruben) that was published in 2008 by Wageningen Academic Publishers.

The second part of the book includes two detailed studies regarding the effects of coffee certification on the internal organisation and operational performance at the cooperative level. Due attention is given to the changes in risk behaviour and market outlet choice that are associated with coffee labelling in Kenya, and the effects of certification on farmers' willingness to invest, engagement into collective action and mutual trust in different types of coffee cooperatives in Ethiopia. The third part of the book focuses on changes in intra-household relationships due to coffee certification. Implications for gender equity in Kenya and for women's bargaining position and trust in Ethiopian coffee cooperatives are discussed against the background of the debates on sustainable livelihoods and gender in development policies.

The editors gratefully acknowledge the cooperation in field research in Kenya by Mzeeh Hamisi Ngutu, Urbanus N. Mutwiwa and Samuel Njuguna of Noble Consultants Company Ltd., and in Uganda by Fred Bagamba from the Department of Agribusiness and Resource Economics at Makerere University. Field research in Ethiopia has been directed by Amsaya Anteneh Woubie. The first round of data collection in Kenya and Ethiopia has been coordinated by prof. Ruerd Ruben, while the second round was coordinated by prof. Paul Hoebink, Bart van Rijsbergen en Willem Elbers. Mirjam Schoonhoven-Speijer and Eveline Dijkdrenth contributed in-depth studies on coffee cooperatives in Kenya, and Christine Plaisier and Annemarie Groot Kormelinck conducted field work in the context of the Ethiopian coffee cooperatives. Funding for the fieldwork in Kenya and Uganda has been provided by Irish Aid through the Solidaridad programme 'Building trade Capacity and Sustainable Livelihoods through Fair Trade and Ethical trade', while the field work in Ethiopia has been supported by the Dutch Science Foundation (NWO-WOTRO) under the 'Cooperatives & Chains' research program. Editorial assistance by Renate Smallegange of Wageningen Academic Publishers is gratefully acknowledged.

Nijmegen/The Hague, August 2014

Paul Hoebink & Ruerd Ruben, editors

Table of contents

List of figures

List of tables

Abbreviations

2SLS	2-stage least squares
APEP	Agricultural Production Enhancement Program
ATT	Average treatment effect on the treated
CA	Cronbach's alpha
CMB	Coffee marketing board
CBD	Coffee berry disease
CIDIN	Centre on International Development Issues Nijmegen
ETB	Ethiopian Birr
ECX	Ethiopia Commodity Exchange
FGD	Focus group discussion
FLO	Fair Trade Labelling Organisation
FT	Fair Trade
GAD	Gender and Development
GAP	Good Agricultural Practices
GPP	Good Processing Practices
IFOAM	International Federation of Organic Agriculture Movements
ISEAL	International Social and Environmental Accreditation and Labelling (alliance)
KSh	Kenyan shilling
NC	Non-certified
NGO	Non-governmental organisation
OLS	Ordinary least square
PO	Producer organisation
PSM	Propensity score matching
RFA	Rainforest Alliance
SCFCU	Sidama Coffee Farmers Cooperative Union (Ethiopia)
SL	Sustainable livelihoods
UCDA	Uganda Coffee Development Authority
UGX	Ugandan shilling
USD	US dollar
Utz	Utz certified
VCM	Voluntary contribution mechanism
WID	Women in Development

Chapter 1

Introduction

Coffee certification in East Africa – searching for impact

Ruerd Ruben and Paul Hoebink
For correspondence: r.ruben@maw.ru.nl

1.1 Motivation

Certification of coffee producers is frequently suggested as a useful strategy for improving the position of smallholders in the market. It started with the launch of the Fair Trade label in 1988 and was followed by several other standards that are promoted either by voluntary agencies and/or by private coffee companies. The label of Utz certified (first called Utz Kapeh) has been launched in 2002 with the aim to enhance responsible coffee certification by established private companies. In recent years, company coffee labels were established by Starbucks (C.A.F.E. Practices) and Nestle (AAA).[1] The 4C Association (originally Common Code for the Coffee Community) provides an entry standard for stakeholders in the coffee sector to address sustainability issues in production and sourcing in a pre-competitive manner.

Various coffee labels rely on rather different strategies for enhancing sustainable production and/or responsible trade. Whereas Fair Trade strongly focuses on reinforcing cooperative organisation and membership representation, Utz certified gives more attention to on-farm improvement of coffee practices for upgrading coffee quality. In a similar vein, Fair Trade guarantees producers a minimum price (and a premium payment for the cooperative); whereas Utz certified relies on free market prices that recognise coffee quality improvements. The procedures for supporting farmers' welfare are thus focusing on different entry points of local livelihoods (Ruben and Verkaart, 2011). In this book, we are mainly interested in tracing the impact of these different strategies for farmers that have been involved in such labelling regimes for a substantial period of time.

---

[1] Civic organisations like Rainforest Alliance provide certification and supervision to several company operated schemes.

Ruerd Ruben and Paul Hoebink (eds.) **Coffee certification in East Africa**
DOI 10.3920/978-90-8686-805-6_1, © Wageningen Academic Publishers 2015

Ruerd Ruben and Paul Hoebink

Coffee certification in East Africa is of a rather recent origin but has been rapidly expanding, representing currently 26% of the world's sustainable certified coffee supply. African coffee production includes both *Arabica* and *Robusta* varieties that are mostly grown by smallholders and marketed through cooperative societies. Production of coffee declined in East Africa from 19.5 million bags in 1997 to only 17.5 million bags in 2008, mainly due to poor management practices, ageing of the coffee trees and losses due to damage by insect pests and diseases (Salami *et al.*, 2010). Coffee prices are strongly fluctuating but show a general declining tendency during the last five years. Coffee marketing regimes are also rather different between the three countries involved in the field studies: in Ethiopia coffee trade is dominated by the state, while in Kenya coffee is exchanged at central auctions and in Uganda a free market regimes (with sometimes limited competition) prevails. This is reflected in different degrees of price transmission: coffee prices in Kenya generally respond better to world prices compared to prices in Uganda and Ethiopia.

Empirical studies on the effects of standards for smallholders are notably scarce. Even while in recent years many papers and journal articles have been published based on anecdotal evidence regarding the perceived benefits of coffee labelling for smallholders, sound proof regarding the effects of labelling for farmers' livelihoods and rural communities based on representative field data and in-depth field interviews is still limited. Our earlier study on 'The impact of Fair Trade' (Ruben, 2008) is generally acknowledged as a benchmark for empirical impact assessment of Fair Trade coffee, but was mainly focussed on Latin American cooperatives that are usually far more specialised in coffee production compared to most producers in East Africa. Moreover, in recent years there has been a proliferation of coffee standards (see Section 1.2), while consumer demand is increasingly oriented towards higher quality premium segments.

This book is intended to deepen our understanding on the role and functions of different certification regimes, and is based on three innovative features: (a) longitudinal field data on changes in coffee farming and their effects on household welfare; (b) in-depth interviews and behavioural experiments regarding risk attitudes, trust and investments of cooperative farmers; and (c) detailed discourse analyses regarding gender roles and female bargaining power within coffee-producing households. We focus attention on the effects of Fair Trade and Utz certified standards comparing their performance with likewise noncertified farmers. Together, this material may be helpful to enhance our insights into the dynamics of coffee certification and the responses of farmers and cooperatives to these challenges.

International standards for impact assessment ask for a comparison of performance on selected outcome indicators, with measurements over time (before-after) and compared with a counterfactual (with-without). We could rely on a representative random sample of smallholders (members of certified and non-certified cooperatives or individual farmers) that allows for such matched comparison. Welfare effects of certification are assessed from survey data at coffee-system and farm-household level (part 1). Hereafter, also relevant group- and village-level externalities at cooperative level are analysed (part 2). Finally, attention is focussed on intra-household distributional effect and gender equity (part 3). In all studies, due attention is given to initial selection criteria for engaging farmers into certification (e.g. are targeted farmers poor people and are they located in less-favoured areas?).

The articles in Part 1 are based on a unique set of balanced panel data from coffee producers in Kenya and Uganda that were visited twice over a period of four years (2009 and 2012) for the collection of detailed data on their production and farming activities, commercial engagement and linkages at cooperative and village level. The survey focuses on six different impact pathways (see Section 1.3): (a) coffee fields (land, labour and input use in coffee, coffee yields, coffee renovation, etc.), (b) farming systems (returns from other crops, off-farm work), (c) household livelihoods and intra-household organisation (income, expenditures, health, savings), (d) cooperative organisation (technical assistance, trade services), (e) village and community networks (water and sanitation, social capital) and (f) changes in value chains (coffee prices, sales). This multi-level framework enabled us to disentangle the effects of certification and to identify strong and weak points of different labelling regime.

Welfare impact of certification can be approached with a wide range of indicators. Most studies focus on coffee yields, prices and (net) revenues, but – given the diversity of on/off-farm activities – net full household income provides an indicator that better enables to consider possible substitution effects and appreciates tendencies in the dependency of household income on coffee revenues. Other important welfare aspects refer to changes in wealth (assets, access to credit, savings) and adjustments in household expenditures patterns.

Part 2 considers the institutional effects of certification, paying attention to the internal functions provided by the cooperative framework (e.g. technical assistance, finance) and the external functions in the marketing setting (e.g. traders selection; price bargaining). Satisfaction with the cooperative is likely to be influenced by perceptions regarding democratic accountability and the degree of internal cohesion. Moreover, local/regional externalities and village-wide effects could occur if non-certified farmers are able to reap the benefits of overall price increases, knowledge spill overs or premium investment in common goods (i.e. community drinking water, schools, road improvement, etc.).

Finally, part 3 focuses on another dimension of impact analysis, paying attention to behavioural implications. Risk attitudes and willingness to invest are considered in the literature as key indicators for pathways out of chronic poverty. In addition, intra-household distribution of task, responsibilities and decision-making are important to consider changes in gender bargaining power that strongly influence prospects for in-depth investments in health, housing and education and thus life-time intergenerational wealth. Similarly, in-depth investments in coffee renovation and soil conservation are key for improving land productivity and coffee quality over time.

Otherwise, investments in education or cattle husbandry are indicative for tendencies towards future income diversification.

The remainder of this introduction is structured as follows: first we discuss the tendencies towards increasing proliferation of coffee standards (Section 1.2), followed by a detailed analysis of different impact pathways of certification (Section 1.3). Hereafter, we summarise the existing evidence on the impact of coffee certification (Section 1.4). In Section 1.5 we outline the critical issues for reaching impact and Section 1.6 presents the key challenges for future policies and programs on certification.

1.2 Proliferation of coffee standards[2]

Forty five years ago, cane sugar was launched as an alternative for beet sugar, which was highly subsidised under the Common Agricultural Policy of the European Union. In 1969 the first 'world shop' was opened and soon dozens of them would offer products on sale from the so-called Third World as acts of solidarity and as an alternative to conventional trade. Some 25 years, ago Fair Trade coffee was launched under the label of Max Havelaar,[3] named after the protagonist in the famous novel of the same name, a 'resident' and colonial civil servant in Indonesia who resisted the exploitation of the Javanese population in coffee production.[4]

Certification was originally perceived as a strategy for strengthening the position of coffee smallholders in the value chain. The basic idea behind certification was to encourage supply chain partners to engage in direct sales transactions under long-term contractual arrangements based on trust regarding product quality and delivery reliability. It was expected that shortening the supply chain through direct interactions with exporters and processors would reduce the transaction costs and market risks and enhance knowledge on good agricultural practices, thus providing suitable incentives for quality upgrading (selling at better prices on premium market segments) and for maintaining scheduled deliveries (to avoid fluctuations occasioned by side sales).

A key dimension of certification refers to the improved certainty for smallholders regarding access to output markets, expected prices and on-time payments. Various labels are essentially different in their strategies for enhancing farmers' welfare through output price certainty (Fair Trade) or input provision and knowledge upgrading (Utz). The original Fair Trade proposition included provisions on pre-finance by processing companies that would enable farmers to escape from advanced pre-harvest sales at low prices to traditional intermediaries. Most private labels (Utz) rely, however, on market prices and try to increase farmers' income through quality upgrading that is recognised with higher action prices.

---

[2] This section is largely based on: Ruben and Verkaart (2011).

[3] Roozen and Van der Hoff (2001) discuss the birth of the Max Havelaar concept. Fridell (2004) provides a historical description of Fair Trade efforts in the broader political sense.

[4] Novel on Dutch colonialism by Multatuli (a pseudonym of Eduard Douwes Dekker).

Coffee certification in East Africa

Institutional dimension of strengthening cooperative performance represents an important element in the certification strategy. Cooperatives or farmers associations are consider key for increasing the scale of production, to maintain the quality standards, and to guarantee the reliability of smallholders as preferred suppliers in the value chain. In practice, it appears sometimes difficult to disentangle the effects of cooperation (i.e. reaching scale) from the effects of certification since both mechanisms are highly intertwined.

Globalisation of international commodity trade is increasingly accompanied by procurement arrangements that aim to guarantee food safety, product quality and reliability of sourcing. Based on the establishment of long-term partnerships along the supply chain, these standards may also include codes of behaviour for information sharing, service provision and trust building to support agency coordination and reduce transaction costs (Reardon *et al.*, 2001). During the last few decades, three major categories of standards have emerged in the coffee sector (see Table 1.1 for an overview):

1. *Voluntary standards* to support practices of Fair Trade (FLO – Fair Trade Labelling Organisation), organic production (IFOAM – International Federation of Organic Agriculture Movements), responsible trade (Utz certified) and sustainable trade (Rainforest Alliance).
2. *Company standards*, like C.A.F.E. Practices by Starbucks and Nespresso AAA by Nestle that aim to guarantee sustainable sourcing under private labels.
3. *Sector-wide standards,* like the Common Code for the Coffee Community (4C Association) agreed upon by national coffee associations, trade unions, non-governmental organisations (NGOs) and key industry players to guarantee minimum sector-wide sustainability standards.

Voluntary and company standards are based on a detailed prescription of preferred production, processing and handling practices and involve independent verification. Some standards also include tracking and tracing regimes. To some extent, private standards have become the predominant basis for product differentiation in markets that are increasingly driven by quality-based competition. Standards take the form of technical specifications, terms and definitions and principles through which goods are categorised or included in product groupings. Thus, in the context of agricultural and food products they permit the identification and preservation of product and process characteristics through the supply chain in a consistent manner over time. This is most critical in the case of credence attributes that relate to the way in which products are produced and handled rather than the intrinsic characteristics of the product itself (Henson and Traill, 1993; Hobbs *et al.*, 2002). Private standards have arguably become a critical element of strategies to differentiate products and firms, that requires the consistent supply of food safety and quality attributes supported by branding and certification (Berges-Sennou *et al.*, 2004).

Table 1.1. Proliferation of coffee labels.

Type	Year of introduction	Main characteristics
Voluntary		
Fair Trade	1988	Its objective is to improve the livelihood of farmers by offering a fair and stable price to cooperatives or associations that are certified; promotes sustainable practices.
Organic (IFOAM)	1990 (US)	Prohibits to use agrochemicals and enhance soil fertility by recycling and sustainable crop rotation.
Rainforest Alliance (RFA)	1993	Organic production under shade trees, certified by the Rainforest Alliance, also with respect to workers and decent wages.
Utz (started as Utz Kapeh)	2002/1997	Empower farmers with Good Agricultural Practices. Minimise pesticides, water and reduce soil erosion. Traceability of coffee.
Bird-friendly	1998	Not only organic but also with shade trees and certified by the Smithonian Migratory Bird Centre.
Sector wide		
4C Association	2007	Entry-level focusing on continuous improvement of economic, social and environmental conditions of production and processing
Company based		
Starbucks (C.A.F.É. Practices)	2004	Accountability: price paid to the farmer; social responsibility: humane working conditions; environmental stewardship: reduce water use and agrochemicals, preserve biodiversity. Emphasis on high quality beans.
Nespresso (AAA)	2006	Together with the Rainforest Alliance the AAA Sustainable Quality Programme with conservation of resources, being good neighbours and improving quality of beans. In 2009 target to bring 80% of farmers under certification.

1.2.1 Voluntary standards

Fair Trade (FT) emerged in the 1960s as an alternative marketing system, established to challenge existing trade relations dominated by large international buyers and to empower Southern producers (Renard, 2005). FT is usually presented as a trading partnership based on dialogue, transparency and respect, seeking greater equity in international trade. In practice, FT producers can sell their production at pre-defined and guaranteed minimum floor prices, receiving an additional premium for deliveries to FT market outlets which should be used for community purposes (Ruben, 2008). The Fair Trade Labelling Organizations International (FLO-Cert) is the independent organisation responsible for inspection and certification of producer organisations and traders. Key requirements for producers for obtaining FT certification are that they should be smallholder producers depending mainly on family labour and organised in cooperatives operating under democratic lines. FT mainly aims to eliminate the role of middlemen along the chain and create a kind of social conscience amongst retailers and consumers. Accordingly, the philosophy behind FT is based on significant ethical and solidarity dimensions that differ substantially from the neo-classical paradigm which considers minimum prices as a price distortion that affects well-functioning markets. This is often considered a major constraint for fully involving multinationals and supermarkets into FT programs.

Utz certified – previously known as Utz Kapeh (meaning good coffee in a Maya language) – was developed by a Dutch Foundation with initial support from the global retailer Ahold (Farnsworth and Goodman, 2006). It is a market-based certification program focussed on improved farm management, input efficiency and coffee traceability, while also demanding good performance on social and environmental issues. Utz has developed a set of standards for third party verification that is aligned with GlobalGAP certification system for the sourcing of fruit and vegetables led by European retailers (Muradian and Pelupessy, 2005). Unlike FT, Utz is not limited to producer cooperatives and is also open to plantation production (Tallontire and Vorley, 2005). Another difference with FT is that Utz does not embrace the concept of minimum prices but offers a flexible, negotiable price premium Utz claims to offer stability to preferred suppliers and aims to move beyond the FT-niche by mainstreaming certified responsible coffee (Bitzer *et al.*, 2008).

FT coffee occupies a niche market that is on average less than two percent of consumption in Western markets. Experts assume that especially FT coffee may have hit a glass ceiling unable to grow beyond a socially conscious but limited consumer base (Giovannucci and Koekoek, 2003). Consequently, FT has remained an option available to only a limited number of producers. In contrast, Utz is the fasted growing certification initiative in the world (Lazaro *et al.* 2008). Many farmers sell their coffee via multiple markets, i.e. dividing their produce over the FT, Utz and conventional outlets. Multi-certification presents a suitable strategy for diversifying sales to different buyers with differing quality and delivery requirements.[5] Otherwise, certification can become a de facto market requirement and simultaneously raise market entry barriers for coffee growers.

Rainforest Alliance (RFA) started in the late 1990s a coffee certification program with support from the United Nations Development Programme and the Global Environment Facility. It aims to integrate productive agriculture, biodiversity conservation and human development, certifying both large and smallholder coffee producers in tropical countries. RFA farmers should avoid child labour, maintain non-discriminatory hiring practices and must pay legal minimum wages. Sustainability criteria are developed with partners in the Sustainable Agriculture Network to help conserve biodiversity and labour standards intend to improve local people's lives. RFA coffee farms must have plans to maintain or restore natural forest cover to achieve minimum shade coverage (i.e. at least 70 trees per hectare) and maintain native

---

[5] Since FT usually buys only a part of certified production, sales to other outlets are also required to guarantee recovery of the investments.

species. Moreover, farmers are not allowed to alter natural water courses, and should maintain buffer zones of natural vegetation between crop areas and human settlement areas. Standards also prohibit activities such as trafficking in wild animals, destruction of ecosystems, dumping untreated wastewater, and other harmful practices.

1.2.2 Company standards

Recently, the number of private labels for producing and delivering sustainable and responsible coffee trade has further increased. Starbucks started in 2004 a programme under the title C.A.F.E. (Coffee and Farmer Equity) Practices to evaluate, recognise, and reward producers of high-quality sustainably grown coffee. C.A.F.E. Practices involves coffee sourcing guidelines developed in collaboration with the NGO Conservation International and implemented through Scientific Certification Systems, a third-party evaluation and certification firm. C.A.F.E. Practices seeks to ensure that Starbucks sources sustainably grown and processed coffee by evaluating the economic, social and environmental aspects of coffee production against a defined set of criteria. Starbucks defines sustainability as an economically viable model that addresses the social and environmental needs of all the participants in the supply chain from farmer to consumer. Compliance is promoted not via a regulatory code specifying and enforcing minimum standards, but rather via an incentive system designed to promote progressive change, in which performance against specified standards of sustainable practices are rewarded by provision of preferential contracts and in some cases the payment of price premiums (MacDonald, 2007). Currently, almost 185,000 producers participate in the C.A.F.E. Practices program.

In a similar vein, the Nespresso AAA Sustainable Quality Program of Nestlé has been developed with a focus on high quality (AA = coffee quality and the third A stands for sustainability). The compliance with the standard is verified by Rainforest Alliance. It features social and environmental practices of coffee that is mainly purchased from Latin-America, and some farms in Africa and Asia. Nespresso makes no distinction in terms of a premium for meeting the AAA standard, but claims that the eligible producers receive well above the market price for a combination of quality and sustainability.

Company standards are generally considered to be helpful for improving coffee production systems, but are less influential in changing the control and accountability relationships within the supply chain. Moreover, they hardly favour farmer and worker organisation, and are less able to engage non-supply chain agents in programs for improving social and physical infrastructures (MacDonald, 2007).

1.2.3 Sector-wide standards

The German Coffee Association and the German government's international development agency (GTZ) initiated in 2007 the Common Code for the Coffee Community (4C Association). It aims to foster sustainability in the 'mainstream' green coffee chain and to increase the quantities of coffee meeting basic sustainability criteria. This multi-stakeholder initiative is based on participation of national coffee associations, trade union representatives and NGOs, as well as key industry players, including Nestlé, Sara Lee/Douwe Egberts, Tchibo and Kraft (now Mondelēz International). The 4C entry-level standard builds on basic good agricultural and management practices and intends to eliminate the most unacceptable practices and to encourage continuous improvement.

The 4C distinguishes itself from Fair Trade, Rainforest Alliance and Utz certified by relying on 'verification' rather than 'certification' of standards compliance, in order to achieve an entry level benchmark for sustainable coffee production across the mainstream industry. In summary it entails 3 yearly third party verification and annual self assesment of progress to ensure improvements are made. To balance between reducing the burden and credibly ensuring compliance. One of the key funcitons of the 4C Association is that it concentrates on collaboration with other standards. It has a number of benchmarking agreements (complete and currently running) – including with Fairtrade International, Utz certified and Rainforest Alliance.[6]

The 4C Association met increasing criticism with respect to: (1) the difficulties of imposing uniform ecological standards to different local agro-ecological settings; (2) the unequal distribution of costs and benefits between producers and downstream actors; (3) limited popular participation in assessing suitable management regimes; and (4) the implicit scale advantages favouring plantations over smallholder producers (Neilson and Pitchard, 2007). The incremental costs of compliance may reduce sustainability prospects if farmers feel obliged to reduce shade trees and wildlife reserves. While smallholders bear the largest share of compliance costs, they tend to loose options for bargaining on quality and product differentiation.

In recent years, coffee certification schemes such as FT and Utz have triggered a number of developments in the East African smallholder coffee sector. These include increased awareness of good agricultural practices, improved processing practices and attention for environmental concerns, better working conditions, record keeping, traceability and cooperative governance. International prices for coffee were initially high in 2010/2011 but started to decline again from 2011 onwards (Box 1.1.).[7] Demand for certified coffee remained, however, considerably lower than the available supply. In 2012, less than one third of the certified coffee in Kenya (28% for Utz, 30% for FT) was sold as certified coffee (i.e. using the Fair Trade or Utz certified label).

---

[6] Figures presented by 4C are confusing about existing overlaps with other initiatives. Only a small fraction of the available verified 4C coffee has actually been purchased by its members.

[7] For a concise overview on the functioning of international coffee market, see e.g. Daviron and Ponte (2005); Bacon *et al.* (2008).

Box 1.1. The international coffee market.

Since the demise of the International Coffee Agreement in 1989 the international coffee market has been one of the most volatile agricultural markets. The deregulation of the international market, the entrance in the market of new producers, in particular Vietnam, technological innovations which made international roasting companies more flexible, all had their negative influence on world market prices. Prices went up during the 1990s for a short period due to production problems, particularly in Brazil, but then went to an all-time low in 2004-2005. In the last years prices went up and down, due in particular to production problems in the largest coffee producer, Brazil. In the meantime coffee markets became more differentiated, due not only to a growing demand for speciality coffees but also as a result of certification.

The International Coffee Organisation reported in its August 2013 that coffee prices were at its lowest level in four years. It reached with USD 1.1645/lb its lowest level since September 2009, but 2010 and 2011 showed a steep rise. In particular the three Arabica groups (Colombian milds, other milds and Brazilian natural) showed no big decreases. Coffee prices however had a steep rise in the beginning of 2014 going to USD 2.0975/lb in March.

This is symptomatic for the international coffee market which shows its up and downs, related to frost, drought or other production problems, new consumer demands and supply of high (quality) production by new producers entering the international markets. It is important to note that coffee prices first went up and then decreased during the research period under consideration.

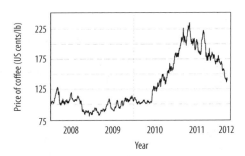

1.3 Impact pathways

A major difficulty for fully understanding the net effects and dynamic implications of coffee certification refers to the fact that simultaneously different mechanisms are in force that influence several dimensions of farm-household welfare. Certification not only provides incentives for adjusting coffee production systems (at plot level), but could also change land use (at farm-level) and labour allocation (at household level). In addition, most certification systems rely on social enforcement through engagement with farmers cooperatives (group level) and also involve external relationships with other neighbouring farmers (community level). Finally, supply chain networks with traders and processors influence the pricing and marketing aspects of certification regime (value chain/market level). This complex multi-layered framework of different interlinked mechanisms trough which certification may influence farm-household welfare deserves further analysis.

In order to be able to better disentangle the net effects of certification we rely on an analytical framework that distinguishes these different impact levels. Thorough appraisal of the effects of certification requires systematic insights into different pathways through which certification influences farm-household welfare. Main differences in impact pathways between the two coffee certification regimes can thus be understood through their intended incidence on either coffee production systems and market signals (Utz certified) or cooperative organisation and community development (FT).

The original Fair Trade proposition offers farmers guaranteed minimum prices and an additional premium for community-level investments. Key attention is given to training for capacity development (often in partnerships with NGOs) in order to reinforce farmers' loyalty with the cooperative organisation and to strengthen the cooperative bargaining position vis-à-vis traders and processors. Utz certified – sometimes labelled as Responsible Trade – relies on strictly market-based prices, but intends to enhance farm-household welfare through coffee systems upgrading at plot level (e.g. improved agricultural practices; tree renovation, etc. with reliance on Farmers Field Schools) that is expected to result in better quality coffees that can receive a premium price at the market. In essence, Fair Trade expects that exogenous price certainty provides incentives to farmers to enhance their market integration, whereas Utz certified expects that farming system intensification results in endogenous market price improvements. Both standards do not engage in providing access to finance and limit their attention only to the coffee plots.[8]

We rely on a distinction between impact levels to discuss the effects of coffee certification as reported in the available literature. This more detailed approach is considered as a welcome addition to existing comprehensive overview studies (Blackman and Rivera, 2010; Le Mare, 2008; Nelson and Pound, 2009) since it permits more thorough insights into the – sometimes contradictory – effects that might occur at different system levels. Distinguishing between impact pathways also enables a more balanced appraisal of the net welfare effects that specific types of (small-scale and marginal) producers might expect from engagement in each of the certification regimes.

---

[8] The essential difference between both approaches has been characterised by Petkova (2006) as 'top down' versus 'bottom up' certification.

The first impact level concerns the coffee plot. Utz certified (and organic) certifications usually require investments for coffee upgrading and improved plot management practices.[9] Valkila (2009) and Valkila and Nygren (2010) point to the requirements of input and labour intensification for obtaining certification that lead to higher costs and lower net margins. Calo and Wise (2005) find that price premiums paid to certified farmers generally fails to cover the added costs associated with crop maintenance (assuming market rates for labour). Renard (2005) and Ruben and Zúñiga-Aras (2011) argue that Fair Trade coffee certification offers – compared to private labels – few incentives for quality upgrading. Apparently, guaranteed prices are not sufficient to mitigate prevailing risk-aversive behaviour, and targeted training programs offer better prospects for enhancing the adoption of good agricultural practices. Most plot-level investment are, however, limited to improving variable input use and optimising tree density, whereas in-depth investments in coffee tree renovation are still scarce (Ruben and Verkaart, 2011; Rueda and Lambin, 2013).

The second impact level focuses on farm-level effects. Since most impact studies are limited to plot-level information, insight into wider farm-level effects is generally limited. Ruben (2008) registers that certified farms tend to specialise more on coffee production and may neglect food crops and/or reduce engagement in off-farm employment. In a similar vein, Philpott *et al.* (2007) provide evidence of scarce biodiversity and limited shading on certified coffee farms, whereas Van der Vossen (2005) shows that certified coffee production competes for labour and nutrients with other farm activities. While specialisation could reinforce internal economies of scale and scope, substitution mechanisms might absorb a large part of the net benefits. The usually modest and sometimes non-significant income effects from certification are likely to be associated to land and labour substitution.

The third impact level refers to household-level effects, where the generation of income and decision on expenditures take place. Most empirical studies conclude that net income effects of certification are rather modest, partly due to higher production costs and otherwise occasioned by low market prices (Barham *et al.*,2011). Even with small net income effects, Ruben and Fort (2012) find significant livelihood improvements in credit access and durable expenditure that are related to reduced risk aversion. Arnould *et al.* (2009) and Becchetti and Constantino (2008) observe positive changes in education and health outcomes related to Fair Trade certification. Bolwig *et al.* (2013) use a Heckman selection model to unravel the revenue effect from certification and conclude that the largest effects are due to engagement in coffee processing. Improvements in intra-household relationships have been rarely observed (Kasente, 2012; Lyon, 2008).

The fourth impact level is related to the cooperative. The certification agreement is almost always reached at group level and the cooperative association is the linking pin between the individual farmers and the market. Arnould *et al.* (2009) distinguish the

---

[9] Many of these trainings are provided within the framework of so-called farmers field schools (FFS).

impact of Fair Trade certification from that of cooperative membership and conclude that most direct economic effects are related to cooperative membership and less influenced by market exchange arrangements. Sáenz Segura and Zúñiga-Arias (2008) also find that membership of cooperatives is the single most important factor driving income differences between certified and non-certified farmers. Elder *et al.* (2012) further analyse the effects of Fair Trade on social capital and conclude that factors like trust in leadership, democratic internal organisation and women' participation are crucial for obtaining positive outcomes from certification. Ruben and Heras (2012) register for coffee cooperatives in Ethiopia that autonomy from the state is a vital requirement for improved business performance, while Jena *et al.* (2012) conclude that certification of Ethiopian coffee cooperatives has limited impact on small-scale coffee producers' livelihoods mainly due to low productivity, an insignificant price premium, and poor access to credit and information from the cooperative.

The fifth impact level concerns the community. An important side-effect from certification that is frequently registered refers to spatial externalities accruing to neighbouring farmers. Such spillovers are found by Ruben and Fort (2012) as a consequence of knowledge exchange networks at community level that lead to rapid diffusion of improved cultivation practices, but also occur due to the fact that the Fair Trade premium is usually invested for collective goods at village level (road improvement, schools and health care facilities, water and sanitation facilities) that equally benefit non-certified producers. Similar effects – albeit with more unequal village-level distribution – are registered by Arnould *et al.* (2009) with reference to schooling and health outcomes. Local participation in certification schemes is sometimes biased towards better-off farmers, and hired workers depending on wage payments do not always equally benefit (Williams, 2013).

The sixth and final impact level refers to the relations with the market and supply chain networks. Mendez *et al.* (2010) confirm that Fair Trade certified farmers receive better prices and higher coffee revenues, but sales to certified markets were far too small for reaching sustainable livelihood effects. This is confirmed by De Janvry *et al.* (2012) while showing that in Central America – due to over-certification – less than a quarter of the certified coffee can be sold under premium conditions. Whereas farmers incur substantial costs for obtaining certification it becomes increasingly important to guarantee access to premium outlets.[10] Certification has brought, however, little changes into agency relations throughout the value chain and the nature of contracts (i.e. distribution of value added shares) has not been substantially modified (Muradian and Pelupessy, 2005; Valkila *et al.*, 2010).

Together, these different impact pathways permit a balanced appraisal of the results of farmers' engagement with coffee certification. In some case, positive synergies between impact at different system level might occur (e.g. cooperative strengthening resulting in improved bargaining position in value chains), but in other occasions

---

[10] Certification costs may involve initial payments of € 1,500-3,000 followed by yearly tariffs of € 700-1,200.

trade-offs between effects have been registered (e.g. upgrading and specialisation in coffee production might lead to reduced resource availability for other farm and non-farm activities). It is therefore of key importance to fully understand these multiple and sometimes contradictory effects of certification within the wide farm, family and cooperative/village context.

1.4 Insights from impact analyses

In the last fifteen years the impact of certification on farmers' lives, income and welfare has come more and more under scrutiny. Nearly all labelling organisations launched their own impact studies, but coffee has been by far the most popular. We counted some 40 studies on coffee alone, mostly based on cross-section data from Fair Trade farmers but biased towards field data from Latin America.[11] There are still few studies addressing the impact of multiple certification schemes or comparing the impact of several standards on farmers welfare.[12]

The first generation of studies consisted mainly of interviews with cooperative leaders, sometimes also with members of cooperatives. Later on, more quantitative methodology was used with surveys of farmers, and in several cases also with a control groups of farmers who did not produce under the certification schemes (so-called counterfactual). Only a few studies are based on substantial field data, and longitudinal studies are almost absent. The emphasis in most studies is on the prices that farmers received for their produce and additionally on welfare effects of price premium for local families and rural communities.

Many studies face serious methodological problems due to the an absence of base-line data. Some studies try to correct this by also surveying control groups. Ruben *et al.* (2009) presents an overview of the key limitations met in several studies. They seldom correct for differences between households in terms of endowments, land size or location. This means that there is no correction for more active, better-off farmers that are likely to be amongst the first to participate in certification schemes. Correction for self-selection is thus of primary importance to differentiate between the impact of labels and the characteristics of farmers.

Table 1.2 provides a concise summary of different types of impact evaluations conducted on Fair Trade coffee certification schemes, indicating the field data collection approach and the sampling approach.

The outcomes of this research provides a rather mixed picture. Some studies conclude that there are substantial effects on the prices that farmers receive. Romero Gonzalez

---

[11] On bananas and tea might around five (valid) impact studies are registered; for handicrafts, nuts, spices and herbs there are only 1-2 studies available (Nelson and Pound, 2009).

[12] Le Mare (2008) presented a first concise overview of evaluations and tried to summarise the outcomes. Nelson and Pound (2009) followed a year later with what she called a 'comprehensive overview'.

Table 1.2. Impact evaluations of Fair Trade coffee schemes.

Type of Study	Authors	Methodology used
Qualitative	Utting (2005)	Fieldwork in northern Nicaragua; no detailed account of methodology
	Murray *et al.* (2006)	Based on interviews with seven cooperatives in Mexico, Guatemala, El Salvador
	Jaffee (2007)	Ethnographic study of the coffee chain from coffee shops in the States to small coffee farmers in Oaxaca, Mexico
	Valkila (2009)	Interviews with 120 farmers, cooperative leaders, experts, coffee companies, labelling organisations in Nicaragua
Mixed methods	Bastin and Matteucci (2007)	Survey among 120 coffee farmers and focus group and expert interviews
	Bacon and Flores (2007), Bacon (2008)	Survey of 228 farmers of seven cooperatives surveyed, group interviews, interviews with coop leaders
	COSA (2013)	Survey of a sample of 351 farms and control group in Daklak province, Vietnam plus stakeholder workshop and focus group interviews
Quantitative	Arnould *et al.* (2009)	Survey among 1,200 coffee farmers in three countries (Nicaragua, Guatemala, Peru) with control group
	Ruben *et al.* (2009)	Survey with 700 coffee and banana farmers in Peru and Costa Rica (using control groups)
	Mendez *et al.* (2010)	Survey (matched) among 469 households in four countries (Guatemala, El Salvador, Nicaragua, Mexico)
	Ceval (2012)	Six case studies in four countries; several (unmatched) surveys with in total 3,750 respondents, plus group and other interviews in a very short field research

(2010) found that coffee farmers in Uganda received a price for their coffee that was three times higher compared to conventional farmers. Fair Trade-certified farmers received 12% of the price paid for a packet of coffee in Spanish supermarkets, while conventional farmers received only 5% of that price. Several other studies also confirm that advantages of selling certified coffee are the chance of receiving a better price, but also the impact of training and better connections with stable market outlets are acknowledged.

The effects of Fair Trade certification on coffee producers and organisations have been analysed in several earlier reports and articles. Detailed case studies from coffee cooperatives in Costa Rica (Ronchi, 2002), Nicaragua (Bacon, 2005; Bacon *et al.*, 2008b) and Mexico (Calo and Wise, 2005; Jaffee, 2007; Milford, 2004) found that Fair Trade initially strengthened producer organisations and concluded that – during the coffee crisis of the early 1990s – Fair Trade accomplished its goal of improving the returns to smallholder producers and positively affecting their quality of life and the strength of the organisations. Other research stressed that Fair Trade initiatives improved the well-being of small-scale coffee farmers and their families, particularly due to better access to credit facilities and external funds as well as through training and improved capabilities to enhance the quality of the product (Murray *et al.*, 2006; Taylor, 2005). Fair Trade certified farmers were also successful in improving their production, were satisfied with prices obtained, and showed improvements in food consumption and living conditions (Becchetti and Costantino, 2006).

The European Fair Trade Association provides an overview of Fair Trade impact studies that were realised since 2000, but none of these studies is based on sufficient field work or a rigorous counterfactual comparison. Most attention is given to positive effects on producers' organisations – focusing on the process of capitalisation from the Fair Trade premium payments – while little attention is given to the individual and household-level implications (Taylor, 2005; Raynolds *et al.*, 2004). Other studies refer to the effects on prices and productivity and the role of Fair Trade for improving competitiveness (Becchetti and Constantino, 2006). Major constraints that are identified relate to the difficulties of involving farmers in marketing decisions.

Recent studies by Valkila (2009) and Valkila and Nygren (2010) that focus on organic Fair Trade farmers in northern Nicaragua are more critical. FT organic coffee production has lower yields and requires higher labour efforts, and therefore the increase in farmer incomes from this low-intensity coffee production is very modest, because little coffee is produced by marginalised farmers. Farmers thus remain in poverty despite being connected to Fair Trade organic markets (see also Bacon *et al.*, 2008a). Evidence suggests that participation in alternative trade networks reduces exposure and vulnerability to variable commodity prices. In a similar vein, Raynolds (2002) also points to the price premium as a critical element to offset other adverse conditions that affect the quality of life. Farmers linked to coffee cooperatives selling to alternative markets received higher average prices and felt more secure regarding their land tenure. However, three quarters of all surveyed farmers reported a decline in their quality of life during the last few years. Responses to the questions about perceived changes in the quality of life showed no significant difference between farmers participating in conventional and alternative trade networks. These findings and the results of the focus groups suggest that income from coffee sales to alternative markets is not enough to offset the many other conditions (e.g. higher input costs, steadily increasing consumer prices, gasoline and communication costs) that provoked the perceived decline in the quality of living conditions.

Comparative studies from Peru and Costa Rica indicate that compliance with FT standards leads to only fairly modest changes in farm production methods and household income, but that greater certainty regarding prices and market outlets has important positive effects on access to finance and investment attitudes (Ruben, 2008; Ruben and Fort, 2012). Using a difference analysis with propensity score matching approach, Ruben *et al.* (2009) show that FT farmers consistently invest more in education and house upgrading, and also appear to be significantly less risk-averse. Otherwise, standards for responsible and sustainable trade focus attention on better farm management practices and quality upgrading as major strategies for strengthening farm-household welfare (Ruben and Zúñiga-Aras, 2011). This implies that knowledge dimensions that guarantee compliance with technical standards and behavioural incentives that favour loyalty to the producer organisation become more relevant.

Other cross-country studies by Arnould *et al.* (2009) and Mendez *et al.* (2010) that apply a rigorous appraisal of certification impacts reach similar conclusions: direct economic and income effects are at best rather modest, whereas observed changes in livelihoods and related education and health outcomes are more strongly related to cooperative membership than to market exchange arrangements. Mendez *et al.* (2010) confirm that certified farmers receive higher prices and coffee revenues, but that sales to certified markets were too limited to reach sustainable livelihood effects. This is empirically demonstrated by De Janvry *et al.* (2012) showing that in Central America – due to over-certification – less than a quarter of the certified coffee can be sold under premium conditions. Whereas farmers incur substantial costs for obtaining the FT certification (with initial payments of € 1,500-3,000 followed by yearly tariffs of € 700-1,200) it becomes increasingly important to guarantee access to premium outlets.

The recent evidence regarding the impact of certification points to the critical importance of the embeddedness of coffee standards in improved global production networks (Coe *et al.*, 2008). This asks for a more detailed assessment of the broader market and supply chain structures and the institutional networks surrounding the coffee sector. In addition to the value chain perspective, due attention should be given to horizontal dimensions of agency relationships, in particular to the prospects for improved smallholder cooperation and the space provided by (inter)national economic and political regimes.

Recent surveys come to the conclusion that price and welfare effects are limited, for a number of reasons. In particular, poor and small farmers sell only limited amounts of coffee and only a part of it under certified schemes (Arnould *et al.*, 2009; Mendez *et al.*, 2010; Ruben *et al.*, 2009; Valkila, 2009). Thus, very often coffee sales are only a share of their income. As a result, welfare effects turn out to be limited but measurable. In particular, when investments for producing certified coffee are higher and prices are insecure, the final income effects may be negligible. This is also because one of the problems coffee farmers mostly face is the limited access to credit (e.g. Bastin and Mateucci 2007). Strengthening the organisation of coffee farmers is found to be an important benefit of certification (Ruben *et al.*, 2009). Table 1.3 provides a concise summary of major findings from more robust impact studies.

1.5 Critical issues for reaching impact

Reaching the desired impact from coffee certification depends on a number of internal and external conditions that enable (or constrain) the functioning of the earlier-outlined impact pathways. The registered outcomes at farm-household, family or cooperative level appear to be highly susceptive to individual, local and regional differences in terms of risk preferences, organisation of the marketing system and the

Table 1.3. Stylised results from coffee impact studies.

Outcome	Examples	Conclusions/reasons
Very positive	Utting (2005)	All small producers interviewed acknowledged major changes, greater stability and security
	Murray *et al.* (2006)	Considerable income effects, access to training, improvements in quality, higher production, but lack of a clear understanding of Fair Trade certification
	Romero Gonzalez (2010)	Coffee farmers under certification in Uganda received three times the price that conventional farmers receive
Positive	Jaffee (2007)	Producers receive clear and substantial benefits, economic, social and environmental, but Fair Trade prices have lost value and is not sufficient
	COSA (2013)	Already high producing farms in Vietnam have reduced use of agrochemicals and synthetic fertilisers, which means significantly lower cash costs for inputs
Limited/modest effects	Arnould *et al.* (2009)	Limited but measurable effects on social welfare
	Bacon (2005; 2008)	Fair Trade farmers are less vulnerable and receive higher prices, but only 40% is sold via alternative markets and 74% of farmers reported a decline in their quality of life
	Valkila (2009)	Positive effects but limited due to low production; effects of organic production unclear, heavier workload
	Ruben and Fort (2012); Ruben *et al.* (2009)	Direct effects on net incomes are modest, but benefits in strengthening farmers organisations and capitalising farmers
	Mendez *et al.* (2010)	Higher prices, but because of low production and low sales under certification limited effects
Mixed results	Pirotte *et al.* (2006)	Nicaraguan cooperatives have gained strength, but FT failed to reach the poorest sector; Fair Trade pushed up auction prices, but lacks visibility.

life cycle of cooperative development. Understanding these system interactions is of crucial importance for capturing the potential impact of coffee certification.

Following the major impact pathways as outlined in Section 1.3, we can derive the following critical issues that influence the effectiveness of coffee certification at different scale levels:

1. *Production systems and livelihoods.*
   In general, involvement in certification creates enhanced knowledge on good agricultural practices and initially leads to increasing production and higher yield levels. Many of these effects tend to disappear over time as non-certified (NC) producers catch up their input use as well. Consequently, the volume effects of

certification are largely 'socialised' over time. Price levels paid to Utz certified farms remain more positive compared to FT certification in Kenya, and are usually better than prices for non-certified producers. In Uganda, far less effects on changes in coffee systems are registered due to stronger price equalisation tendencies that are provoked by the free market regime.

Interestingly enough, while most certified farmers maintain a strong specialisation on coffee, non-certified farmers also invest in other (food) crops, livestock and – mainly in Uganda – engage into non- and off-farm employment. Particularly in Kenya, given the relatively low coffee prices, this leads to more wealth accumulation and stronger income diversification amongst non-certified farmers that positive contributes to their subjective appreciation of welfare changes.

2. *Household welfare effects.*
   Wealth differences and expenditure effects that are still registered in the baseline were largely absorbed over time. In Kenya, Fair Trade producers catch up with NC farmers in terms of credit use, but savings are generally declining. Utz certified farmers maintain their relative advantage in expenditure levels compared to Fair Trade farmers that already existed from the very beginning, but the differences with non-certified farmers becomes either considerably smaller (in Kenya) or eventually disappears (in Uganda).

   The underlying strategy of certification is based on improvements in quality performance and/or sustainability of production systems that should pay-off in terms of higher net revenues. Kilian *et al.* (2006) explore the differences in production costs and price premiums for organic and fair-trade coffee systems in Central America and argue that Fair Trade-certified cooperatives were able to pay a significantly higher price for coffee to their members compared with the mainstream market. Lazaro *et al.* (2008) conclude in a similar study for Tanzania that only large-scale coffee producers have managed to meet the costs of compliance with the Utz standard, since the price premiums are perceived inadequate for covering the higher production and certification costs. Stellmacher and Grote (2011) point to the dilemma that certification aims at paying higher producer prices, but higher prices encourage farmers to intensify their production and might therewith contribute to processes of forest depletion and loss of biodiversity.

3. *Behavioural implications.*
   Certification is thought to exercise decisive influence on farmers risk and investment attitudes and could also influence cooperative trust and intra-household gender relationships. Gaming experiments in Kenya (Schoonhoven-Speijer and Ruben, Chapter 5) demonstrate that behavioural change only occurs if cooperative trust and loyalty are sufficiently guaranteed. Certification hardly reduced the incidence of external shocks and certified farmers remain risk-averse as long as the cooperative framework cannot offer sufficient guarantees and trust. Wollni and Zeller (2007) find, however, that farmers engaged in cooperatives are more likely to grow specialty coffee and participate in high-quality market outlets. These results are particularly valid for areas where farmers income is more dependent on coffee and thus less alternative livelihood options are available. In a similar vein, field experiments in Ethiopia confirm that better-performing

cooperative exhibit more trust and enhance willingness to invest collectively, but individual investments are far more dependent on risk attitudes (Plaisier, Chapter 6). In addition, certification only influences decision-making procedures in the public domain and women's bargaining position in the private domain remains largely unaffected, unless women are accepted as full members of the cooperative and are included in the board (Dijkdrenth, Chapter 7 and Groot Kormelinck, Chapter 8).

4. *Institutional effects.*
   Certified farms are generally fairly satisfied with the technical assistance provided by their cooperatives, but few significant changes in organisational integration are observed in Kenya and some decline in Uganda. Interestingly, in some cases certification leads to reduced membership of other organisations, thus limiting the local networks wherein smallholders are usually involved.

The certified market is only able to absorb a quarter to less than half of total coffee production, and cooperatives are therefore forced to sell a large share of certified coffee on conventional markets. As shown in the Ethiopia study (Woubie *et al.*, Chapter 4) multi-certification then provides an attractive alternative. Moreover, many members are frequently involved in side sales ('hawking') to receive earlier payments. These side sales range from 50% in the case of Sidama (Ethiopia) to at least 25% in the coffee cooperatives in Kenya and Uganda.

The registered effects are strongly dependent on specific local circumstances and influenced by particular events in the life-cycle of projects, cooperatives and farm-households. It is therefore important to register four general factors that influence outcomes of certification programs:

- *Country marketing regimes.* The coffee marketing regimes in Ethiopia (state exchange) and Kenya (auction) are far more centralised compared to the prevailing free market in Uganda, with corresponding effects on price transmission. Farm-gate coffee prices in Kenya are more aligned with world prices compared to prices in Uganda and Ethiopia. Moreover, cooperative legislation leads to stronger state interference in Ethiopian cooperatives (Ruben and Heras, 2012) and a tendency towards individualisation in the Uganda case. It is likely that individual behavioural responses and trust attitudes are aligned to these tendencies.
- *Regional market integration.* Marked differences in local and regional conditions strongly influence prices and market opportunities. Where (Fair Trade) certification sometimes focuses on relatively poor farmers living in marginal regions, initial effects are likely to be considerable, but these effects tend to disappear or are dispersed once regional market integration has been strengthened and other farmers equally benefit. As shown in the Kenya case study (van Rijsbergen *et al.*, Chapter 3), initial returns from certification are highest in remote areas characterised by high dependence on coffee farming where less alternative livelihood options are available. Utz certification tends to focus more on farmers located in higher potential areas that exhibit more options for quality improvement. Figure 1.1 shows large differences in the attractiveness of coffee marketing margins compared to the

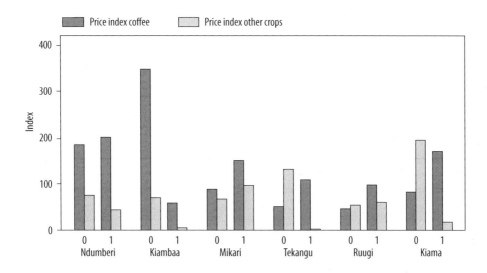

Figure 1.1. Price ratio between coffee and other crops in Kenya (index at $t_0 = 100$).

output/input price ratio of other crops between regions and cooperatives in Kenya. In the poorer Kiambu region (Ndumberi, Kiambaa and Mikari cooperatives), the coffee marketing margins for Utz certified farms (Ndumberi) remained stable, but for Fair Trade certified farms (Kiambaa) coffee prices strongly reduced over time, and Non-certified farmers (Mikari) benefitted most from changes in prices of other crops. In Nyeri district (Tekangu, Rugi and Kiama cooperatives) these changes are far less profound, while differences in net margins are generally in favour of certified and non-certified coffee.

- *Cooperative life cycle.* Considerable differences are observed between cooperatives in terms of internal organisation, trust and quality of service provision. It is likely that some self-selection has taken place when the initial selection of cooperatives for certification was made. In some cases (Kulika coop, Uganda), this was based on accumulated experience from earlier projects. Side sales are strongly related to cooperative trust. Whereas the provision of technical assistance is generally appreciated, scores for cooperative bargaining power (force index) and for social coherence (identification index) remain generally low. Life-cycle effects of cooperative development may also involve disincentives (Francesconi and Ruben, 2014). Since demand for FT coffee is limited and standards tend to be easily met by conventional farmers, rapid growth in membership can increase organisational inefficiency (or coordination costs), thus offsetting the intended benefits of FT certification. Certified cooperatives that do not control membership growth may be more likely to degenerate and collapse than conventional cooperatives.
- *Household behaviour.* Since the final diff-in-diff estimates are presented as matched comparisons, heterogeneity in individual farm-household characteristics is outweighed. Nevertheless, farmers still differ in intrinsic (non-observable)

characteristics that cannot be fully included in the estimates. In particular, differences in risk attitudes and entrepreneurial abilities are likely to be related to options for household income diversification and/or trust in cooperative insurance. Given the relatively limited changes in the latter two indicators, long-term behavioural effects of certification may still remain below potential.

1.6. Implications and outlook

The articles included in this book provide new evidence about the impact of coffee certification based on unique field surveys and in-depth interviews. To the best of our knowledge, this is the first rigorous impact study that relies on balanced panel data with a four years' time interval (for Kenya and Uganda, see Chapter 2 and 3). Moreover, for coffee producers in Ethiopia special attention is given to effects of the phenomenon of multi-certification (Chapter 4). This data is complemented with several in-depth field studies in Kenya and Ethiopia focussing on particular aspects of the performance of cooperative members: changes in risk attitudes forthcoming from certification (Chapter 5), the impact of trust on farmers' willingness to invest (Chapter 6), changes in gender relationships at the cooperative and household level (Chapter 7), and gender bargaining power and trust relationships (Chapter 8).

The registered effects of and the comparison between different labelling regimes provides room for further discussion on the potential long-term implications of the coffee certification for smallholder welfare. The following critical factors influence the outcome of certification:

- *Certified coffee sales.* The effect of the price premiums associated with FT and Utz on the total income of farmers is modest and fairly limited. On average, coffee makes up roughly only one third to a quarter of farmers' total income in Kenya, whereas less than one third of the FT and Utz certified coffee in Kenya is sold as certified. The expected gross effect from certification involves thus less than 10% of farm-household income (see also De Janvry *et al.*, 2012). Moreover, given the high costs of certification, net income effects will be even lower.
- *Catching-up effects.* Farmers selected for FT or Utz certification are usually found in sub-optimal production areas. Consequently, initial gains from certification are usually high, but these tend to disappear once other non-certified farmers catch up in the process. Most initial gains from trade are therefore gradually disappearing due to spatial externalities. This points to important certification effects in the beginning of the coffee life cycle that tend to even out over time. Maintaining the competitive advantage thus requires further actions for deepening the impact of certification.
- *Self-selection.* Certification programs tend to select potential participants in areas where famers' organisation is likely to be effective. It is difficult to disentangle the effects of cooperative reinforcement from the outcomes of certified market exchange. Experimental evidence suggests, however, that reinforcing cooperative strength precedes the generation of individual welfare effects. Initial selection of

marginal coffee producers as target groups guarantees some interesting pay-offs in the early stage of certification, but these effects are rapidly lost if no further development of dynamic competitive advantages takes place.

- *Cooperative consolidation.* Membership of coffee cooperatives proved to be a key mediating variable for reinforcing the use of good agricultural practices. However, reliance on only production knowledge turns out to be insufficient for guaranteeing long-term welfare gains. In general, certification proved of little help for reinforcing improved marketing and bargaining skills amongst cooperative members. Female members are still at a large distance from cooperative governance positions and deserve to be incorporated as full members.
- *Incomplete contracts.* Most delivery contracts for certified coffee remain incomplete in the sense that provisions for adequate pre-finance are hardly ever included or applied. This means that most deliveries are paid only after considerable time and pre-finance by traders and processors is not available. Given the immediate cash requirements of many poor coffee farmers, this leads to important side sales that have a strong depressing effect on income security.
- *Chain governance.* Many certification programs were able to exercise a decisive influence on the strengthening and improvement of coffee production systems, but hardly changes anything in the structure of the value chain. The share of primary producers in the final consumer's price of (certified) coffee still remains low (approximately 6-8%) and has not structurally been changed.[13] This is partly due to over-certification and otherwise influenced by the increasing quality segmentation on the coffee market. Real changes in the division of added value between supply chain parties has not taken place under the influence of certification.

Summarising the outcomes, three major general conclusions can be drawn regarding the future perspectives for coffee certification.

First, it appears that different certification regimes have other effects on farming systems and enterprise development. Whereas Fair Trade clearly enhances further specialisation in coffee production and more engagement in dry coffee processing, Utz certified enhances input-intensification of coffee production and multi-certification enhances coffee renovation and diversification of coffee outlets. This may point towards a kind of life cycle for certification that starts with enabling farmers to produce larger volumes for the Fair Trade market and gradually shifting emphasis to improving yields and quality that are demanded by Utz certified outlets. Multi-certification may become an option for diversifying outlets and risks and to tackle problems of over-certification.

Farmers with Utz certified coffee production tend to focus on input intensification and quality upgrading. Investments in knowledge and improved cropping practices

---

[13] Calculations using the average price for dry coffee in our sample (KSh 73.16/kg equals € 0.61/kg) and consumer prices for coffee in the Netherlands (€ 8.34/kg for ground coffee), resulting in a 7.3% of the Dutch retail price going to the coffee farmer. See also Johannessen and Wilhite (2010).

are considered critical for remaining competitive in the long run. Multi-certification can be useful to enable farmers to engage with the transition from the 'protected' Fair Trade segment towards more demanding – and potentially more rewarding – 'Responsible Trade' market outlets. Since direct income effects become rather limited, indirect incentives forthcoming from cooperative fringe benefits and outlet security considerations are vital to maintain farmers involved in certification programs.

Other important differences between Fair Trade and Utz certified programs are found in the field of cooperative development and community outreach. Fair Trade focuses particularly on strengthening of the internal cooperative organisation, whereas Utz certified addresses mainly administrative and management aspects of the cooperative enterprise. Similarly, the Fair Trade premium offers global outreach and social service provision for rural communities, while Utz certified focuses more attention on market linkages and knowledge sharing.[14]

The FT regime proves to be especially suitable to assist local farmers' organisations in getting initial access to the market, but incentives for further upgrading of production systems and quality performance appear to be rather restricted. In fact, cooperatives with longer FT engagement may become over-specialised in coffee and tend to neglect investments in upgrading (Ruben, 2008). Therefore, in subsequent phases further alignment with private brands might be a useful step to guarantee sustained market participation and to increase capacities for adapting to increasingly stringent market demands. The price premium may eventually disappear and can then be replaced by a quality performance premium.

Second, none of the certification regimes has been able to generate substantial changes in the structure of the coffee value chain. Primary coffee producers still receive a small share of retail price and options for providing pre-finance (as part of the contract) have hardly improved. Coffee cooperatives could slightly reinforce their service provision to members and improve their bargaining position towards traders, but at the same many farmers increasingly rely on side-sales ('hawking') to outside agents to overcome market outlet constraints. Over time, non-certified coffee producers demonstrate to be able to reach similar output and yield levels and initial advantages of certification tend to disappear gradually. Moreover, some improvements in village service provision are registered particularly for Fair Trade certified producers, but linkages of coffee farmers with other social or community organisations generally deteriorated.

Supply chain relationships broadly vary between Fair Trade and Utz certified cooperatives. Utz farms are generally better able to enforce member loyalty and control

---

[14] This also reflects differences between top-down and bottom-up pathways for market segmentation that give priority to either consumer-oriented labels for marketing purposes or business-to-business standards for upgrading purposes. Whereas the former are mainly used to open-up market access (thus facilitating options for redistribution of value shares throughout the chain; see Vagneron and Roquigny, 2011), the latter aim at dynamic market development (i.e. increasing the total value within the chain).

internal free-riding problems, particularly when input deliveries and farm training are linked to obligatory sales through the cooperative. Utz contracts tend to focus on farm management, production practices and quality compliance, while neglecting broader community-level constraints. On the other hand, cooperative participation is better safeguarded under Fair Trade standards, where farmers are entitled to decide jointly about the distribution of premium payments. FT contracts devote more attention to community-wide issues and favour the creation of external bargaining power.

Third, broader societal structures and institutional networks surrounding the coffee sector clearly influence the outcomes of the certification process. In countries where a competitive free market regime is prevailing (Uganda), Utz certified quality advantages can be directly translated into better prices. Bypassing traditional private buyers can thus become a major benefit. Otherwise, the regime of vertically integrated exporters, sales through cooperative unions and state-controlled auctions (Kenya, Tanzania) make it more difficult to bargain attractive price margins (Baffes, 2006; Krivonos, 2004). Pre-arranged sales under certified conditions may then offer major advantages.

Critical conditions for further dovetailing different regimes of coffee standard would include the expansion of capacities and explicit learning objectives into the standard-setting and verification procedures. This might enable smallholder farmers to switch attention from targets of volume and scale towards criteria of quality and reliability, while reinforcing internal management and cooperative loyalty. Such progress standards can substantially reduce market imperfections and might provide useful incentives for coffee producers to remain competitive in a highly dynamic market environment.

In conclusion, a dynamic picture emerges from the experiences with coffee certification in East Africa that is far away from the image that is created on the back of the coffee package. While different standards certainly provide incentives to coffee farmers for improving production, yields or quality, due attention needs to be given to more substantial changes in the value chain structure, the strengthening of cooperative organisations and the creation of local competitive market conditions. There is still a much to do in the field of coffee certification!

References

Arnould, E., A. Plastina and D. Ball (2009). market disintermediation and producer value capture: the case of Fair Trade coffee in Nicaragua, Peru and Guatemala. *Journal of Public Policy and Marketing* 28(2): 186-201.

Bacon, C. (2005). Confronting the coffee crisis: can Fair Trade, organic, and specialty coffees reduce small-scale farmer vulnerability in Northern Nicaragua? *World Development* 33(3): 497-511.

Bacon, C. (2008). Confronting the coffee crisis; can Fair Trade, organic and specialty coffees reduce the vulnerability of small-scale farmers in Northern Nicaragua. In: C.M. Bacon, V.E. Méndez, S.R. Gliessman, D. Goodman and J.A. Fox (eds.) *Confronting the coffee crisis, Fair Trade, sustainable livelihoods and ecosystems in Mexico and Central America*, Cambridge: MIT Press, pp. 177-205.

Bacon, C. and M.E. Flores (2007). *Estudio de Impacto del Sistema de Café de Comercio Justo en America Latina y el Caribe*. Nicaragua: Coordinadora de Pequeños Productores de Commercio Justo de Café en Latina America y el Caribe.

Bacon, C.M., E. Méndez, S.R. Gliessman, D. Goodman and J. Fox (eds.) (2008b). *Confronting the coffee crisis. Fair Trade, sustainable livelihoods and ecosystems in Mexico and Central America.* Cambridge, MI, USA: MIT Press, pp. 155-178.

Bacon, M.C., V. Méndez, M.E. Flores Gómez, D. Stuart and S.R. Díaz Flores (2008a). Are sustainable coffee certifications enough to secure farmer livelihoods? The millennium development goals and Nicaragua's Fair Trade cooperatives. *Globalizations* 5(2): 259-274.

Baffes, J. (2006) Restructuring Uganda's coffee industry: why going back to basics matters. *Development Policy Review* 24(4): 413-436.

Barham, B.L., M. Callenes, S. Gitter, J. Lewis and J. Weber (2011). Fair Trade/organic coffee, rural livelihoods, and the 'agrarian question': Southern Mexican coffee families in transition. *World Development* 39(1): 134-145.

Bastin, A. and N. Matteucci (2007). Financing coffee farmers in Ethiopia: challenges and opportunities. international conference on rural finance research: moving results into policies and practice. *Savings and Development* 31(3): 251-282.

Becchetti, L. and M. Constantino (2006). *Fair Trade on marginalized producers: an impact analysis on Kenyan farmers*. Working paper CEIS 220/ECINEQ2006. Rome, Italy: University of Rome.

Bechetti, L. and M. Constantino (2008). The effects of Fair Trade on affiliated producers: an impact analysis on kenyan farmers. *World Development* 36(5): 823-842.

Berges-Sennou, F., P. Bontems and V. Requillart (2004). Economics of private labels: a survey of literature. *Journal of Agricultural and Food Industrial Organization* 2(1): 1-23.

Bitzer, V., M. Francken and P. Glasbergen(2008). Intersectoral partnerships for a sustainable coffee chain: really addressing sustainability or just picking (coffee) cherries? *Global Environmental Change* 18(2): 271-284.

Blackman, A. and J. Rivera (2010). *The evidence base for environmental and socioeconomic impacts of 'sustainable' certification*. Washington, DC, USA: Resources for the Future.

Bolwig, S., L. Riisgaard, P. Gibbon and S. Ponte (2013). Challenges of agro-food standards conformity: lessons from East Africa and policy implications. *European Journal of Development Research* 25: 408-427.

Calo, M. and T.A. Wise (2005). *Revaluing peasant coffee production: organic and Fair Trade markets in Mexico*. Medford, MA, USA: Tufts University, Global Development and Environment Institute.

Center for Evaluation (CEval) (2013). *Assessing the impact of Fair Trade on poverty reduction through rural development – final report Fair Trade impact study*. Saarbrücken, Germany: Saarland University.

Coe, N.M., P. Dicken and H. Hess (2008). Global production networks: realizing the potential. *Journal of Economic Geography* 8(3): 271-295.

COSA (2013). *Vietnam coffee: A COSA survey of Utz certified farms.* Philadelphia, PA, USA: Committee on Sustainability Assessment.

Daviron, B. and S. Ponte (2005). *The coffee paradox: global markets, commodity trade and the elusive promise for development.* London, UK: Zed Books.

De Janvry, A., C. McIntosh and E. Sadoulet (2012). *Fair Trade and free entry: can a disequilibrium market serve as a development tool?* Available at: http://irps.ucsd.edu/assets/001/503924.pdf.

Elder, S.D., H. Zerriffi and P. Le Billon (2012). Effects of Fair Trade certification on social capital: the case of Rwandan coffee producers. *World Development* 40(11): 2355-2367.

Farnworth, C. and M. Goodman (2006). *Growing ethical networks: the Fair Trade market for raw and processed agricultural products.* Background paper for the World Development Report 2008. Available at: http://tinyurl.com/o8c7nww.

Franscesconi, N. and R. Ruben (2014). Fair Trade's theory of change an evaluation based on the cooperative life cycle framework and mixed methods. *Journal of Development Effectiveness* 6(3): 268-283.

Fridell, G. (2004). The Fair Trade network in historical perspective. *Canadian Journal of Development Studies* 25(3): 411-428.

Giovannucci, D.S. and F.J. Koekoek (2003). *The state of sustainable coffee: a study of twelve major markets. international coffee organization.* London, UK: International Institute of Sustainable Development.

Henson, S.J. and W.B. Traill (1993). Economics of food safety. *Food Policy* 18(2): 152-162.

Hobbs, J.E., A. Fearne and J. Spriggs (2002). Institutional arrangements and incentive structures for food safety and quality assurance in the food chain. In: Hooker, N.H. and E. Murano (eds.). Interdisciplinary food safety research. Boca Raton, FL, USA: CRC Press, pp. 43-68.

Jaffee, D. (2007). *Brewing justice. Fair Trade coffee, sustainability and survival.* Berkeley, CA, USA: University of California Press.

Jena, P., T. Stellmacher and U. Grote (2012). The impact of coffee certification on small-scale producers' livelihoods: evidence from Ethiopia. *International Association of Agricultural Economists (IAAE) Conference, Foz do Iguaçu, Brazil,* August, 2012. Available at: http://tinyurl.com/kwal37d.

Johannessen, S. and H. Wilhite (2010). Who really benefits from Fair Trade? An analysis of value distribution in Fair Trade coffee. *Globalizations* 7(4): 525-544.

Kasente, D. (2012). Fair Trade and organic certification in value chains: lessons from a gender analysis from coffee exporting in Uganda. *Gender and Development* (20): 111-127.

Kilian, B., C. Jones, L. Pratt and A. Villalobos (2006). Is sustainable agriculture a viable strategy to improve farm income in Central America? A case study on coffee. *Journal of Business Research* 59(3): 322-330.

Krivonos, E. (2004). *The impact of coffee market reforms on producer prices and price transmission.* Policy Research Working Paper No. 3358. Washington, DC, USA: World Bank.

Lazaro, E., J. Makindara and F.T.M. Kilima (2008). *Sustainability standards and coffee exports from Tanzania.* Copenhagen, Denmark: DIIS Working paper.

Le Mare, A. (2008). The impact of Fair Trade on social and economic development: a review of the literature. *Geography Compass* 2(6): 1922-1942.

Lyon, S. (2008). We want to be equal to them: Fair-trade coffee certification and gender equity within organizations. *Human Organization* 67(3): 258-268.

MacDonald, K. (2007). Globalising justice within coffee supply chains? Fair Trade, Starbucks and the transformation of supply chain governance. *Third World Quarterly* 28(4): 793-812.

Méndez, V., C. Bacon, M. Olson, S. Petchers, D. Herrador, C. Carranza,L. Trujillo, C. Guadarrama-Zugasti, A. Cordon and A. Mendoza (2010). Effects of Fair Trade and organic certifications on small-scale coffee farmer households in Central America and Mexico. *Renewable Agriculture and Food Systems* 25(3): 236-251.

Milford, A. (2004). *Coffee, co-operatives and competition: the impact of Fair Trade*. Bergen, Norway: Chr. Michelsen Institute.

Muradian, R. and W. Pelupessy (2005). Governing the coffee chain: the role of voluntary regulatory systems. *World Development* 33(12): 2029-2037.

Murray, D.L., L.T. Raynolds and P.L. Taylor (2006). The future of Fair Trade coffee: dilemmas facing Latin America's small-scale producers. *Development in Practice* 16(2): 179-191.

Neilson, J. and B. Pritchard(2007). Green coffee? The contradictions of global sustainability initiatives from an Indian perspective. *Development Policy Review* 25(3): 311-331.

Nelson, V. and B. Pound(2009). *The last ten years: a comprehensive review of the literature on the impact of Fair Trade*. Greenwich, UK: Natural Resources Institute.

Petkova, I. (2006). 'Shifting regimes of governance in the coffee market: From secular crisis to a new equilibrium? *Review of International Political Economy* 13(2): 313-339.

Philpotts, S.M., P. Bichier, R. Rice and R. Greenberg (2007). Field-testing ecological and economic benefits of coffee certification programs. *Conservation Biology* 21(4): 975-985.

Pirotte, G., G. Pleyers and M. Poncelet (2006). Fair-trade coffee in Nicaragua and Tanzania: a comparison. *Development in Practice* 16(5): 441-451.

Raynolds, L. (2002). Consumer/producer links in Fair Trade coffee networks. *Sociologia Ruralis* 42(4): 404-424.

Raynolds, L.T., D. Murray and P.L. Taylor (2004). Fair Trade coffee: building producer capacity via global networks. *Journal of International Development* 16(8): 1109-1121.

Renard, M.C. (2003). Fair Trade: quality, market and conventions. *Journal of Rural Studies* 19(1): 87-96.

Renard, M.C. (2005). Quality certification, regulation and power in Fair Trade. *Journal of Rural Studies* 21(4): 419-431.

Romero Gonzales, A.M. (2010). *La cadena de valor del café de comercio justo de Uganda*. Intermón-Oxfam.

Ronchi, L. (2002). *The impact of Fair Trade on producers and their organisations: a case study with Coocafe in Costa Rica*. Brighton, UK: University of Sussex.

Roozen, N. and F. van der Hoff (2001). *Fair Trade. Het verhaal achter Max Havelaar-koffie, Oké-bananen en Kuyichi jeans*. Amsterdam, the Netherlands: Van Gennep.

Ruben, R. (ed.) 2008. *The impact of Fair Trade*. Wageningen, the Netherlands: Wageningen Academic Publishers.

Ruben, R. and R. Fort (2012). The impact of Fair Trade certification for coffee farmers in Peru. *World Development* 40(3): 570-582.

Ruben, R. and J. Heras (2012). Social capital, governances and performance of Ethiopian coffee cooperatives. *Annals of Public and Cooperative Economic* 83(4): 463-484.

Ruben, R. and S. Verkaart (2011). Comparing Fair and responsible coffee standards in East Africa. In: B. Helmsing, and M. Vellema (eds.) *Value chains, social inclusion and economic Development*. London, UK: Routledge, pp. 61-81.

Ruben, R. and G. Zúñiga-Aras (2011). How standards compete: comparative impact of coffee certification in Northern Nicaragua. *Supply Chain Management* 16(2): 98-109.

Ruben, R., R. Fort and G. Zúñiga-Aras (2009). Measuring the impact of Fair Trade on development. *Development in Practice* 19(6): 777-788.

Rueda, X. and E.F. Lambin (2013). Responding to globalization: impacts of certification on Colombian small-scale coffee growers. *Ecology & Society* 18(3): 21.

Sáenz Segura, F. and G. Zúñiga-Arias (2008). Assessment of the effect of Fair Trade on smallholder producers in Costa Rica: A comparative study in the coffee sector. In: R. Ruben (ed.) *The impact of Fair Trade*. Wageningen, the Netherlands: Wageningen Academic Publishers, pp. 117-135.

Salami, A., A,B. Kamara and Z. Brixiova (2010). Smallholder Agriculture in East Africa: trends, constraints and opportunities. *African Development Bank, Working Paper* 105.

Stellmacher, T. and U. Grote (2011). *Forest coffee certification in Ethiopia: economic boon or ecological bane?* Working Paper Series 76. Bonn, Germany: Zentrum für Entwicklungsforschung, University of Bonn.

Tallontire, A. and B. Vorley (2005). Achieving Fairness in trading between supermarkets and their agrifood supply chains. London: UK Food Group.

Taylor, P.L. (2005). In the market but not of it: Fair Trade coffee and forest stewardship council certification as market-based social change. *World Development* 33(1): 129-147.

Utting, C. (2005). Does Fair Trade make a difference? The case of small coffee producers in Nicaragua. *Development in Practice* 15(3-4): 584-598.

Vagneron, I. and S. Roquigny (2011). Value distribution in conventional, organic and Fair Trade banana chains in the Dominican Republic. *Canadian Journal of Development Studies* 32(3): 324-338.

Valkila, J. (2009). Fair Trade organic coffee production in Nicaragua – sustainable development or a poverty trap? *Ecological Economics* 68(12): 3018-3025.

Valkila, J. and A. Nygren (2010). Impacts of Fair Trade certification on coffee farmers, cooperatives, and laborers in Nicaragua. *Agriculture and Human Values* 27(3): 321-333.

Valkila, J., P. Haaparanta and N. Niemi (2010). Empowering coffee traders? The coffee value chain from Nicaraguan Fair Trade farmers to Finnish consumers. *Journal of Business Ethics* 97: 257-270.

Van der Vossen, H. (2005). A critical analysis of the agronomic and economic sustainability of organic coffee production. *Experimental Agriculture* 41: 449-473.

Williams, P. (2013). Fair wages & fair prices. a report for the European Fair Trade association. Available at: http://tinyurl.com/ofqlg9r.

Wollni, M. and M. Zeller (2007). Do farmers benefit from participating in specialty markets and cooperatives? The case of coffee marketing in Costa Rica. *Agricultural Economics* 37(2): 243-248.

Chapter 2

The impact of Utz certification on smallholder farmers in Uganda

Willem Elbers, Bart van Rijsbergen, Fred Bagamba and Paul Hoebink
For correspondence: w.elbers@maw.ru.nl

2.1 Introduction

Sustainability standards like Fair Trade (FT) or Utz certified are widely regarded as a promising way of improving smallholder coffee farmer welfare. As yet, the impact of certification remains poorly understood. The current chapter presents the findings of the study regarding the impact of Utz certification in Uganda.[15] The study is based on two waves of data collection carried out in 2009 and 2012 with farmers belonging to two cooperative organisations that received support from the Dutch Non-Governmental Organisation (NGO) Solidaridad: Kulika (located in Kamuli district) and Ankole Coffee Processors Ltd. (located in Ibanda district). This study aims to provide a broad comparison between farmers and their organisations selling Utz certified or conventional coffee. In line with this objective, the guiding research question is: *What is the impact of Utz involvement at producer and producer organisation level?*

The central issue in impact evaluations is the ability to address the counterfactual issue: What would have happened if the target group had not participated? This hypothetical situation cannot be observed empirically and thus needs to be constructed for correctly analysing the net impact of a programme and the attribution to this result by policy. To measure the impact, the study combines two types of quantitative analysis:
1. 'with and without' assessment of the results achieved by cooperatives that received programme support compared to other likewise cooperatives without this support;
2. 'before and after' analysis of the results of the support comparing the initial (baseline) and the final (endline) situation.

Primary data was collected at two moments in time (2009 and 2012) through single farm visit interviews using structured questionnaires administered to respondents

---

[15] The study was carried in cooperation between the Centre for International Development Issues Nijmegen (CIDIN) and Dr. Fred Bagamba, School of Agricultural Science, Makerere University, Kampala.

Ruerd Ruben and Paul Hoebink (eds.) **Coffee certification in East Africa**
DOI 10.3920/978-90-8686-805-6_2, © Wageningen Academic Publishers 2015

(mainly the household head). A farm household was defined as a social entity that collectively makes productive and consumptive decisions and often eats from the same pot.

Table 2.1 provides information on the different groups in Ibanda and Kamuli districts that were part of the survey. In both regions, we sampled farmers in the treatment (intervention) group and a comparator treatment group. After the second round, we could count 573 farmers that were interviewed twice.[16]

Table 2.2. provides information on the progress of coffee certification in each of the sample cooperatives. In each district, always one cooperative counts with Utz certification for several years. There is also a control group with no engagement into certification. Many Utz certified farmers that were part of the Kulika project were previously participating in a similar project, the Agricultural Production Enhancement Program (APEP). Section 2.4 explains how this is taken up in the survey design of Kamuli district.

To contextualise and explain the survey findings, we also carried out qualitative research. The latter included focus group discussions (FGDs) with Utz certified farmers and non-certified farmers, as well as semi-structured interviews with representatives of relevant stakeholders. The qualitative research focused on three key topics: production, quality and income. These topics were discussed in relation to a number of other issues including farming practices, market competition and prices, market awareness, sales options and considerations, farmer satisfaction and perceived benefits of certification. These topics and the questions asked during the FGDs and interviews were based on a review of the academic literature on (the impact

Table 2.1. Number of farmers included in the Uganda case study.

Group		2009	2012
Ibanda district			
Old Ankole	treatment	98	97
New Ankole	treatment	95	90
Conventional	control	124	115
Kamuli district			
Kulika 1	treatment	65	60
Kulika 2	treatment	63	55
Mbulamuti	control	85	82
Nawanyaru	control	82	74
Total		612	573

---

[16] Only 39 cases were lost after the second round; this attrition rate of 5% is considered fairly limited. No systematic pattern of attrition was observed.

Table 2.2. Sample composition by degree and years of certification (2009-2012).[1]

Counties	Cooperatives	2009	2010	2011	2012
Ibanda	Old Ankole	Utz	Utz	Utz	Utz
	New Ankole	none	Utz	Utz	Utz
	Conventional	none	none	none	none
Kamuli	Kulika 1	APEP + Utz	APEP + Utz	APEP + Utz	APEP + Utz
	Kulika 2	Utz	Utz	Utz	Utz
	Mbulamuti	APEP	APEP	APEP	APEP
	Nawanyaru	none	none	none	none

[1] Utz = Utz certified; APEP = Agricultural Production Enhancement Program.

of) Utz certified coffee. The open-ended nature of the group discussions/interviews also allowed for issues not covered by the interview guide to be explored. A total of 16 FGDs were carried out; 8 in Kamuli district and 8 in Ibanda. In each focus group discussion 15 to 25 farmers participated. In total 8 semi-structured interviews were conducted. All (focus group) interviews were recorded and transcribed for analysis. To further contextualise the findings and identify possible challenges, the available project documentation (e.g. original proposal, progress reports, and evaluations) was also reviewed.

The remainder of this chapter is structured as follows. Section 2.2 offers a characterisation of the Ugandan coffee sector. Section 2.3 discusses the findings in Ibanda district while section 2.4 presents the findings in Kamuli district. Both sections discuss direct welfare effects, indirect effects and institutional implications. Section 2.5 revisits the main research question and outlines the conclusions of the study.

Note that the research findings are discussed separately for Ibanda and Kamuli districts. This was done because merging the findings would have resulted in a distorted image of the impact of Utz certification. The Utz intervention in Kamuli district was part of an EU project that ultimately did not prove to be sustainable. As explained in more detail in Section 2.4, the project to some extent collapsed between the two waves of data-collection in 2009 and 2012. As such, in the case of Kamuli district, it is impossible to disentangle the effects of Utz certification from the effects of the project-failure.

2.2 Coffee sector in Uganda

Coffee, together with tea and cotton, constitute Uganda's traditional exports. Coffee has been historically Uganda's largest source of export revenues since it overtook cotton in the mid-1950s. Over half a million households distributed over two thirds of the country depend on coffee as a source of income (Compete, 2002). The sector provides income for an even larger number of people, along the value chain, as hired farm labour and in businesses such as processing, input supply, trading and transport. For many of these households, coffee is the only source of income.

There are two main types of coffee, both of which are grown in Uganda: Arabica, which has a milder taste and tends to be more expensive, and higher yielding Robusta, which is widely used in instant coffee and in stronger roasts. Whereas the Arabica coffee (*Coffea arabica*) varieties originated in Ethiopia, the Robusta species (*Coffea canephora*) are indigenous to Africa's equatorial forests, where coffee cherries were eaten as fruit or added to foods (Sayer, 2002). Uganda is considered to be the second home for coffee. Robusta coffee has long been known to the Baganda who used it in the ritual of 'blood-brotherhood'. Coffee chewing still retains some ritual significance. Wild varieties are still found in the foothills of the Rwenzori Mountains in Western Uganda, where they are harvested as specialty 'eco' coffee and marketed as 'Kibaale wild'.

The Robusta type dominates coffee production in Uganda and is demanded by roasters, as a component in certain blends due to its special taste qualities (You and Bolwig, 2003), which is a result of being grown at higher altitudes than most Robusta coffees in the world (Ponte, 2001; CFC, 2001). It is mainly grown in the central region at altitude ranging from 1000-1,500 m where temperatures are favourable (24-30 °C). It is especially demanded by European roasters and commands a considerable premium over the world Robusta reference price. Ideal temperatures for Arabica are 15-25 °C, which in Uganda are found in highland areas especially around the slopes of Mt. Elgon and the Rwenzori Mountains.

Commercial coffee marketing in Uganda started in 1912 when the crop was bought from farmers by private traders, processed and exported. The crop was originally grown by European and Asian farmers but was abandoned to smallholders as prices fell in the 1920s. In 1929, the British Government restructured the sector by setting up a coffee board (which later became the Coffee Industry Board in 1943) to handle export and quality control. The coffee board was modified in 1953 to become Coffee Marketing Board (CMB) whose roles were expanded to encompass regulatory and marketing functions, in addition to advising government on reorganisation of the whole sector.

During colonial times, farmers established village-based cooperatives as a means of avoiding exploitation by middlemen and private coffee traders. From the 1940s, they developed strategic control over the supply and export of coffee. Up to the 1960s, some private traders (e.g. Bugisu Union) were still able to export coffee. In 1969, the Coffee Marketing Board Act was passed that made the CMB the sole exporter of all Uganda coffee, but cooperatives were allowed to buy coffee from farmers, process the coffee and sell to the CMB. In 1977, private traders were allowed, by the coffee amendment decree, to internally purchase and process coffee, thereby breaking the monopoly that had been given to the CMB and cooperatives by the 1969 Act.

There were certain advantages in CMB's monopoly. Coffee was a major earner of foreign exchange and a source of government revenue, and thus it was in the interest of government to manage and control the collection of proceeds from coffee export. Even when the contribution of other export crops (e.g. cotton, tobacco and tea) significantly declined, the relative contribution of coffee increased tremendously, from about 40% of the export earnings in the early 1970s to 95% in 1989 (Buchanayandi, 1996). Uganda's coffee improved in quality and it was a premium reference for other world Robusta coffees.

The monopoly of the CMB, however, came with a number of disadvantages that resulted in the poor performance of the sector:
1. Farmers were paid low prices through producer fixed margins, about 20% of the world price during that period.
2. Farmers had problems marketing their coffee in time, which led to massive stockpiling of coffee.
3. Shortage in crop finance that led to non-cash payment to farmers. In some cases, farmers were not paid at all.
4. Limited funding of research and extension institutions that led to further decline in coffee production and productivity.

To avert the decline in coffee production and reverse the trend towards a production peak of 213,000 metric tonnes in 1972/73, government implemented the Coffee Rehabilitation Programme, with funding from the European Union (EU). The assumption was that farmers would automatically increase production provided that they had access to relevant inputs and extension advice. However, the share of the world price received by farmers remained low and the marketing system remained inefficient. There were modest gains in productivity, but welfare gains remained below expectations (Buchanayandi, 1996). Specifically, the efforts failed to improve the smallholder farmer incomes as prices remained low or even declined. As the economy was beginning to pick up, the collapse of the International Coffee Agreement prompted world prices to crash by more than half the previous level (Sayer, 2002).

There were also other factors at play that contributed to the decline in coffee production and productivity. Political instability in the 1970s led to a collapse in coffee marketing and consequent weakening of the cooperative structures. During the 1970s and 1980s, Uganda's economy faced both domestic and international constraints that negatively affected coffee production and export. The situation worsened with the liberalisation of coffee export marketing, which led to the collapse of most of the cooperative unions. The cooperatives lacked the business structures and market knowledge to survive in the new competitive environment. As a result, both the quality and price of Uganda coffee had been driven down in the pursuit of quantity.

General economic mismanagement and poor incentives to farmers led to widespread neglect of coffee gardens, aggravating the problem of the already declining yields and quality due to the old age of the existing trees (Otim and Ngategize, 1993). In addition, Uganda had to face stiff competition over the years from producers like India, Philippines, Thailand and Indonesia, among others, which had increased their production levels and captured growing share of the internal market, resulting in downward pressure on prices at the world market. Moreover, demand did not increase in the consuming countries at the rate at which production had been increasing. The combined effect was a slump in coffee prices, especially for Robusta. The Ugandan government adopted policy measures that would improve competitiveness, profitability and viability of coffee production and export.

In addition to macroeconomic management, the government implemented sector-specific coffee policies that targeted increasing production at household level, including encouraging farmers to replant old trees with new improved high-yielding clonal coffee, the liberalisation of producer prices and marketing operations, and abolition of export taxes on agricultural produce. The government also restructured the CMB into a limited company, the CMBL, and instead created another body, the Uganda Coffee Development Authority (UCDA) to take over the regulatory functions within the coffee sector.

Despite the above efforts, Uganda continued to suffer unfavourable terms of trade. Prices for export crops continued to plummet at the world market. The lowest level ever recorded for coffee prices was in the 2001-2002 period. This was attributed to structural changes in the global market, including production innovations in Brazil and booming supply from Vietnam, and partly due to changes in corporate strategies among the largest roasters, including the way coffee is blended (Lazaro and Makindara, 2008).

In the early 1990s, the government adopted reforms towards the abolition of the monopoly previously enjoyed by CMB. Parastatal marketing had been corrupt and inefficient. Farmers had to wait until export sales had been made before they would get paid and most times received poor and occasionally no returns. A newly-created UCDA took over the regulatory functions and CMB remained with only the marketing/trading functions. CMB continued to export coffee but as a limited company until it was finally dissolved.

The UCDA was entrusted with five functions: (1) research and development, (2) quality control, (3) promotion, (4) policy formulation, and (5) statistics and monitoring. Price controls were removed to allow farm gate prices and margins to be determined by market forces. The percentage share of the world price paid to the farmer increased and coffee export proceeds were left entirely to the exporters. The restriction on rail transport was lifted and the process of licensing coffee sector participants was simplified. Quality control and certification were delegated to sector participants. It was envisaged that as the industry grew, it would become self-regulating. Instead of setting minimum export prices, UCDA provided indicative prices calculated on the basis of market information and published daily, to guide farmers and exporters. These prices were in no way binding.

However, new problems arose, which negatively affected the coffee sector. The government was under pressure to liberalise the coffee sector, with those putting pressure on the government arguing that it would benefit the farmers through increased earnings. However, exports became dominated by multinational companies or agents of overseas financiers whose profit-oriented decisions were not necessarily in the interest of the country. Moreover, the cooperative unions and societies of the parastatal era had fulfilled a function that is still missed today, that of providing processing facilities and credit for inputs, organising blanket spraying, fixing a buying price and providing easy access to the market (Sayor, 2002).

With privatisation, farmers, buyers, processors and exporters were free to operate and contract as they pleased. Inexperienced local traders were interested in making short-term profits without concern for quality, tarnishing the reputation of Ugandan coffees. Uganda's coffee had always been paid a premium by international importers because of its neutral taste, which allowed it to be blended with other more expensive coffees, thus reducing costs without compromising the cup quality (Compete, 2002). The large exporters that dominated the sector focused more on volume rather than quality.[17] The result of this situation was a decrease of the overall quality of coffee exported from Uganda, as most growers did not see better prices paid for better quality coffee. Uganda risked losing out if buyers began to see a trend of declining production and/ or falling quality.

Despite the inevitable upheavals brought by the liberalisation process, exports reached their highest ever levels of 4 million bags (240,000 tonnes) during the years 1995-1997 as the consequence of a combination of higher international prices and a much greater farm gate share of the export prices (Bussolo et al., 2007). Since then, volumes have fallen, primarily because of the occurrence of coffee wilt disease and the 2000-2005 coffee crisis when international coffee prices reached all-time lows. During the past decade, Uganda's annual coffee exports averaged just below 2.8 million bags, with a high of 3.2 million bags and a low of 2 million bags (Figure 2.1).

By 2001, it had been realised that to exploit the market opportunities, Uganda needed to focus resources on developing farmer associations that could act as conduits for delivering capital and/or services to producers. Specifically, the sector needed to create a better link between price and quality. There is a need to refocus resources on production of high quality/high value Arabica, whose market is far from saturation, and on value addition for the Robusta coffee. Specifically, resources could be focused on organising farmer associations to engage in semi-washed or fully washed Robusta, which can be sold at a premium although the markets are small. The key is to provide training to the associations so that they can be sustainable and run their business under the competitive environment.

---

[17] In that sense, the macro-economy does not favor Utz with its emphasis on improving quality.

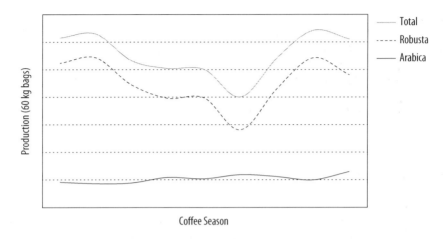

Figure 2.1. Uganda coffee export production trends (2000-2009) (UCDA Data Bank).

One of the possible avenues for increasing the value of agricultural exports is through sales to emerging, niche and value added markets such as specialty Fair Trade, organic, Rainforest Alliance, and Utz certified coffee. Certification enables farmers to develop a relationship with exporting companies, thus improving their market access. It also enables farmers to access services such as extension, training and provision of inputs. However, Utz certification has had unknown impacts on the income and welfare of farmers due to the fact that most schemes are new and little research has been carried out on them (Lazaro and Makindara, 2008). This field study was carried out to assess the impact of Utz certification on smallholder farmers in two districts of Uganda: i.e. Kamuli (located in East Uganda) and Ibanda (located in West Uganda).

2.3 Findings from Ibanda district

In Ibanda district, Western Uganda, the cultivation of coffee is an important source of income available to rural families. The benefits from coffee production have been far from optimal, however, among other reasons due to poor coffee farming practices, coffee wilt disease and the lack of reliable buyers. In 2005 the Dutch NGO Solidaridad started working with Ankole Coffee Processors Ltd., a registered private coffee export company, to address this situation.

In the years 2005-2010, Ankole was supported to organise farmers operating in the area and assisted the farmers in attaining Utz certification through the adoption of good agricultural practices. A selection of farmers was trained in sustainable coffee husbandry practices, proper harvesting and dry processing procedures. In addition, they were provided with equipment, seedlings, technical information and education to approach coffee farming as a business. Furthermore, farmers were organised into producer organisations (POs) and zones. Every 20-30 farmers were organised in a PO, and every 5-8 POs made a zone, depending on the distance from one farmer to another. The producer organisation leaders and zone leaders played a key role in the project as they conducted meetings with farmers, mobilised them, and kept records. During the project a total of 2,000 farmers were certified under the Utz arrangement. In 2010, Solidaridad provided (one-off) pre-finance to Ankole to enable faster payments to farmers and to sideline middlemen (this loan was subsequently repaid).

2.3.1 Survey design

Three groups of farmers were studied in Ibanda, as shown in Table 2.3 'Old Ankole' members are farmers that are member of Ankole since 2006, while 'New Ankole' members are farmers that are members since 2009. 'Conventional' farmers were selected from within the same communities. Comparing 'Old Ankole' with 'New Ankole' and 'Conventional' in a single year (2009 or 2012) provides us with an indication of the effect of farmers working together under the Utz code of conduct. A comparison of the difference in 'Old' and 'New Ankole' over the time period 2009-2011 is likely to give us an assessment of the price difference effect for organised farmers trained under the Utz code of conduct.

In turn, the comparison of the difference in 'New Ankole' for the period 2009-2012 with the difference in 'Conventional' over the same period, should give us the total effect of being Utz certified. An important underlying assumption for this research design is that Ankole would start selling the coffee of their certified farmers as Utz starting in the 2009-2010 season. Unfortunately this did not happen. As such, estimation of the counterfactual and attribution to the intervention in impeded. Figures for the three different groups of farmers in Ibanda are presented in the next paragraphs. We again present the data after logarithmic transformation for convenience.

2.3.2 Comparison 1. Old Ankole versus New Ankole

Old Ankole farmers have significantly more coffee trees than New Ankole farmers in 2009 as well as in 2012. No significant differences are observed for production per acre or per tree for both years. Old Ankole farmers produced significantly more coffee in 2009, but this difference disappeared in 2012. Old Ankole farmers also earn more money from coffee in 2009 and also in 2012. No significant differences in differences were observed in terms of income or production (Table 2.4).

Table 2.3. Impact evaluation strategy in Ibanda district.

	Old Ankole	New Ankole	Conventional
2009	Utz	none	none
2012	Utz	Utz	none

Table 2.4. Impact of Utz certification (Old Ankole versus New Ankole farmers).[1]

Outcome variable	2009			2012			diff-in-diff[1]
	New Ankole	Old Ankole	diff[1]	New Ankole	Old Ankole	diff[1]	
	mean	mean	mean	mean	mean	mean	mean
Income							
Coffee income (×1000)	561.6	893.7	332.1**	1,042.0	1,485.8	443.8**	111.7
Dry coffee income (×1000)	534.9	860.4	325.5**	869.9	1,411.1	541.2**	215.7
Cherry coffee income (×1000)	22.6	7.8	-14.8	42.0	40.1	-1.8	12.9
Salary income (×1000)	260.8	666.7	405.9*	24.0	93.7	69.7	336.2
Total income (×1000)	1305	2,475	1,170.5**	1,740.6	2,363.1	622.5	548.0
Production							
Coffee area (acres)	1.17	1.46	0.285*	2.15	4.53	2.37	2.09
Number of coffee trees	297	533	237**	448	669	221**	-15.9
Coffee trees per acre	333	391	57.5	322	383	61.2	3.8
Coffee yield (kg/acre)	657	698	40.9	797	916	119	78
Coffee yield (kg/tree)	2.09	2.18	0.0943	3.29	3.23	-0.0555	-0.15
Coffee cherry harvested (kg)	532	823	291**	922	1107	185	-106
Coffee sold in cherry form (kg)	56.2	23.5	-32.7	219	139	-80.6	-47.9
Dry coffee sold (kg)	328	466	139	259	417	158***	19.7
Cherry coffee price (UGX/kg)	68.8	38.5	-30.4	167	130	-36.8	-6.41
Dry coffee price (UGX/kg)	1,210	1,222	11.8	221	317	95.2	83.4
Investments							
Made house improvements	0.22	0.282	0.0618	1.74	1.53	-0.21**	-0.272**
Investment new coffee (×1000)	15.9	25.1	9.2	12.7	45.4	32.8*	23.6
Perceptions and participation							
Economic situation vs. 5 years ago	1.58	1.33	-0.249*	1.95	1.6	-0.348**	-0.10
Economic situation vs. 5 years later	1.28	1.18	-0.10	1.46	1.31	-0.151	-0.05
Number of organisations	2.33	2.46	0.134	1.19	1.31	0.113	-0.02
Satisfaction technical assistance	4.78	7.96	3.18**	2.74	4.4	1.66***	-1.52*
Satisfaction trade assistance	4.26	7.51	3.26**	3.01	4.26	1.25**	-2.01**
Identification index	2.59	4.17	1.58**	1.81	2.35	0.533	-1.05**
Force index	2.64	4.19	1.55**	1.82	2.34	0.525	-1.02**
Willingness to pay ac (×1000)	6,969	6,138.0	-830.7	15,378	12,792	-2,586	-1,755
Willingness to rent ac (×1000)	526.9	528.7	1.8	281.8	885.6	603.8**	602.0*
Risk							
Risk index	1.99	2.02	0.0361	2.18	2.12	-0.0614	-0.0975

[1] Significance:* P<0.1; ** P<0.05; *** P<0.01.

No differences were observed in terms of wealth (not reported in Table 2.4). Looking at investments we see that New Ankole farmers started to invest more in house improvements over time, compared to Old Ankole farmers. Although the 'difference in difference' is not significant, we observe a significant difference in 2012 in investment in new coffee, while this difference was not observed in 2009.

The most significant difference in difference estimates are observed in the domain of perceptions and participation. While Old Ankole farmers were more satisfied with technical and trade assistance from Ankole, identified themselves more with the organisation and scored higher on the force index, differences between the two groups got smaller in 2012 (satisfaction) or even disappeared (identification and force index). Another significant difference is the difference in willingness to rent an acre, where Old Ankole farmers became much more willing to rent an acre compared to New Ankole farmers.

2.3.3 Comparison 2: Old Ankole versus conventional

Comparing Old Ankole farmers with conventional farmers we do not observe differences in production over time. Income from dry and cherry coffee is higher for Old Ankole farmers in 2012, while income from cherry coffee was higher for conventional farmers in 2009. This change over time is significant (Table 2.5).

No significant differences were observed in terms of wealth (not reported in Table 2.5), while conventional farmers made more investments in house improvement over time compared to Old Ankole farmers. This corresponds with the trends observed in perceptions and participation variables. Both groups of farmers became more optimistic about their economic situation now and in the future, but the difference over time for the conventional farmers is significantly more compared to the difference for Old Ankole farmers. Conventional farmers also got more satisfied with technical and trade assistance, identified themselves more with the organisation and scored higher on the force index, while the Old Ankole farmers scored less on these subjects over time.

2.3.4 Comparison 3: New Ankole versus conventional

Comparing New Ankole with conventional farmers does not show significant differences in 2009 or in 2012 (Table 2.6). Comparing over time shows 'difference in difference' for coffee yield per acre and coffee trees per acre, where conventional farmers increased both compared to New Ankole farmers. All other variables do not show significant differences between these groups, except for perceptions and participation. New Ankole farmers scored higher than conventional farmers in 2009 on many variables. Over time all significant differences from 2009 disappeared, mostly because conventional farmers scored higher on, for instance, topics such as satisfaction, identification and the cooperative force index, while New Ankole farmers scored lower on these topics.

Table 2.5. Impact of Utz certification (Old Ankole versus conventional farmers).

Outcome variable	2009			2012			diff-in-diff[1]
	Conventional	Old Ankole	diff[1]	Conventional	Old Ankole	diff[1]	
	mean	mean	mean	mean	mean	mean	mean
Income							
Coffee income (×1000)	541.8	872.8	331.0*	1,154.7	1,447.8	293.1	-37.9
Dry coffee income (×1000)	507.5	837.7	330.2*	1,018.5	1,369.0	350.5*	20.3
Cherry coffee income (×1000)	33.8	8.2	-25.5**	15.6	42.3	26.7*	52.3***
Salary income (×1000)	515.4	670.3	154.9	66.6	98.8	32.2	-122.7
Total income (×1000)	1,664.4	2,455.6	791.3	1,855.3	2,372.6	517.4	-273.9
Production							
Coffee area (acres)	1.37	1.4	0.0317	1.84	4.64	2.8	2.77
Number of coffee trees	382	478	96.2	484	625	140	44.2
Coffee trees per acre	321	381	60.5	390	384	-6.57	-67
Coffee yield (kg/acre)	513	709	196	1,241	929	-312	-509
Coffee yield (kg/tree)	2.4	2.25	-0.145	5.13	3.18	-1.95	-1.81
Coffee cherry harvested (kg)	596	828	232	1,128	1,066	-61.8	-294
Coffee sold in cherry form (kg)	90.2	24.8	-65.4**	157	146	-11.1	54.3
Dry coffee sold (kg)	251	467	216**	327	398	71.2	-145
Cherry coffee price (UGX/kg)	62.6	40.5	-22	94.7	137	42.4	64.5
Dry coffee price (UGX/kg)	1,383	1,24	-142	356	334	-21.9	120
Investments							
Made house improvements	0.271	0.284	0.013	1.8	1.530	-0.27***	-0.29**
Investment new coffee (x1000)	11.5	15.8	4.3	20.0	37.5	17.5	13.2
Perceptions and participation							
Economic situation vs. 5 years ago	1.38	1.34	-0.0445	1.98	1.59	-0.386***	-0.341*
Economic situation vs. 5 years later	1.11	1.16	0.0522	1.64	1.26	-0.378***	-0.431***
Number of organisations	1.85	2.39	0.544***	1.07	1.28	0.214	-0.33
Satisfaction technical assistance	1.05	7.97	6.92***	3.22	4.14	0.919	-6***
Satisfaction trade assistance	0.966	7.49	6.52***	3.07	3.96	0.894	-5.63***
Identification index	0.645	4.15	3.5***	1.71	2.26	0.543*	-2.96***
Force index	0.656	4.16	3.51***	1.66	2.26	0.604*	-2.9***
Willingness to pay ac (×1000)	5,565	6,102	536	15,769	12,6	-3,169	-3,705
Willingness to rent ac (×1000)	475.4	514.1	38.7	1045.1	917.5	-127.6	-166.3
Risk							
Risk index	1.97	2.03	0.0541	2.24	2.11	-0.13**	-0.181***

[1] Significance:* $P<0.1$; ** $P<0.05$; *** $P<0.01$.

Table 2.6. Impact of Utz certification (New Ankole versus conventional farmers).

Outcome variable	2009			2012			diff-in-diff[1]
	Conventional	New Ankole	diff[1]	Conventional	New Ankole	diff[1]	
	mean	mean	mean	mean	mean	mean	mean
Income							
Coffee income (×1000)	506.7	538.2	31.5	1,112.9	1,079.9	-33.1	-64.5
Dry coffee income (×1000)	472.1	512.6	40.5	962.2	913.2	-49.1	-89.6
Cherry coffee income (×1000)	33.9	21.8	-12.0	25.1	36.8	11.7	23.8
Salary income (×1000)	457.0	252.9	-204	74.4	23.2	-51.2	153
Total income (×1000)	1,582	1,272	-310	1,775.6	1,718.4	-57.2	52.6
Production							
Coffee area (acres)	1.34	1.24	-0.103	1.78	2.45	0.663	0.77
Number of coffee trees	350	291	-59	457	415	-42.6	16.4
Coffee trees per acre	309	317	8.01	389	289	-99.8**	-108*
Coffee yield (kg/acre)	539	617	78	1,241	785	-456	-534*
Coffee yield (kg/tree)	2.46	2.07	-0.386	5.66	3.6	-2.06	-1.67
Coffee cherry harvested (kg)	608	526	-81.5	1,113	937	-176	-95
Coffee sold in cherry form (kg)	90.9	57.9	-33	182	228	46.6	79.6
Dry coffee sold (kg)	243	315	72.1	317	266	-51.3	-123
Cherry coffee price (UGX/kg)	68.7	67.5	-1.2	126	151	25.6	26.8
Dry coffee price (UGX/kg)	1,341	1,193	-147	363	261	-101	45.9
Investments							
Made house improvements	0.29	0.23	-0.06	1.77	1.74	-0.03	0.03
Investment new coffee (x1000)	9.9	15.4	5.5	19.1	13.8	-5.3	-10.8
Perceptions and participation							
Economic situation vs. 5 years ago	1.36	1.54	0.17	1.94	1.96	0.03	-0.15
Economic situation vs. 5 years later	1.13	1.26	0.14	1.59	1.43	-0.16	-0.30*
Number of organisations	1.77	2.26	0.49***	1.12	1.19	0.069	-0.42*
Satisfaction technical assistance	1.18	4.56	3.38***	3.22	2.94	-0.279	-3.66***
Satisfaction trade assistance	1.01	4.06	3.05***	3.03	3.31	0.278	-2.78***
Identification index	0.68	2.45	1.77***	1.69	1.89	0.204	-1.57***
Force index	0.673	2.51	1.84***	1.68	1.88	0.198	-1.64***
Willingness to pay ac (×1000)	5,424	6,767	1,342*	15,117	16,061	944.9	398
Willingness to rent ac (×1000)	419.8	514.2	94.4	1,081.4	296.5	-785**	879**
Risk							
Risk index	2	2	-0.0002	2.22	2.17	-0.05	-0.05

[1] Significance:* *P*<0.1; ** *P*<0.05; *** *P*<0.01.

2.3.5 Production and quality

As shown by the survey results, coffee production of the 'New Ankole' farmers has grown significantly between 2009 and 2012. Not only have these farmers brought more of their land under coffee production, the adoption of improved farming practices has also contributed to higher yields. A farmer explains:

> I have been planting more coffee and increased the land size under coffee production. [...] Because of the pruning, mulching, pest control and harvesting mature coffee, I get better yields (FGD).

Interestingly, one of the side-effects of the increased coffee production in the area is that several new coffee factories have been established in recent years.

Problems such as low yields, the lack of reliable buyers and the prevalence of diseases like coffee wilt undermined the attractiveness of coffee farming in the area. During the FGD, it became clear that Ankole has played a major role in making coffee farming more attractive to farmers. A farmer expressed that:

> I have got motivation to grow coffee again after I had lost all that I had in the beginning (FGD).

Several farmers pointed out that they previously were not into coffee but decided to go into coffee farming because of the opportunities it offers. The following factors emerged as the most decisive in enhancing the attractiveness of coffee farming:

- *Decent coffee prices.* Ankole has been reported consistently offering higher coffee prices than other buyers in the area. Before Ankole was active, farmers had no alternative besides selling their coffee to middlemen who offered poor prices. At the time of fieldwork (June 2012), Ankole offered UGX 4,700 for high quality [processed Robusta] coffee, while other buyers offered UGX 4,300.[18]
- *Reliability.* Ankole buys high quality coffee throughout the season. As a result, farmers have the certainty that the investments they put into producing high quality coffee will result in a payoff. Furthermore, farmers have trust in Ankole's weighing system which, unlike that of the middlemen, provides accurate readings.
- *Free seedlings*. Since 2005 Ankole has been offering free seedlings to both certified and non-certified farmers. According to the staff of Ankole, the production of seedlings has quadrupled since the project started.
- *Transport cost-sharing.* Ankole offers a transport cost-sharing arrangement to the farmers from whom its buys coffee. It pays UGX 1.000 for each bag of 60 kg of coffee. Ankole is the only buyer in Ibanda district which offers this arrangement.[19]

---

[18] UGX = Ugandan Shilling, valued at 2,45 UGX/USD (January 2012)

[19] There are two ways in which coffee is transported to the factory (Ankole). First, Ankole has divided its working area in zones and has fixed buying days when its vehicles collect coffee from the different zones. Second, farmers also organise the transport themselves and pool resources to hire trucks.

- *Cheap milling charges.* Unlike other factories in the area which charge UGX 200 per kg for the milling of coffee, Ankole offers the service at UGX 50.
- *Husks are returned.* Ankole is the only factory which gives coffee husks back to farmers after the milling. To farmers this is attractive as they can use the husks as manure for the production of matoke (cooking bananas).

Both the staff of Ankole and the farmers themselves point out that good agricultural practices (e.g. pruning, mulching, hygiene when drying) have been widely adopted in the project area. As a consequence, they claim that the size and weight of berries has increased. When asked why they adopted good farming practices, farmers gave the following reasons:

- *Trainings and follow-up field visits.* Ankole has carried out numerous trainings on good farming practices. Besides enhancing the capacity of farmers, farmers have seen for themselves that good farming practices result in higher yields. Furthermore, the follow-up field visits that have been carried out to monitor farmers' compliance with good farming practices were also mentioned as having an encouraging effect (the trainings and field visits stopped in 2010).
- *Quality as a condition.* Ankole only buys high quality coffee. As such, maintaining good farming practices is a prerequisite in order to sell to Ankole.
- *Promise of a premium price.* When Ankole started training farmers in good farming practices, farmers were promised that certification would result in higher prices. While this was initially an incentive to farmers to adopt good farming practices, the premium price unfortunately has never been realised. As such, the promise of receiving a premium price and the value of certification has lost its former attractiveness to farmers.[20]

2.3.6 Middlemen

Besides motivating farmers to produce high quality coffee, the presence of Ankole as a reliable buyer offering decent prices throughout the season has the major advantage that farmers are (largely) able to bypass middlemen. Selling to middlemen is associated with two kinds of problems. First, they offer considerably lower prices than Ankole; at the time of field work this was up to UGX 400 per kg. Second, many of them reportedly use weighing scales that have been tampered with. Consequently, farmers selling to middlemen get paid less for their coffee and lose income.[21]

Middlemen, which are referred to locally as 'shake shake people', have not been completely side-lined however. The main reason for this is that middlemen pay immediately with cash, while there is always a waiting period with Ankole. After

---

[20] It remained unclear during the fieldwork why Ankole has not yet sold coffee under the certified arrangement. During an interview, the management of Ankole attributed this to the fact that certified coffee is delayed a lot in terms of payment while offering little in terms of margin.

[21] Selling to middlemen has the advantage that they are less concerned with quality. Hence, farmers tend to send their lower quality coffee to middlemen as Ankole would not accept such coffee.

selling their coffee, farmers mostly get paid within one or two days, although this can take up to eight days. A farmer explains that:

When you have immediate cash needs, selling to Ankole is not always an option so you are left with no alternative but to sell at the prevailing prices [offered by middlemen] (FGD).

Another reason why farmers sell to middlemen is that for farmers living further away from Ankole, the costs of transporting coffee are high. A farmer points out that:

> Sometimes the produce is not big enough to justify someone's efforts of travelling long distances to the factory. So then you are more inclined to sell to the shake shake people (FGD).

2.3.7 Income and welfare impact

Due to farmers' increased production, and the presence of a reliable buyer offering decent prices (Ankole), the income of farmers has increased considerably. During the FDGs, farmers indicated they have used their increased income for expenses in such areas as school fees, medical bills, housing, farm investments and savings. The FGDs also suggest a change in the farmers' economic mind-set and strategy. A farmer explains that:

> There has been a change in the traditional beliefs. The people in this area used to be involved with cattle only. Now people start to mix with coffee (FGD).

Farmers point out that there has been a shift from subsistence farming to commercial farming. In addition, they explain that in general people have started to operate in a more entrepreneurial way. For example, farmers have used their increase in income to invest in other enterprises such as animal rearing or starting a small retail shop. According to the farmers, such economic diversification has not only given them added income but also reduced risk. Another consequence is that there has been a growing demand for credit in the area, as farmers seek to invest in business opportunities.

2.3.8 Conclusions

The research in Ibanda district suggests that coffee has become an (even more) important source of income for farmers in the project area. The survey data shows that total coffee income increased for all farmers over the last three years. The provision of free seedlings, transport-cost sharing, and cheap milling charges have all contributed to the attractiveness of coffee farming and maintaining good farming practices.

The changes in the 'New Ankole' group show the positive effect of Utz certification. The fact that many of the services offered by Ankole were not restricted to certified farmers only is beneficial to the farmers involved, but impeded the measurement of impact. Furthermore, the effects of Utz certification have been indirect. Farmers have not benefited from a premium price, but mainly from the trainings that resulted in higher quality and production (and subsequently income). Most important for the positive changes observed has been the reliability of Ankole as a coffee buyer. Farmers have the certainty that they can sell their coffee throughout the coffee season at a decent price. Because Ankole only buys high quality coffee, farmers can be sure that investing in their farms and maintaining good farming practices results in a payoff.

Even when a reliable buyer is present, timely payment is crucial for the ability of farmers to bypass middlemen. While farmers sell most of their produce to Ankole, there are still farmers in the project area who sell to middlemen. This is because farmers that sell to Ankole have to wait several days before getting paid. When they have urgent cash needs, however, this is something they cannot always afford.

Ankole Coffee Processors Ltd. is a business venture and therefore looks at farmers as suppliers of coffee and concentrates on out-competing other coffee buyers. Maintaining the interest of the farmers' organisations was very challenging after the period in which they received support from Solidaridad had ended.

2.4 Findings from Kamuli district

2.4.1 Introduction

Coffee has traditionally been a cash crop in Kamuli district, Eastern Uganda. Due to poor farming practices, the quality of coffee and yields had gone down in earlier years. Due to a lack of access to the export market, coffee was sold at low prices to middlemen operating in the area. In the 2006-2010 period, the project 'Establishing an export market for certified responsible coffee with smallholder producer in Uganda' has been implemented at Kisozi sub-county in Kamuli district.[22] This project was implemented by the NGO Kulika Uganda with support from the EU and the Dutch NGO Solidaridad. It had the following main goals:
- improving productivity and quality;
- obtaining certification from Utz certified, a certification programme for responsible coffee production;
- organising farmers so that they become empowered to sell coffee without the interventions of middlemen and directly access the international market for responsible coffee.

The beneficiaries of the project were subsistence smallholder coffee farmers and their families. Initially, Ibero Uganda Ltd., a major international coffee export company,

---

[22] The project covered all nine parishes of Kisozi sub-county namely Kisozi, Namaganda, Kakunyu, Nankandulo, Lwanyama, Kakira, Kiyunga, Magogo, and Butembe.

was the certificate holder and provided the market component of the project, thereby enabling the coffee producers' access to the export market. When the project ended in 2010, Ibero discontinued its involvement. With the support of Solidaridad, Kulika continued supporting the farmers by buying and marketing the coffee and becoming the Utz certificate holder.

Since the start of the project, a total number of 3,512 coffee farmers were trained in coffee management practices and sustainable agriculture. During the trainings, the focus was on quality coffee production in conformity with Utz certified standards and providing farmers with fair coffee prices by giving them direct access to the export market. Grouping the farmers was an important part of the project. At the village level, farmers were organised into POs. A total of 141 POs were created, each comprising of about 15-30 members and headed by a democratically elected chairperson. These chairpersons, who act as key farmers in the project, used their newly acquired knowledge and skills to train the members of their respective POs in good farming practices.

Each PO has its own demonstration garden, which functions as a field training school where group meetings and practical trainings are conducted. To centralise the buying of coffee and create economies of scale, 9 Depot Committees were created, each of which represented between 10-20 POs. More recently, a farmers' company (BUTPCO) was established to ultimately take over the responsibilities of Kulika and become the certificate holder. At the time of fieldwork in June 2012, this company was expected to buy, process and sell the coffee for the 2012-2013 season with the support of Kulika.

2.4.2 Survey design

Four different groups of farmers were studied in the research, as shown in Table 2.7. Many Utz certified farmers within the Kulika project were previously part of a similar project (APEP) which may have already affected the same type of indicators to be measured in this study. We therefore selected a group of farmers that were also part of the APEP programme but did not participate in the Kulika project (Mbulamuti) and a group of farmers that were also part of the APEP programme and participated in the Kulika project (Kulika 1). Even though most farmers from the Kulika project were part of the APEP programme, some of them did not participate in it. We also looked at these farmers (Kulika 2) and used farmers from a neighbouring sub-county (Nawanyaru) as a control group for these farmers.

In the cross-sectional setting, the comparison of the Kulika 1 farmers with the Mbulamuti farmers allows us to estimate the marginal effect of Utz certification on farmers with previous training and organisation by APEP. On the other hand, the comparison of the Kulika 2 farmers that did not have the APEP training with the similar and organised farmers from the Nawanyaru sub-county isolates the (pure) effect of Utz certification by the Kulika project. Note that the data does not allow us to isolate the effects of Utz throughout time (panel-effect). This is because no Utz

Table 2.7. Impact evaluation strategy in Kamuli district.

	Kulika 1	Kulika 2	Mbulamuti	Nawanyaru
2009	APEP + Utz	Utz	APEP	none
2012	APEP + Utz	Utz	APEP	none

intervention occurred at the control groups (Mbulamuti and Nawanyaru) between the two waves of data-collection. In reporting the results we use transformations of the actual numbers (log transformation) because comparison by order of magnitude using logs is much more effective statistically as well as easier to gauge.

2.4.3 Comparison 1: Kulika 1 versus Mbulamuti

If we compare the income and production data from the APEP groups, we observe some significant differences in 2009 (Table 2.8). Mbulamuti farmers sell more coffee in cherry form, receive a higher price for cherry coffee and have a higher income from cherry coffee, compared to Kulika 1 farmers. Kulika 1 farmers received a better price for dry coffee in 2009. Most of these effects disappeared in 2012, except for the difference in price for cherry coffee, which was still higher for the Mbulamuti farmers in 2012. Looking at the difference in difference estimates, only the amount of coffee sold in cherry form is statistically significant. Mbulamuti farmers sold less coffee in cherry form in 2012, compared to 2009, while Kulika 1 farmers increased selling of cherry coffee in these 3 years.

These findings can be contextualised with findings from the qualitative study, where farmers reported positive effects on quality and production of coffee due to participation in Kulika but these gains were realised only during the project implementation. There were no statistically significant effects on coffee prices (both cherry and dry), implying that Kulika 1 farmers were not paid better prices by adopting Utz recommended practices. This result is consistent with observations from the qualitative study in which it was reported that middlemen used Kulika prices as a base to offer slightly higher prices. Thus, although Kulika involvement resulted in higher prices for farmers, this offered no advantage to the Kulika farmers since non-Kulika farmers also benefited, as this prompted the middlemen to offer similar or slightly higher prices. Besides, Ibero, the coffee exporting company, was the same company that participated in an earlier project (APEP) and benefited both the Kulika and Mbulamuti farmers.

We did not observe significant differences in wealth (not reported in Table 2.8) or investments between these two groups in 2012, nor did we observe change over time. In 2009 we observed a significant difference in investment in new coffee between the two groups. However this effect disappeared in 2012.

Table 2.8. Impact of Utz certification (Kulika 1 versus Mbulamuti farmers).

Outcome variable	2009			2012			diff-in-diff[1]
	Mbulamuti	Kulika 1	diff[1]	Mbulamuti	Kulika 1	diff[1]	
	mean	mean	mean	mean	mean	mean	mean
Income							
Coffee income (×1000)	200.3	168	-32.3	221.1	247.5	26.4	58.7
Dry coffee income (×1000)	128.8	118.6	-10.2	156	203.8	47.8	58
Cherry coffee income (×1000)	67.3	22.6	-44.7***	45.7	28.7	-17.1	27.6
Salary income (×1000)	32.5	200.1	167.7	83.5	2.3	-81.2	-248.8
Total income (×1000)	313.4	548	234.6	437.7	815	377.4	142.8
Production							
Coffee area (acres)	1.05	0.92	-0.127	3.8	1.04	-2.75	-2.63
Number of coffee trees	383	389	5.98	355	402	47.3	41.4
Coffee trees per acre	405	484	79.4	367	420	52.9	-26.5
Coffee yield (kg/acre)	612	442	-171	370	370	0.504	171
Coffee yield (kg/tree)	1.76	0.93	-0.829	1.18	1.67	0.487	1.32
Coffee cherry harvested (kg)	564	500	-64.5	340	289	-51	13.4
Coffee sold in cherry form (kg)	175	61.3	-114***	118	97.4	-20.2	94*
Dry coffee sold (kg)	130	127	-3.52	160	157	-3.19	0.336
Cherry coffee price (UGX/kg)	237	136	-102**	252	127	-124**	-22.9
Dry coffee price (UGX/kg)	439	595	157*	521	733	212	56
Investments							
Made house improvements	0.376	0.372	-0.004	1.74	1.6	-0.136	-0.132
Investment new coffee (×1000)	389	4,605	4,216**	496	15,558	15,062	10,846
Perceptions and participation							
Economic situation vs. 5 years ago	1.63	1.33	-0.306*	1.81	1.77	-0.045	0.262
Economic situation vs. 5 years later	1.49	1.23	-0.254*	1.23	1.53	0.302**	0.556***
Number of organisations	1.71	1.51	-0.199	1.09	1.16	0.071	0.27
Satisfaction technical assistance	6.34	7.65	1.31**	0.231	6.4	6.16***	4.86***
Satisfaction trade assistance	5.76	7.07	1.31**	0.198	5.86	5.66***	4.36***
Identification index	3.72	4.12	0.398*	0.158	3.71	3.55***	3.15***
Force index	3.64	4.07	0.421*	0.115	3.58	3.46***	3.04***
Willingness to pay ac (×1000)	2,398.4	2,289.7	-108.7	2,737.3	2,849	111.7	220.4
Willingness to rent ac (×1000)	131	133.9	2.9	117.5	123	5.56	2.5
Risk							
Risk index	2.01	1.92	-0.088	2.19	2.11	-0.077	0.0113

[1] Significance: * P<0.1; ** P<0.05; *** P<0.01.

There were statistically significant positive effects on perception and participation variables, probably because Kulika maintained its presence and support in terms of training and farm inputs. While Mbulamuti farmers were more optimistic about the future economic situation in 2009 compared to Kulika farmers, this changed in 2012 with Kulika farmers being more optimistic compared to Mbulamuti farmers. Kulika farmers were more satisfied with technical and trade assistance in 2009 compared to Mbulamuti farmers, and this difference only got larger. Kulika farmers also identified themselves more with the organisation and, according to the results of force index, Kulika is more efficient, reacted better in the face of events, and is more profitable, peaceful and trustworthy, compared to Mbulamuti.

2.4.4 Comparison 2: Kulika 2 versus Nawanyaru

Looking at the production and the income variables, we observe similar trends for Kulika 2 versus Nawanyaru (conventional farmers) to those observed in Comparison 1 (Table 2.9). While Nawanyaru farmers sold more cherry coffee in 2009, this changed in 2012 and the difference in difference between the two groups is significant. While there were no significant differences in 2009 in terms of yields, in 2012 Kulika farmers produce significantly less coffee per tree compared to Nawanyaru farmers. While collecting data in the field with Kulika farmers, we observed indeed many abandoned coffee plots with trees that were not pruned for a long time and weeding was not done anymore. Looking at income from dry coffee and total income from coffee we did not observe differences in 2009, while Kulika farmers significantly earn less money from coffee in 2012 compared to Nawanyaru farmers. Although the difference-in-difference is not significant, these findings are in line with the trend. The phasing out of Kulika activities and the pulling out of Ibero could be partly responsible for the change in behaviour where Kulika farmers are reverting to sale of more of their coffee in cherry form, a practice they had abandoned. Without the existence of the market that demands quality, it may not make economic sense to follow practices that would demand more labour and other resources. Besides, most farmers are economically poor, which forces them to sell their coffee early, and to any buyer, to meet their immediate financial needs. Considering results on perceptions and participation, we observe similar trends. Kulika farmers were more satisfied in 2009 and remained more satisfied compared to Nawanyaru farmers. They also scored higher on the degree of cooperative identification and the appreciation of cooperative force. The only difference in difference estimate that is significant is the number of organisations people belongs to, which declines for both groups between 2009 and 2012, but the decline is significantly higher for the conventional farmers.

2.4.5 Institutional changes

There have been a number of organisational and financial changes throughout the project period. In the first few years (2006-2010) Ibero was the certificate holder responsible for buying, processing and selling the coffee of the registered farmers. After the project ended in March 2010, Kulika took over the role of Ibero, with the

Table 2.9. Impact of Utz certification (Kulika 2 versus Nawanyaru farmers).

Outcome variable	2009			2012			diff-in-diff[1]
	Nawanyaru	Kulika 2	diff[1]	Nawanyaru	Kulika 2	diff[1]	
	mean	mean	mean	mean	mean	mean	mean
Income							
Coffee income (×1000)	311.3	242.8	-68.5	379.7	173.9	-206**	-137.3
Dry coffee income (×1000)	229.8	195.3	-34.5	324.0	129.3	-195**	-160.2
Cherry coffee income (×1000)	48.4	23.2	-25.2**	34.3	44.4	10.1	35.3*
Salary income (×1000)	62.7	199.6	136.9	0.5	97.3	96.7	-40.2
Total income (×1000)	430.2	655.5	225.3	568.2	470.6	-97.6	-322.9
Production							
Coffee area (acres)	0.829	1.09	0.265	1.03	1.21	0.179	-0.09
Number of coffee trees	522	413	-109	368	313	-54.4	54.4
Coffee trees per acre	484	383	-101	330	285	-45.2	55.7
Coffee yield (kg/acre)	695	709	14.2	349	260	-88.8	-103
Coffee yield (kg/tree)	2.09	1.76	-0.33	1.63	1.12	-0.51*	-0.187
Coffee cherry harvested (kg)	650	562	-87.2	354	210	-144	-57.2
Coffee sold in cherry form (kg)	131	53.3	-77.3**	115	92.3	-22.7	54.6
Dry coffee sold (kg)	229	178	-50.3	262	121	-141**	-90.6
Cherry coffee price (UGX/kg)	191	119	-72.2*	209	243	34.4	107
Dry coffee price (UGX/kg)	627	715	88.9	807	751	-55.8	-145
Investments							
Made house improvements	0.216	0.375	0.159*	1.56	1.75	0.189	0.03
Investment new coffee (×1000)	1,838	9,075	7,237	575	7,618	7,043*	-194
Perceptions and participation							
Econ. sit. versus 5 years ago	1.79	1.47	-0.317*	1.84	1.73	-0.117	0.2
Econ. sit. versus 5 years later	1.41	1.32	-0.082	1.39	1.28	-0.116	-0.034
Number of organisations	1.5	1.5	0.001	0.792	1.42	0.633**	0.632**
Satisfaction technical assistance	2.8	7.92	5.13***	1.04	6.07	5.04**	-0.093
Satisfaction trade assistance	2.44	6.78	4.33***	0.72	4.9	4.18**	-0.155
Identification index	1.61	3.83	2.22***	0.748	3.43	2.68**	0.452
Force index	1.62	3.83	2.21***	0.649	3.29	2.65**	0.432
Willingness to pay ac (×1000)	2,229.6	1,986.8	-242.8	2,605.1	2,745.7	140.7	383.5
Willingness to rent ac (×1000)	138.1	145.4	7.2	152.0	144.2	-7.9	-15.1
Risk							
Risk index	1.97	2.09	0.119*	2.11	2.2	0.089	-0.0304

[1] Significance: * P<0.1; ** P<0.05; *** P<0.01.

support of Solidaridad. In 2010, Kulika sold the coffee to Ugacof Ltd., who exported it as Utz certified coffee. In 2011, however, the coffee was sold as conventional coffee. Since the end of the project, the number of Kulika staff has been vastly reduced due to financial constraints. At the time of 2nd round of fieldwork (June 2012), for example, only three staff members of Kulika remained active. In more practical terms, this meant that since 2010 Kulika has become less and less active in terms of activities and contact with farmers. Because Kulika aims to phase out its involvement in the project area, it established a farmers' company (BUTPCO) in 2011, which is to take over the role of Kulika. This company will be responsible for a number of tasks, including carrying out farmer certification, promoting group production and the buying, processing and selling of coffee. Kulika staff explained that in terms of sustainability, much will depend on whether the newly established company will have the capacity to operate independently.

2.4.6 Quality and production

The qualitative research suggests that the project had positive effects on the quality and production of coffee in the period it was implemented (2006-2010). Before the project started, coffee was no longer an important cash crop for most farmers and some had given up on coffee farming altogether, partly because of the prevalence of coffee wilt disease. Many farmers sold their coffee 'green', meaning that the coffee was sold when the berries were not yet ripe. Also, it was common practice to dry coffee berries on the ground. When the project started, farmers learned about the importance of adopting good farming practices in areas such as sustainable coffee production, hygiene and sanitation, marketing, record-keeping and environmental conservation. Amongst other things, farmers were trained on how to selectively pick, dry and store the coffee properly.

> Before Kulika came, we used to harvest all the berries on the plant at the same time, not minding the ripe and raw ones. But now we only pick the ripe ones, making the harvesting period much longer (FGD).

According to Kulika staff and interviewed farmers, the project has led to widespread adoption of good farming practices, and as a result, an improvement of the quality of coffee produced in the project area. Farmers also explained that their production increased during the project-period due to higher yields per tree, more land that was brought under coffee production and a higher coffee tree stand per acreage as a result of gap filling and replanting.[23]

---

[23] For reasons that will be explained further below, many of the benefits associated with improved quality and production, however, did not appear to be sustainable.

2.4.7 Competition from middle men

Group interviews also revealed that the presence of Ibero/Kulika as a buyer had a positive effect on the prices offered for coffee in the area. Once Ibero/Kulika start buying, middlemen are forced to match the price that is offered, resulting in income benefits for farmers. In 2011, for example, coffee sold to middlemen yielded UGX 600 per kilo. When Kulika started buying coffee at UGX 1,800, however, the middlemen matched immediately, even to the point that they offered higher prices than Kulika. A staff member of Kulika explains that:

> They [middlemen] are listening as to how much we are buying and give an added price. So when we start from 2,000, they will come to 2,100. When we go to 2,100, they will go to 2,300, so they go ahead of us (interview staff member Kulika).

While beneficial for the farmers, the matching behaviour of the middlemen has also made things more complicated for Kulika. Because middlemen are paying high prices, it has been difficult to realise high volumes and make accurate buying predictions.

2.4.8 Incentives

The project provided a number of incentives to make coffee-farming and adopting good farming practices attractive to farmers. During the FGDs, the following incentives emerged as the most decisive ones:

- *Higher yields.* The prospect of achieving higher yields formed a major incentive for farmers to adopt good farming practices. As a farmer explains:

> We used to think that whenever you grow a coffee plant, it would cater for itself, that you just have to wait for earning money. When Kulika came we learned that a coffee plant ought to be cared for. We saw that plants which had been cared for yield more than the ones not cared for (FGD).

- *Higher prices.* Farmers were told that producing better quality coffee would result in higher prices. For example, in 2011 selling to middlemen yielded between 500-600 UGX per kg, while Kulika offered 1,500-1,800 UGX per kg of dried coffee beans. Farmers were also told that certified coffee would result in a premium price, but this never materialised.
- *Trainings and follow-up visits.* Farmers received training and their knowledge and skills on coffee farming were enhanced. Additional follow-up visits were carried out by Kulika staff to assess the performance of the farmers and provide feedback. The trainings and farm visits encouraged farmers to implement the skills and knowledge learned.
- *Provision of inputs.* To stimulate farmers to adopt good practices, demonstration plots and coffee and shade tree seedlings nurseries were established and

competitions were organised in which farm tools, equipment, planting materials and agro-chemicals were distributed to the best-performing farmers.

2.4.9 Delays in buying

Perhaps the biggest problem with the project that emerged during the FGDs is that the coffee has been consistently bought too late in the season. In Kamuli district, the harvesting season runs from July till December. Table 2.10 shows that, throughout the years, certified coffee is bought increasingly towards the end of the coffee farming season.

The late buying of coffee – initially by Ibero and later by Kulika – has major consequences for the project. Due to high levels of poverty in the area and the need of farmers to meet their cash needs, most farmers simply cannot wait that long to sell their coffee. A farmer explains:

> When we have urgent problems like sickness or school fees, we have no choice but to sell to the middlemen because Kulika buys too late (FGD).

The project manager of Kulika estimated that in 2011 project farmers sold 85% of their coffee to middlemen. What makes the selling of coffee to middlemen so problematic is that they offer very poor prices while farmers are not in a position to negotiate. Besides Kulika there are no other buyers in the project area offering decent prices for high quality.

Furthermore, there is an absence of competition between middlemen who, according to farmers, make price agreements. Transporting coffee to other areas was not considered a feasible option by farmers due to high transport costs. In summary, farmers have no choice but to sell their coffee at a low price. What makes the situation even worse is that the middlemen are known to work with tampered weighing scales. The late buying of coffee means that the positive effects of the presence of Ibero/Kulika as a buyer (see above) only apply for a limited amount of time each year.

Table 2.10. Month of coffee buying in Uganda.

Year	Month	Buyer
2007	September	Ibero
2008	October	Ibero
2009	November	Ibero
2010	December	Kulika
2011	December	Kulika

2.4.10 Loss of attractiveness

Farmers explained that it has become progressively less attractive for them to engage in coffee farming and maintain good farming practices. The main problem is that in their eyes Ibero and Kulika have not appeared to be reliable buyers. Since the project started, coffee has been bought late in the season and this has worsened over time. Due to the absence of alternative buyers offering decent prices, farmers have been forced to sell their produce to middlemen. The consistently late buying of coffee has undermined farmers' confidence in Kulika as a reliable buyer. This confidence is further undermined by the declining support offered by Kulika (trainings, follow-up visits, provision inputs) since 2010 and the news that it is phasing out in the area.

Farmers also pointed out that when selling to middlemen, better quality does not always result in a better price. Coffee berries that are still green yield the same price as those that have been dried. Because farmers sell most of their produce to middlemen, their motivation to maintain good farming practices has been undermined. This was confirmed by Kulika staff who explained that it had been difficult to motivate farmers to maintain good farming practices. As one farmer expresses:

> Imagine drying your coffee for nine days and getting almost the same price like someone who just dried for three days. [...] This means quality is not paying [...] Therefore, doing all the work [maintaining good farming practices] is not worth the effort (FGD).

Overall, the qualitative research suggests that farmers are less inclined to maintain good farming practices. This is also reflected in the available statistics which show that farmers have been dropping out of Utz certification since the project ended (Table 2.11). This was also apparent during the fieldwork in which numerous coffee plots were encountered that had not been maintained.

Table 2.11. Utz certified farmers in Uganda (2007-2011).

Year	Number of certifications
2007	3,044
2008	3,088
2009	3,234
2010	3,288
2011	2,731

2.4.11 Conclusions

The results from the field research in Kamuli district provide a mixed image. On the one hand, the project successfully provided incentives to make coffee farming and the adoption of good practices attractive by means of trainings, follow-up visits, demonstration plots, coffee and shade tree seedlings nurseries and the provision of farming materials. Farmers saw for themselves that the adoption of good practices resulted in higher yields, according to the qualitative data. The qualitative analysis also showed that the attractiveness of coffee farming and maintaining good practices deteriorated when the project ended. The quantitative data captures the 2009-2012 period and the positive effects reported in the qualitative data refer to the 2006-2010 period.

The positive effects reported in the interviews could not be captured in the quantitative data, which showed declining yields and declining total production. This trend was observed for both treatment and control groups. The findings suggest that the positive effects reported in the qualitative data were mainly limited to the period of project implementation (2006-2010), and could therefore not be found in the quantitative data from the 2009-2012 period. In other words, the project benefits do not seem to have been sustainable.

Thus far, the project has not succeeded in creating sustainable incentives for farmers to engage in coffee farming and maintain good farming practices. The second problem has been the lack of a reliable buyer that purchases coffee throughout the farming season at a decent price. In the months Ibero/Kulika buys coffee, the monopoly of middlemen in the area is successfully broken and farmers get substantially higher prices for their coffee. Most of the season, however, farmers have no alternative to selling to middlemen due to the delay in coffee buying. For the farmers it became less attractive over time to maintain good (but time-consuming) farming practices and engage in coffee production. The decreasing attractiveness of maintaining good farming practices has been further accelerated by the decline in the support offered by Kulika and the news that Kulika is phasing out its support.

2.5 General conclusions and outlook

This chapter investigates the impact of Utz certification at producer and producer organisation level. Two targeted coffee cooperatives in Uganda were studied during a three year period – Kulika in Kamuli district and Ankole Coffee Processors Limited in Ibanda district. The outcomes of the research proved to be rather positive for Ibanda district and more mixed results are registered for Kamuli district.

2.5.1 Ibanda district: Ankole

The Ankole case suggests that coffee has become an important source of income for farmers in the area and shows the positive impact of Utz certification. The provision of free seedlings, transport-cost sharing, and cheap milling charges have all contributed to the attractiveness of coffee farming and offer incentives for maintaining good farming practices. The reliability of Ankole as a coffee buyer has been essential in bringing about the positive changes observed. Farmers have the certainty that they can sell their coffee throughout the coffee season at a decent price. Because Ankole only buys high quality coffee, farmers can be sure that investing in their farms and maintaining good farming practices pays off.

Even when a reliable buyer is present, minimum delay in payment is crucial for the ability of farmers to bypass middlemen. While farmers sell most of their produce to Ankole, there are still farmers in the project area who sell to middlemen. This is because farmers that sell to Ankole have to wait several days before getting paid. When they have urgent cash needs, however, this is something they can ill afford. Farmers' perceptions were negatively affected between the period 2009 and 2012, probably because they anticipated greater benefits which did not materialise after the withdrawal of Solidaridad support.

Another interesting finding is the observed change in attitude from subsistence farming to a more entrepreneurial approach towards farming, which seems directly related to the Utz certification. This also results in a large demand for credit facilities. Although credit is provided by Ankole, it is far too little to meet the demand.

2.5.2 Kamuli district: Kulika

Looking at Kulika, the project successfully provided incentives to make coffee farming and the adoption of good agricultural practices attractive by means of trainings, follow-up visits, demonstration plots, coffee and shade tree seedlings nurseries and the provision of farming materials. Farmers saw for themselves that the adoption of good practices resulted in higher yields, according to the qualitative data.

However, this is not reflected in the quantitative performance data that show declining yields and declining total production. Kulika participated in an EU-funded project that ended in 2010. The coffee trader involved in that project (Ibero) pulled out at the end of the project. The findings suggest that the positive effects reported in the qualitative data were mainly limited to the period of project implementation (2006-2010), and could therefore not be traced in the quantitative data that cover the 2009-2012 period. In other words, it seems that the project benefits have not been sustainable. However, farmers' perceptions about assistance provided and participation in organisations remained positive for Kulika farmers, largely because Kulika maintained a presence even after the withdrawal of Ibero. There were no serious coffee buyers offering better services than Kulika. Instead the middlemen buying coffee in the area are most interested in short term gains, do not offer competitive prices and are mindless of coffee quality.

The main problem – when Ibero withdrew – has been the lack of a reliable buyer that purchases coffee throughout the farming season at a decent price. Throughout the project period, coffee has been consistently bought too late in the season. For the farmers it became less attractive over time to maintain good farming practices and engage in coffee production. This has been reinforced by the decline of the support offered by Kulika and the news that Kulika is phasing out its support. Recently a farmers' company (BUTPCO) was established to ultimately take over the responsibilities of Kulika and become the certificate holder. Much will depend on the success of this newly established company.

References

Buchanayandi, T.N. (1996). The impact of coffee market liberalization: the Uganda experience.' Improving coffee management system in Africa. In: Proceedings of IAC workshop, Kampala, Uganda, September 6, 1995. African Crop Science Society, pp. 7-12.

Bussolo, M., O. Godart, J. Lay and P. Thiele (2007). The impact of coffee price changes on rural households in Uganda. *Agricultural Economics* 37(2-3): 293-303.

Common Fund for Commodities (CFC) (2001). *Characteristics of the demand for robusta coffee in Europe.* Technical Report 4. Amsterdam, the Netherlands: Common Fund for Commodities.

Compete (2002). The path forward in Uganda's coffee sector. Paper for the COMPETE Presidential Conference on export competitiveness, Kampala, February 2001. Available at: http://tinyurl.com/q58gkvx.

Lazaro, E.A. and J.A. Makindara (2008). Sustainable coffee exports from Tanzania. SAFE Policy Brief 3. Available at: http://tinyurl.com/q96fr8f.

Otim, S. and P.K. Ngategize (1993). Uganda coffee supply response and export demand: an econometric analysis. *African Crop Science Journal* 1(2): 175-182.

Ponte, S. (2001). *Coffee markets in East Africa: local responses to global challenges or global responses to local challenges?* CDR Working Paper 01.5. Copenhagen, Denmark: Centre for Development Research.

Sayer, G. (2002). *The impact of falling world prices on livelihoods in Uganda.* Coffee futures, Uganda coffee report for Oxfam. Unpublished research report for Oxfam GB. Oxford, UK: Oxfam GB.

You, L. and S. Boldwig (2003). *Alternative growth scenarios for Ugandan coffee to 2020.* Environment and Production Technology Division (EPTD) 98. Washington, DC, USA: International Food Policy Research Institute (IFPRI).

Chapter 3

The effects of coffee certification in Kenya

Bart van Rijsbergen, Willem Elbers, Luuk van Kempen, Ruerd Ruben, Paul Hoebink with Mzeeh Hamisi Ngutu, Urbanus Mutwiwa and Samuel Njuguna
For correspondence: bart-van.rijsbergen@minbuza.nl; b.vanrijsbergen@maw.ru.nl

3.1 Introduction

Sustainability standards like Fair Trade (FT) or Utz certified (Utz) are widely regarded as a promising way of improving smallholder coffee farmer welfare. As yet, the impact of certification remains poorly understood. This chapter presents the findings of the study regarding the impact of FT and Utz in Kenya.[24] The study was carried out in the Kiambu and Nyeri districts of Kenya (Figure 3.1). The study is based on two waves of data collection carried out in 2009 and 2013 with farmers belonging to six cooperative societies: Ndumberi, Tekangu, Kiambaa, Mikari, Rugi and Kiama. This chapter aims to answer the following central research question: *What is the impact of FT/Utz involvement at producer and producer organisation level in Kenya?*

To address this question, we used both quantitative and qualitative methods. We aimed to provide detailed descriptions of both processes and outcomes from the coffee certification program through a triangulation of methods and data sources. It is important to note that we do not only analyse data from the six coffee cooperatives but particularly focus on the net effects derived from certification, which means that attention is focussed at differences derived from specific certification regimes. Primary data was collected from 600 farmers through two rounds of farm visit interviews in 2009 and 2013, using structured questionnaires administered to respondents (mainly the household head). A total of 493 of the same farmers were revisited in the 2013 wave.[25] The sample size composition is depicted in Table 3.1, while detailed

---

[24] This study was carried out within the framework of the Irish Aid programme 'Building Trade Capacity and Sustainable Livelihoods through Fair Trade and Ethical Trade' in East Africa'. Field work was carried out in cooperation between the Centre for International Development Issues Nijmegen (CIDIN) and Noble Consultants Limited with support from Solidaridad East and Central Africa (SECAEC).

[25] Analysis of attrition will be part of a separate analysis.

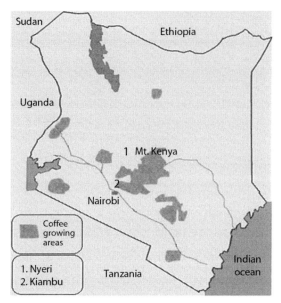

Figure 3.1. Kenya coffee producing areas and location of case studies.

Table 3.1. Sample composition: number of farmers included in study.

Cooperative		2009	2013
Kiambu district			
Ndumberi	treatment	80	62
Kiambaa	control	100	74
Mikari	control	120	93
Nyeri district			
Tekangu	treatment	80	77
Rugi	control	100	85
Kiama	control	120	102
Total		600	493

descriptions of the treatment (certified farmers) and control groups (non-certified farmers) are reported in Annex A.1, Table A.2 and general information on Kiambu and Nyeri districts is provided in Annex A.1, Table A.3.

With regard to the quantitative component, the study combines:
1. 'with and without' assessment of certification by comparing FT and Utz (treatment) with non-certified (control) cooperatives in different sites; and
2. 'before and after' analysis of certification by comparing treatment and control cooperatives at the baseline (2009) with ex-post survey (2013) outcomes.

We thus rely on a 'difference in difference' estimator, while correcting for selection bias by using propensity score matching (PSM). This gives a balanced comparison of the net effects of certification, after matching for intrinsic farm household characteristics that influence the likelihood of being certified (Annex A.1, Table A.4). The distribution of the PSM scores after matching (Annex A.1, Table A.5) indicates that both sub-samples provide an adequate base for comparison.

The sample taken in both districts consists of three cooperatives with different trajectories of certification in force (Table 3.2). In Kiambu district, attention is focussed on FT and Utz (double) certification that is compared with non-certified cooperatives, while in Nyeri district mainly Utz certified cooperatives are compared with not-certified farmers and an incipient FT certified cooperative.[26]

In this study, four different panel-data estimations are reported, taking the certification status of the cooperatives in 2013 into account (Table 3.2):
• A comparisons of changes in performance over time, comparing FT cooperatives with non-certified (NC) cooperatives (change at Kiambaa cooperative versus change at Mikari cooperative.
• A comparison of change at Rugi cooperative (recent FT certification) versus change at Kiama cooperative), in order to capture the effect of FT.
• A comparison of the change in performance over time for an Utz certified cooperative (Tekangu) and a non-certified cooperative (Kiama), in order to capture the effect of Utz.
• A comparison of the change in performance over time between an Utz certified cooperative (Tekangu) and a FT cooperative (Rugi), in order to capture the difference between Utz and FT benefits.

Table 3.2. Fair Trade and Utz certification of the cooperatives in the study (data for the impact analysis was collected in 2009 and 2013).

District	Cooperatives	2009	N	2010	2011	2012	2013	N
Kiambu	Ndumberi	FT + Utz	80	FT + Utz	FT + Utz	FT + Utz	FT + Utz	62
	Kiambaa	none	100	none	FT	FT	FT	74
	Mikari	none	120	none	none	none	none	93
Nyeri	Tekangu	Utz	80	Utz	Utz	Utz	Utz	77
	Rugi	none	100	none	none	none	none / FT	85
	Kiama	none	120	none	none	none	none	102

---

[26] Rugi cooperative was about to become FT certified when the 2013 survey was carried out. Rugi's board had received training in good management practices while its farmers had been trained in good agricultural practices. The cooperative, however, had not yet sold its coffee as FT certified. As such, the survey data from the 2013 round provides useful information for assessing the effects of FT trainings but not for assessing the impact of FT prices. Furthermore we need to remark that the relative position of Rugi versus Kiama was more difficult at baseline, looking at baseline data.

To contextualise the survey findings and understand the processes underlying certification, further in-depth qualitative research was carried out in January and February 2013. This included focus group discussions (FGDs) with Fair Trade certified farmers, Utz certified farmers and non-certified farmers. A total of 13 FGDs were carried out; in each FGD 15 to 25 farmers participated. In addition, semi-structured interviews were conducted with representatives of relevant stakeholders, including board members of the cooperatives. This research focused on production, quality and income parameters and the main problems experienced by farmers and cooperative Boards.[27] All FGDs and semi-structured interviews were recorded and transcribed for analysis.

The outline of the remaining sections of this chapter is as follows. Section 3.2 offers a brief characterisation of the Kenyan coffee sector. Section 3.3 presents the main findings of the fieldwork and the results of the data-analysis, focussing respectively on direct welfare effects and indirect spill-over effects. Section 3.4 outlines the institutional implications of certification, followed by an assessment of the key challenges at farm-household level (Section 3.5) and cooperative level (Section 3.6). Section 3.7 puts the findings in a regional perspective and finally Section 3.8 revisits the main research questions and outlines the policy conclusions of the study.

3.2 The Kenyan coffee sector

The findings of the study can be contextualised by providing an overview of the historical background and recent development of the Kenyan coffee sector. We therefore discuss the history and importance of coffee farming in Kenya and give an overview of the various coffee varieties that are grown. The processes of coffee cultivation and processing are discussed, followed by a review of the organisation of the coffee sector and a summary of the performance of the Kenyan coffee sector (i.e. cultivated area, yield level, volumes produced, prices and quality). Finally, we provide an overview of the organisation of the marketing system and recent trends in terms of pricing.

3.2.1 History and importance

Kenya's economy is dependent on agriculture, with an annual direct and indirect contribution to gross domestic product of 24 and 27%, respectively. Ideal temperate and climatic conditions make the country favourable for the production and development of a variety of crops and livestock. In Kenya, agriculture and forestry continue to be the main drivers of the economy, with its share increasing from 21.4% in 2010 to 24.0% in 2011 (KNBS, 2012). Coffee ranks fourth after tourism, tea and horticulture, in terms of the total export earnings, e.g. coffee accounted for 10% of the total export earnings in 2000 and 6% in 2001.

---

[27] Interview guides are available upon request with the authors.

As one of the most important export crops, coffee plays a crucial role in the livelihoods of millions of rural households in Kenya. A large number of smallholder coffee farmers depend directly on coffee as their primary source of income. Coffee also contributes significantly to foreign exchange earnings and plays a leading role in providing opportunities for employment and demands for infrastructure development. There are a number of famous coffee-producing regions in the world, and Kenya is ranked the 17th largest coffee producer worldwide. Not only is it used in its 'pure' form, but Kenyan coffee is also popular to create blends for the market and the global demand for Kenyan coffee has meant that the industry plays a significant part in the country's economy.

Coffee originated in the Kaffa region of Ethiopia where it grows naturally (NCA USA, 2013). The Holy Ghost Fathers of the French Catholic Church, who planted coffee trees at Bura near Taita Hills in the early 1890s brought the Bourbon seeds to Kenya. At this time, the Protestant Scottish missionaries were experimenting with Mocha seedlings at various stations in Kenya, including Kibwezi (1893) and Kikuyu. In the earlier years only settlers grew coffee, but this was liberalised shortly after independence.

Kenya produces some of the best coffee in the world, notably the 'fully washed mild', more flavourful *Coffea arabica*. This variety performs well due to the well-distributed rainfall, high altitude (1,500-2,000 metres above sea level) and therefore moderate temperatures (averaging 20 °C), with characteristically high equatorial ultraviolet sunlight diffusing through thick clouds, and deep red volcanic soils.

In Kenya, most coffee is grown in the triangular area between Mt. Kenya, the Aberdare Range and Machakos Town – essentially the Central and Eastern Provinces. This area accounts for over 70% of Kenya's coffee production. Table 3.3 provides detailed information on the areas under coffee production in Kenya.

Table 3.3. Area under coffee production and production in Kenya (estimates for 2008-2012) (KCTA, 2012a).

Province	Area in hectares		Production in metric tonnes		Active cooperative societies	
	Cooperatives	Estates	Cooperatives	Estates	Cooperatives	Active grower members
Central	40,636	16,648	17,985	21,123	97	260,048
Coast	80	-	5	-	1	245
Eastern	26,269	3,197	9,625	2,343	131	174,237
Nyanza	7,139	178	1,280	32	40	80,118
Rift Valley	4,206	4,399	1,577	1,465	113	17,963
Western	6,717	183	1,266	34	39	38,213

3.2.2 Coffee varieties grown in Kenya

Kenya predominantly grows the Arabica variety, which is processed using the wet method.[28] Over time, various research activities (led by the Coffee Research Foundation and universities) geared towards selection and breeding have taken place. These activities mainly focussed on addressing issues of coffee berry disease, drought resistance, flavour, leaf rust, mealybug and other pests and diseases. This led to the development of two popular super strains/varieties developed before independence which account for over 90% of Kenya's coffee, namely: (1) Scott Laboratory (SL28) which is Mocha-dominated, not particularly high yielding, drought resistant and superior in taste, and (2) SL 34 which is a high yielder across a variety of altitudes and climate. Other varieties as described by the Coffee Research Foundation are: (3) Kent varieties K7 and K20 planted in Meru in 1934, the former being resistant to leaf rust but of poor flavour and the latter very susceptible to coffee berry disease, and (4) Ruiru 11, released in 1985, which is resistant to coffee berry disease and leaf rust, but its Robusta genes have resulted in a taste that is inferior to the SL varieties.[29] Production characteristics of the main coffee varieties are as shown in Table 3.4.

3.2.3 Coffee cultivation and processing

There are two flowerings in each season and the blossom normally appears shortly after the beginning of the long rains in March and April. The main crop ripens from October until December in most coffee producing districts in Kenya. The second and smaller flowering comes with the short rains in October and November and

Table 3.4. Yield of main coffee varieties grown in Kenya (Coffee Research Foundation, 2013).

Variety	Yield (kg cherry/ tree)	Yield of clean coffee (tonnes/ha)	Outturn (12-20% in Arabica coffee (%)	Grade AA + AB (%)	100 bean weight (g)
SL28	8.52	1.8	18.24	80	20
SL34	6.11	1.35	14.4	62	30
K7	9.05	2.01	14.5	68	24
Ruiru 11	8.39	4.6	17.79	70	25

[28] Globally, there are two primary types of coffee, Arabica and Robusta. Arabica accounts for 70% of world production while Robusta comprises only 30% of the total market. Arabica is considered to be of higher quality and a more aromatic type of the coffee.

[29] Other minor varieties include: (a) Blue Mountain, introduced in Western Kenya from Jamaica in 1913 due to its resistance to coffee berry disease (CBD), (4) Bourbon grown in the Solai area of the Rift Valley, and (b) Batian, released in 2010, which has features similar to SL28 but which is resistant to CBD and leaf rust. In addition it starts production in the 2nd year of planting (other traditional varieties take three years) and its cherry ripening comes earlier than the traditional varieties. The cup is described as well balanced, sweet, and full bodied with a very pleasant aftertaste (Anmer Coffee, 2010; Kimemia, 2011).

is picked in the early part of the season, often starting in the following June. Farm-level operations include planting, weeding, fertilising, pruning, spraying, and picking/harvesting of red cherries.

During the harvest, only ripe red cherries are picked and pulped to remove the outer skin without injuring the bean inside. The cherry is then transported to a wet mill. At the wet mill, the cherries are weighed and pulped to remove the outer skin. Afterwards, the cherries are sorted through water density separation. In 2005, there were 4,021 licensed pulping stations, of which 1,021 belong to the cooperative societies, 2,229 to small estates, 391 to medium estates and 380 to large estates (Kinoti, 2005). After pulping, the beans are fermented for 12 to 72 hours, thoroughly rinsed, then soaked for 16 hours, followed by more rinsing and finally sun-drying down to 12-15% moisture on raised screen beds. The parchment is moved to conditioning bins before transport to the dry mill.

Milling plant operations involve pre-cleaning (removal of light material such as wool and papers), de-stoning (removal of heavy material that may be present in the coffee), hulling (removal of parchment/husks on the coffee) and polishing (removal of the silver skin/seed coat). Grading is also done, which involves arranging the bean sizes as per the grades (AA, AB, C, TT, T, E, PB) with corresponding names of screen sizes. The coffee is then packed in 60 kg sacks and transported to the warehouse. Major coffee millers include Thika Coffee Mills, Kenya Planters' Cooperative Union, Central Kenya Coffee Mills, Sasini Coffee Mills, Kofinaf, and Nyambene.

3.2.4 Organisation and production of the sector

The Kenya coffee sector is characterised by two types of farms: plantations (estates) and cooperatives. The plantation sub-sector consists of about 454 farms, with large estates cultivating about 24,605 ha. The cooperative sub-sector is made up of 422 cooperative unions, representing about 570,824 smallholders cultivating about 85,106 ha, equivalent to about 0.2 hectares apiece (KCTA, 2012a). Only large-scale farmers and estates irrigate their coffee and have 'stable' access to financial services. According to the Economic Survey (KNBS, 2012), the area under estates is about one third that occupied by the cooperatives, as shown in Figure 3.2.

Kenya's coffee cooperative system was formed after the end of World War II and is regulated by the government under the Cooperatives Act. This act requires smallholders to come together and form coffee cooperative societies. The societies vary greatly in size, and merging and splitting are common. Some cooperatives have only one wet mill whilst other have more. Factories typically provide services to 300 to 800 members of a society.

Coffee production has been on a declining trend since 1987/1988 when a record 130,000 MT of clean coffee was produced. In the last five years, the country's production has been declining, despite a temporary increase in 2008/2009 (Figure 3.3). In this

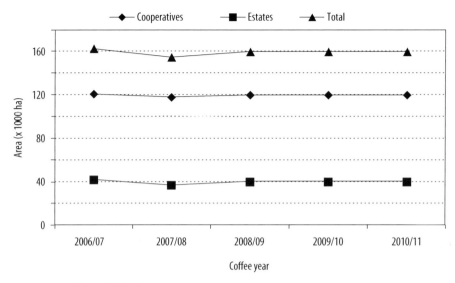

Figure 3.2. Area under coffee bushes in Kenya (2006/2007 to 2010/2011) (KNBS, 2012).

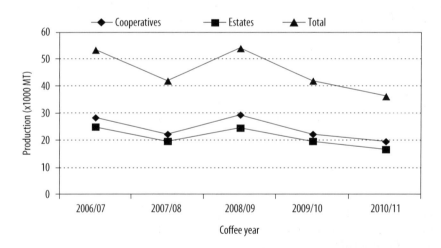

Figure 3.3. Total coffee production in Kenya (2006/2007 to 2010/2011) (KNBS, 2012).

time period the production averaged 45,540 MT, which is only 35% of what was being produced in 1987/1988. The area under coffee declined especially in estates near Nairobi (Figure 3.4). In cooperatives, coffee was stumped (not uprooted) or neglected, hence many fields were not in production. Overall production has been declining as coffee bushes were neglected (cherry not picked for delivery to the factory), due to poor prices in the past, lack of inputs, and mismanagement of the sector.

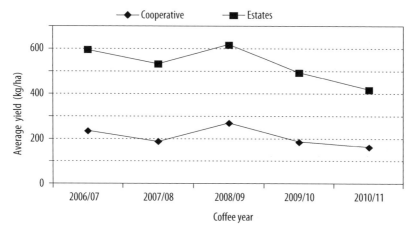

Figure 3.4. Average yields from estates and cooperatives (2006/2007 to 2010/2011) (KNBS, 2012).

Estates are more productive as they are professionally managed and have better access to credit. The average yields shown in Figure 3.4 are very low, compared to average yields for Arabica coffee worldwide of 698 kg/ha and yields of 1,160 kg/ha in neighbouring Rwanda and 995 kg/ha in neighbouring Ethiopia (Condliffe *et al.*, 2008). It is clear that the low yields in smallholder farms is one of the major challenges to be overcome if coffee is to remain a viable farm enterprise.

In recent years, donors have initiated numerous projects to support the smallholder coffee sector in Kenya. While an overview of the impact of donor support on the coffee sector is absent, much attention has been paid to improving the quality and production of coffee (Box 3.1).

3.2.5 Marketing and prices

The major export destinations for Kenyan coffee include Germany (30%), Benelux (12%), USA/Canada (11%), Sweden (9%), Finland (6%) and the United Kingdom (6%) (KCTA, 2012). While domestic consumption of coffee in Kenya remains limited, there has been an increase in recent years. This increase is reflected in the rise of coffee shops such as Savannah, Java, Dorman's and Coffee World. At the same time, the high cost (compared to income levels) of brewed coffee in coffee shops and the high prices exported coffee fetches may not push domestic consumption of locally produced coffee beyond the current 3-4% in the medium term.

In the coffee value chain, so-called marketing agents fulfil an important role. There are two categories of marketing agents, i.e. (1) commercial marketing agents that offer their services purely for commercial purposes, and (2) grower marketing agents which are growers marketing their own coffee. By the year 2009, over 40 companies were registered to participate in coffee marketing. The key players in this latter category

Box 3.1. Coffee certification in Kenya.

Coffee certification schemes such as Fair Trade, Utz and Rainforest Alliance have triggered a number of developments in the Kenyan smallholder coffee sector:

- Increased awareness of Good Agricultural Practices (GAPs), Good Processing Practices (GPP), environmental concerns including activities related to climate change (adaptation and mitigation).
- Improved working conditions, e.g. safety, environmental protection, timely payment of salaries to workers and coffee producers.
- Improved record keeping and traceability.
- Better governance due to capacity building programmes, including more stable leadership (management committees are not replaced overnight as was the case before).
- Better collaboration between producers, traders and roasters thereby increasing sustainable sourcing and marketing of coffee.
- Both traders and roasters have come up with Corporate Social Responsibility projects to assist the producers such as construction of health clinics and supporting women and youth projects.

Source: interview Mzeeh Hamisi Ngutu (Noble Consultants), 15-1-2013

are Coffee Management Services Ltd., Kenya Cooperative Coffee Exporters, Tropical Farm Ltd (K), Sasini (K) Limited, Oakland's Marketing (Kofinaf Co. Ltd.), Grower Marketing Agents, Thika Coffee Mills, Nyambene Coffee Mills and Sustainable Management Services Ltd. Details can be found in the Kenya Coffee Directory (KCTA, 2012b).

There are two coffee marketing systems operating in Kenya:
1. *Central auction system,* commonly referred to as Nairobi Coffee Exchange. This is a market where the licensed coffee dealers purchase coffee through competitive bidding. Before the coffee is brought to the auction, the marketer sends samples to the members of the Nairobi exchange. After the auction, members pay the marketing agents and move the coffee to their own warehouses. The marketing agent in turn pays the farmer (cooperative or estate) via the bank. Coffee auctions are conducted every Tuesday of the week. The auction is under the management of the Kenya Coffee Producers and Traders Association.
2. *The direct sales system,* commonly referred to as the 'Second Window'. The direct sales system requires that a grower directly negotiates with the buyer outside the country and a sales contract is duly signed and registered with the Coffee Board.[30]

---

[30] Direct sales have the potential of being beneficial to smallholder coffee farmers as the cooperative can directly negotiate prices with a buyer while auction prices are fixed by bidding. Other potential benefits of direct sales include a shorter duration between sales date and the time cash is remitted. The actual impact of direct sales on smallholder coffee farmers, however, has not been systematically assessed yet.

The Board registers the contract after carrying out an inspection and analysing the coffee for quality and value as per the contract. Most of the Kenyan coffee is sold at the general auction (Table 3.5). In the 2010/2011 coffee year, marketing agents handled 8% of the total marketed coffee (610,493 bags) while the Nairobi Coffee Exchange handled the rest.

Figure 3.5 provides a breakdown of the volumes of direct sales per marketing agent. While some of the coffee delivered via direct sales is sold as certified, there is no data indicating which part is sold as certified coffee and which part as conventional coffee.

The key distinctions in grading coffee are liquor profile, bean (screen) sizes and the numbers of defects in a standard coffee sample. Consumer purchasing decisions are primarily driven by the liquor distinctions. Roasters prefer beans packed in relatively

Table 3.5. Quantity of Kenyan coffee sold through the auction and direct sales (2006/2007 to 2011/2012) (KCTA, 2013).

Year	Total production (MT)	Auction sales (MT)	Direct sales (MT)
2006/2007	54,340	53,344 (98%)	996 (2%)
2007/2008	41,248	39,448 (96%)	1,800 (4%)
2008/2009	57,336	51,881 (90%)	5,455 (10%)
2009/2010	42,096	36,197 (86%)	5,899 (14%)
2010/2011	36,629	33,680 (92%)	2,949 (8%)
2011/2012	49,003	43,366 (88%)	5,637 (12%)

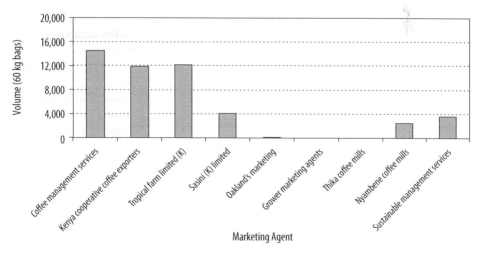

Figure 3.5. Volume of coffee sold via direct sales (2010/2011 coffee year) (KCTA, 2011).

uniform sizes to enhance roast evenness that produces balanced liquor. In Kenya, seven grades (KCPTA, 2013) are adopted for the main coffee (AA, AB, C, E, PB, T and TT), sixteen grades for miscellaneous coffee (F, HE, KB1, KB2, KB3, KB4, KB5 KB6, SB, SC, UG, UG1, UG2, UG3, UG4, UG5) and three grades for unwashed coffee (MH, ML RH). Figure 3.6 shows the volumes of the different grade categories traded at the central auction.

Prices of Kenyan coffee are relatively high compared to world prices (USAID, 2010). Although production has been on the decline, prices have continued to rise steadily over the years (Figure 3.6, 3.7 and 3.8). Prices have increased to a large extent due to superior quality (superior quality but small volumes – demand/supply effects) as well as the world market (disease outbreaks in other countries). The rise of prices is generally viewed as not being sustainable. The price corrected itself after the world market got an increasing supply of mild Arabica coffee from many origins coupled with a deteriorating world economy and coffee price dropped to a low in July 2013.[31]

In the years 2008-2009 to 2011-2012, on average 79.2% of all coffee sold at the Nairobi Coffee exchange was sold as a main coffee grade. A closer look at the prices paid for the different main coffee grades (AA, AB, C, E, PB, T and TT) shows that there are considerable differences between the grades (Table 3.6). Not surprisingly, high quality coffee on average gets a higher price than low quality coffee. For example, AA-graded coffee on average pays between two and three times more than T-graded coffee.

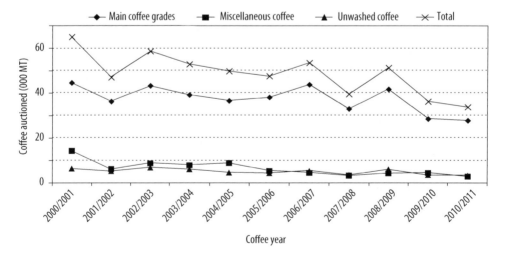

Figure 3.6. Quantity of different grades auctioned (2000/2001 to 2010/2011) (KCTA, 2012).

---

[31] Kenyan coffee prices may also be affected by developments in others countries which are working towards improving the quality of their coffee and introducing new varieties resistant to diseases. Consumers may not be willing to pay more for Kenyan coffee if high quality alternatives are available.

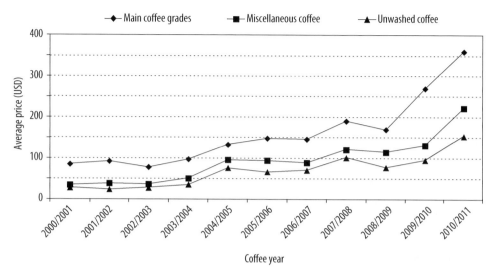

Figure 3.7. Average price of main grades auctioned (2000/2001 to 2010/2011) (KCTA, 2012).

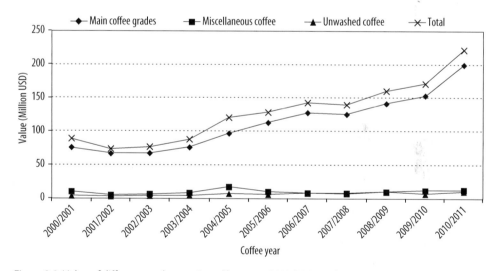

Figure 3.8. Value of different grades auctioned between 2000/2001 and 2010/2011 (KCTA, 2012).

For the year 2010/2011 the price paid by the various marketing agents varied between USD 163 and USD 594 per bag of 50 kg (Figure 3.9).

Inputs make up a large share of the production costs of smallholder coffee farmers. A study by Oikocredit (2011) found that fertilisation and spraying make up respectively 13.4 and 33.4% of the production costs of smallholder coffee farmers. Coffee

Table 3.6. Average prices for main coffee grades (2008-2009 to 2011-2012; in USD) (KCTA, 2012a).

Grade	2008-2009	2009-2010	2010-2011	2011-2012
AA	192.33	343.89	432.59	329.00
AB	176.39	301.08	280.52	253.55
C	155.62	218.07	299.21	198.85
E	209.93	272.49	331.27	342.28
PB	172.45	292.59	379.53	250.88
T	94.58	108.22	194.15	140.75
TT	157.08	241.45	320.14	205.66

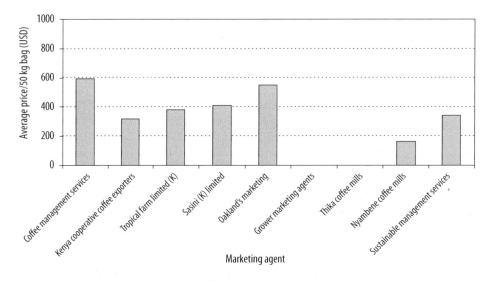

Figure 3.9. Average price per 50 kg bag of coffee (2010/2011) (KCTA, 2011).

production costs have escalated in the recent past mainly due to major increases in the cost of purchased farm inputs. While exact data is unavailable, Table 3.7 shows that the value of purchased agricultural inputs has increased considerably between 2007 and 2011. Currency devaluation, inflation and inefficient input markets have been some of factors behind the increase in costs. Poor road infrastructure also has significantly contributed to the costs of inputs due to high transport costs.

The rising cost of production combined with the inability of most farmers to get access to credit has forced some farmers to abandon coffee farming and/or neglect their coffee trees. Declining farming skills and some instances of adulteration of chemicals and fertilisers are some of the reasons responsible for the declining production. Low and delayed payments have been cited as main causes for the many debts in the farmer

Table 3.7. Value of purchased agricultural inputs (excluding labour) in KSh millions (KNBS, 2012).

Item	2007	2008	2009	2010	2011
Fertilisers	3,594.9	6,160.2	5,680.1	6,021.9	9,397.4
Other agricultural inputs	1,389.0	1,258.4	3,941,0	4,307.0	3,362.1
Livestock drugs and medicines	942.0	857.4	1,856.0	1,467.2	1,382.7
Bags	604.0	428.8	520.8	425.0	267.3
Manufactured feeds	2,038.0	4,849.0	5,543.5	4,453.0	3,910.8
Purchased seed	2,547.7	3661.0	3,182.1	4,227.0	3,337.9
Other material inputs	453.0	651.0	565.8	536.2	592.6

cooperatives due to accrual of interests on loans. To rescue the sector, the Kenyan government released KSh 1 billion coffee debt waiver owed to coffee cooperatives in 2011 (Mwangi, 2011).

3.3 Impact of certification

This section reports the findings from the fieldwork in Kenya. We first focus on direct welfare effects (e.g. production, prices, income), and then discuss indirect effects (e.g. spill-over effects, risk attitudes). In Section 3.4 institutional implications (e.g. organisational capacity and regional externalities) will be outlined. Sections 3.5 and 3.6 discuss the main issues experienced by farmers and cooperative boards.

3.3.1 Direct welfare effects

Farmers from both the FT and Utz certified cooperatives received training on GAP. These trainings focused on a variety of topics, including inputs and nutrition, planting, pruning and maintenance of coffee trees, intercropping, weeding, soil conservation and erosion, rainwater harvesting, spacing, picking and keeping records. Farmers were organised in groups headed by promoter farmers. The promoter farmers monitor the performance of other farmers and pass on their skills to their groups' members.

Tekangu cooperative received donor support to hire its own agronomist to promote good farming practices as part of the Utz certification process. Ndumberi cooperative used Fair Trade premiums and also a grant from Fair Trade's technical assistance fund to hire its own agronomist support in the promotion of good farming practices. Farmers from Ndumberi and Kiambaa cooperative made exposure visits to Tekangu as part of the FT trainings. These visits had important motivating effects because they clearly showed that the application of good farming practices pays off in higher yields.

Overall, farmers pointed out that the trainings had made them more aware of the importance of investing in higher production and better quality. Through the example of 'early-adopters', farmers could see for themselves that employing good farming practices resulted in higher production and quality. As explained by a Board member of Tekangu: 'we could see that farmers that had previously neglected their coffee started to take much better care of their plants when they started to see the benefits [of good agricultural practices]' (FGD Board, 28-1-2013).

In Tables 3.8 to 3.11 we present the outcomes of the difference-in-difference estimates after matching for the four comparisons between treatment (FT or Utz) with the control (no certification or recent FT). Significant differences are clearly indicated for 8 categories of key performance indicators:
1. income effects;
2. production costs for inputs and labour;
3. household expenditures, credit and savings;
4. coffee production, yields and prices;
5. investments in social and productive assets (water, latrines, cattle);
6. investments in house improvement and coffee renovation;
7. appreciation of cooperative services (bargaining power); and
8. behavioural effects (change in gender roles, risk averseness, health).

3.3.2 Production

While farmers of both the FT and Utz certified cooperatives stressed the positive effects of trainings on good agricultural practices during the FGDs, the effects found in the quantitative data are ambiguous. Involvement in FT certification does not influence production volumes in one case (Kiambaa versus Mikari; Table 3.8) and in the other case (Rugi versus Kiama; Table 3.11) certification gives a negative influence on coffee production volumes compared to NC farms. In the case of Rugi it should be noted that farmers had only received trainings on good agricultural practices for one year.

Utz certified farmers showed higher production at baseline (2009) compared to non-certified farmers, but at endline (2013) these effects disappear (Table 3.10). Comparing FT and Utz shows a higher production of dry coffee for Utz farmers in both years (Table 3.11). In 2009 we saw significant differences in input use in coffee between groups; however, these differences disappeared in 2013. We observed a significant change in input use between FT and NC farmers, caused by the NC farmers (Kiama) starting to use more inputs.

3.3.3 Awareness

Overall, the level of awareness amongst farmers regarding FT and Utz appeared to be low (Table 3.12). In the case of Ndumberi, which is both Utz and FT certified, farmers reported that they had received training, but were not able to tell whether the

Table 3.8. Difference in difference – Kiambaa (FT) versus Mikari (control).

Outcome variable	2009			2013			diff-in-diff[1]
	Control	FT	diff[1]	Control	FT	diff[1]	
	mean	mean	mean	mean	mean	mean	mean
Coffee income (×1000 KSh)	19.8	23.6	3.7	11.3	19.8	8.4**	4.7
Coffee income net (×1000 KSh)	12.9	14	1.1	6.5	9.6	3.1	2
Dry coffee income (×1000 KSh)	2.1	3.1	1	1.3	2.7	1.3	0.4
Cherry coffee income (×1000 KSh)	17.8	20.6	2.9	10	14.7	4.7	1.8
Share of income from coffee (%)	4.2	14.5	10.3	5.4	43.2	37.8***	27.5***
Share income coffee vs. cattle[2]	10.1	18.8	8.7	9.4	28	18.6***	9.9
Income other crops (×1000 KSh)	3.8	3	-0.7	0.7	0.2	-0.5	0.2
Income livestock (×1000 KSh)	264	288	24	308	55	-253*	-277
Total income (×1000 KSh)	653	324	-329**	436	126	-310**	19
Input costs coffee (×1000 KSh)	4.1	2.8	-1.4*	4.7	2.8	-2	-0.6
Input costs other (×1000 KSh)	3.4	2.4	-1.0*	3.5	2.1	-1.4	-0.4
Seed costs other (×1000 KSh)	3.2	2.1	-1.1*	1.3	1.8	0.5	1.6**
Hired labour coffee (yes/no)	0.7	0.7	0	2.2	1.3	-0.9**	-0.8*
Credit (×1000 KSh)	79.4	28.7	-50.7**	7.9	20	12.1	62.9**
Expenditure food (×1000 KSh)	4.6	3.9	-0.7	6.2	8.8	2.6*	3.4**
Expenditure energy (×1000 KSh)	1.6	1.8	0.2	3.7	5	1.2	1.1
Expenditure transport (×1000 KSh)	3.8	5	1.1	3.4	0.9	-2.5***	-3.7***
Expenditure total (×1000 KSh)	44.3	49	4.7	58.2	34.9	-23.3	-28
Coffee area (acres)	0.8	0.7	-0.1	1.1	0.7	-0.3	-0.2
Number of mature coffee trees	417	349	-68	545	374	-170*	-102
Coffee trees per acre	534	508	-26	583	611	28	54
Coffee yield (kg/acre)	1.4	1.2	-0.3*	0.8	0.9	0.1	0.4
Coffee yield (kg/tree)	2.6	2.3	-0.3	1.5	1.7	0.2	0.5
Coffee sold in cherry form (kg)	870	938	68	425	332	-94	-161
Dry coffee sold (kg)	62.5	50.9	-11.6	42.7	54.5	11.8	23.4
Cherry coffee price (KSh/kg)	21.4	24.6	3.3***	27.2	52.6	25.4***	22.2***
Dry coffee price (KSh/kg)	33.6	40.7	7.1***	57.1	138	80.6***	73.5***
Have piped water (yes/no)	0	0.4	0.3***	0.4	0.5	0.1	-0.2
Animals in stock	7.7	5.9	-1.8	8.1	5	-3.2**	-1.4
House improvements (yes/no)	1.8	1.7	-0.2**	1.8	1.7	-0.1	0.1
Investment in new coffee (yes/no)	0.1	0.3	0.2*	0.6	0.5	-0.1	-0.2
Economic situation vs. 5 years ago (1-3)	2	1.9	0	1.5	1.4	-0.1	0
Economic situation vs. 5 years later (1-3)	1.6	1.6	0	1.3	1.3	0	0
Number of organisations	1.4	1.3	-0.2	0.5	0.5	-0.1	0.1
Identification index (1-3)	2.7	2.6	-0.1*	2.5	2.4	-0.1	0.0*
Force index (1-3)	2.6	2.4	-0.2	2.1	2.1	0	0.3
Risk (1-3)	2.1	2.1	0	2.2	2.2	0	0
Gender index (5-25)	17.8	18	0.2	14.2	14.2	-0.1	-0.3
Days lost due to poor health (log)	3.4	3.4	0	0.9	1.9	1	1

[1] Significance: *** P<0.01; ** P<0.05; * P<0.1.

[2] Income coffee/(income livestock/100).

Means and Standard Errors are estimated by linear regression. Estimation on the common support. Robust Standard Errors.

Table 3.9. Difference in difference – Rugi (FT) versus Kiama (control).

Outcome variable	2009			2013			diff-in-diff[1]
	Control	FT	diff[1]	Control	FT	diff[1]	
	mean	mean	mean	mean	mean	mean	mean
Coffee income (×1000 KSh)	21.4	34.6	13.2***	38.7	34.4	-4.3	-17.5**
Coffee income net (×1000 KSh)	14.5	20.9	6.4*	27.4	27	-0.4	-6.8
Dry coffee income (×1000 KSh)	1.4	1.9	0.5	4.2	2.4	-1.8***	-2.3***
Cherry coffee income (×1000 KSh)	20	32.7	12.7***	31.6	32	0.4	-12.3
Share of income from coffee (%)	9.6	16.3	6.7**	16.5	23	6.6	-0.1
Share income coffee vs. cattle[2]	31.2	39.2	8.1	93.4	92.6	-0.8	-8.9
Income other crops (×1000 KSh)	6.3	4.4	-1.9*	0.4	0.4	0	2
Income livestock (×1000 KSh)	138	130	-8	48	34	-14	-6
Total income (×1000 KSh)	305	295	-10	222	203	-19	-9
Input costs coffee (×1000 KSh)	4.9	8.3	3.3***	9.3	8.1	-1.3	-4.6**
Input costs other (×1000 KSh)	4	5.4	1.4	3.4	2.6	-0.8	-2.2
Seed costs other (×1000 KSh)	2.9	2.7	-0.2	1.4	0.9	-0.5**	-0.3
Hired labour coffee (yes/no)	0.6	0.7	0.1	1.8	2.4	0.6	0.6
Credit (×1000 KSh)	34.9	15.7	-19.2	4.5	6.6	2.2	21.3
Expenditure food (×1000 KSh)	2.5	2.6	0.1	6.5	6.8	0.3	0.2
Expenditure energy (×1000 KSh)	0.9	0.8	-0.1	5.7	4.3	-1.4	-1.3
Expenditure transport (×1000 KSh)	1.7	1.2	-0.6*	2.3	1.8	-0.5	0.1
Expenditure total (×1000 KSh)	27	21.4	-5.5	42.9	35.7	-7.2	-1.6
Coffee area (acres)	0.4	0.5	0.1**	0.8	0.6	-0.1	-0.2**
Number of mature coffee trees	200	246	46*	210	241	31	-15
Coffee trees per acre	523	495	-29*	411	551	140**	169**
Coffee yield (kg/acre)	1.8	2.3	0.5**	1.6	1.6	0.1	-0.5
Coffee yield (kg/tree)	3.6	5.1	1.5***	3.9	3.6	-0.3	-1.8
Coffee sold in cherry form (kg)	660	1034	374***	565	645	80	-294*
Dry coffee sold (kg)	33.2	39.7	6.5	56.6	39.6	-17.0**	-23.5**
Cherry coffee price (KSh/kg)	29.7	31.3	1.6**	59.1	49.5	-9.6**	-11.2***
Dry coffee price (KSh/kg)	49.1	47.3	-1.8	89.3	76.6	-12.7**	-10.9**
Have piped water (yes/no)	0.2	0.1	-0.1*	0	0	0	0.1
Animals in stock	9.6	8.1	-1.6	10	6.6	-3.4***	-1.8
House improvements (yes/no)	1.8	1.8	-0.1	1.7	1.9	0.2***	0.2**
Investment in new coffee (yes/no)	0.2	0.2	0	0.6	0.4	-0.1*	-0.2*
Economic situation vs. 5 years ago (1-3)	1.7	1.7	0	1.4	1.2	-0.2*	-0.2
Economic situation vs. 5 years later (1-3)	1.2	1.6	0.4***	1.3	1.1	-0.2***	-0.6***
Number of organisations	1.2	1.4	0.3***	0	0.2	0.2***	-0.1
Identification index (1-3)	2.6	2.5	-0.1	2.3	2.4	0.1	0.2
Force index (1-3)	2.5	2.3	-0.1	2.3	2.4	0.1	0.3*
Risk (1-3)	2.3	2.2	-0.1**	2.2	2.2	-0.1	0.1
Gender index (5-25)	17.9	19.2	1.3	14	13.9	-0.1	-1.4
Days lost due to poor health (log)	2.8	3.6	0.7*	0.3	1.1	0.7	0

[1] Significance: *** P<0.01; ** P<0.05; * P<0.1.

[2] Income coffee/(income livestock/100).

Means and Standard Errors are estimated by linear regression. Estimation on the common support. Robust Standard Errors.

Table 3.10. Difference in difference – Tekangu (Utz) versus Kiama (control).

Outcome variable	2009			2013			diff-in-diff[1]
	Control	Utz	diff[1]	Control	Utz	diff[1]	
	mean	mean	mean	mean	mean	mean	mean
Coffee income (×1000 KSh)	22.9	37.2	14.3***	39.4	49.4	10	-4.3
Coffee income net (×1000 KSh)	14.5	22.2	7.7*	26.2	40.5	14.4*	6.7
Dry coffee income (×1000 KSh)	1.4	3.9	2.5***	4.2	5.4	1.1	-1.4
Cherry coffee income (×1000 KSh)	21.6	33.4	11.8***	31.7	42.9	11.2	-0.6
Share of income from coffee (%)	10.4	21.6	11.3**	20.8	31.7	10.9	-0.4
Share income coffee vs. cattle[2]	25.4	57.2	31.8**	89.6	59.3	-30.3	-62.1*
Income other crops (×1000 KSh)	6.4	5	-1.4	0.3	0	-0.3	1
Income livestock (×1000 KSh)	138	121	-17	43	85	43	60
Total income (×1000 KSh)	330	268	-62	182	245	63	125
Input costs coffee (×1000 KSh)	5.1	8.6	3.5***	9.8	9.3	-0.5	-4.0*
Input costs other (×1000 KSh)	4	4.1	0.2	3.6	4	0.4	0.2
Seed costs other (×1000 KSh)	3	2.2	-0.8**	1.3	1.3	0	0.8*
Hired labour coffee (yes/no)	0.6	0.8	0.2***	1.8	1.8	0	-0.2
Credit (×1000 KSh)	37.9	47.5	9.6	0	5	5	-4.6
Expenditure food (×1000 KSh)	2.6	2.7	0.1	6.5	6	-0.5	-0.6
Expenditure energy (×1000 KSh)	0.9	1.4	0.4*	5.6	4.2	-1.4	-1.8*
Expenditure transport (×1000 KSh)	1.8	1.9	0.2	2.1	2.9	0.8	0.7
Expenditure total (×1000 KSh)	28.1	34.1	6	40.5	43.9	3.4	-2.6
Coffee area (acres)	0.4	0.6	0.2***	0.8	0.7	0	-0.2*
Number of mature coffee trees	204	275	71**	218	208	-10	-81**
Coffee trees per acre	525	478	-48***	424	391	-32	15
Coffee yield (kg/acre)	1.9	2.1	0.2	1.9	1.7	-0.1	-0.4
Coffee yield (kg/tree)	3.7	4.4	0.7*	3.7	3.7	0	-0.7
Coffee sold in cherry form (kg)	708	975	267**	587	632	45	-223
Dry coffee sold (kg)	35.5	80.2	44.7***	56.8	72.7	15.9	-28.8*
Cherry coffee price (KSh/kg)	30	34.5	4.5***	58.4	86.6	28.1***	23.7***
Dry coffee price (KSh/kg)	49.3	50.5	1.2	92.4	105	12.8*	11.7*
Have piped water (yes/no)	0.2	0.1	-0.1**	0.1	0	0	0.1*
Animals in stock	9.8	10.3	0.5	9.4	10.6	1.1	0.7
House improvements (yes/no)	1.9	1.7	-0.2**	1.8	1.6	-0.2**	0
Investment in new coffee (yes/no)	0.2	0.3	0.1*	0.6	0.6	0	-0.1
Economic situation vs. 5 years ago (1-3)	1.7	1.6	-0.1	1.4	1.3	-0.1	0
Economic situation vs. 5 years later (1-3)	1.2	1.6	0.4***	1.3	1.3	-0.1	-0.5***
Number of organisations	1.1	1.3	0.1*	0	0.2	0.1*	0
Identification index (1-3)	2.7	2.6	0	2.3	2.4	0.1	0.1
Force index (1-3)	2.5	2.4	-0.1	2.3	2.2	0	0.1
Risk (1-3)	2.3	2.2	-0.1*	2.2	2.3	0	0.1*
Gender index (5-25)	17.9	20.3	2.4**	14.1	14.6	0.4	-2
Days lost due to poor health (log)	2.8	3.8	1.0**	0.5	0.8	0.2	-0.8

[1] Significance: *** P<0.01; ** P<0.05; * P<0.1.

[2] Income coffee/(income livestock/100).

Means and Standard Errors are estimated by linear regression. Estimation on the common support. Robust Standard Errors.

Table 3.11. Difference in difference – Tekangu (Utz) versus Rugi (FT).

Outcome variable	2009			2013			diff-in-diff[1]
	FT	Utz	diff[1]	FT	Utz	diff[1]	
	mean	mean	mean	mean	mean	mean	mean
Coffee income (×1000 KSh)	30.7	37	6.4	35.1	49.5	14.4*	8
Coffee income net (×1000 KSh)	17.7	20	2.3	25.8	37.7	11.9	9.6
Dry coffee income (×1000 KSh)	1.8	3.8	2.0***	2.4	5.3	2.9***	0.9
Cherry coffee income (×1000 KSh)	28.8	33.2	4.3	32.7	42.9	10.2	5.9
Share of income from coffee (%)	17	21.6	4.6	21.5	30.3	8.7	4.2
Share income coffee vs. cattle[2]	34.4	60.5	26.2	83	72.1	-10.8	-37
Income other crops (×1000 KSh)	4.3	4.8	0.5	0.4	0.1	-0.2	-0.8
Income livestock (×1000 KSh)	122	120	-2	28	84	57	58
Total income (×1000 KSh)	287	263	-24	169	249	80	105
Input costs coffee (×1000 KSh)	8.1	8.3	0.2	8.8	9.9	1.1	0.9
Input costs other (×1000 KSh)	5.7	4.1	-1.6*	2.9	4	1.1	2.7**
Seed costs other (×1000 KSh)	2.8	2.2	-0.6*	0.9	1.3	0.4	1.1**
Hired labour coffee (yes/no)	0.7	0.8	0.1	2.4	1.8	-0.6	-0.7
Credit (×1000 KSh)	29.6	20	-9.6	7.1	0	-7.1**	2.5
Expenditure food (×1000 KSh)	2.6	2.7	0.1	6.7	6	-0.7	-0.7
Expenditure energy (×1000 KSh)	0.7	1.4	0.6**	4.2	4.2	0	-0.6
Expenditure transport (×1000 KSh)	1.4	1.9	0.5	1.8	2.9	1.1**	0.6
Expenditure total (×1000 KSh)	23.1	34.7	11.7*	34.8	45.3	10.5*	-1.2
Coffee area (acres)	0.5	0.6	0.1*	0.6	0.7	0.1	0
Number of mature coffee trees	226	273	47	219	205	-14	-61
Coffee trees per acre	494	481	-13	521	401	-120**	-107*
Coffee yield (kg/acre)	2.3	2	-0.3	1.3	1.5	0.2	0.5
Coffee yield (kg/tree)	4.7	4.2	-0.4	3	3.4	0.4	0.8
Coffee sold in cherry form (kg)	898	971	73	662	631	-31	-104
Dry coffee sold (kg)	41.1	74.5	33.4***	39.1	67.2	28.1***	-5.4
Cherry coffee price (KSh/kg)	31.7	34.6	2.8***	51.3	87.6	36.2***	33.4***
Dry coffee price (KSh/kg)	48	50.6	2.5	79.2	106	26.3***	23.8***
Have piped water (yes/no)	0.1	0.1	0	0	0	0	0
Animals in stock	8.5	10.1	1.6	7.5	10.5	3.0**	1.4
House improvements (yes/no)	1.8	1.7	-0.1	1.9	1.6	-0.3***	-0.2**
Investment in new coffee (yes/no)	0.2	0.3	0.1	0.4	0.6	0.2**	0.1
Economic situation vs. 5 years ago (1-3)	1.7	1.6	-0.1	1.2	1.3	0.1	0.1
Economic situation vs. 5 years later (1-3)	1.5	1.6	0.1	1.1	1.3	0.2**	0.1
Number of organisations	1.4	1.3	-0.2*	0.2	0.2	-0.1	0.1
Identification index (1-3)	2.6	2.6	0.1	2.3	2.4	0.1	0
Force index (1-3)	2.4	2.4	0	2.4	2.2	-0.2*	-0.2
Risk (1-3)	2.2	2.2	0.1	2.1	2.2	0.1	0
Gender index (5-25)	19.2	20.1	0.9	14	14.6	0.6	-0.3
Days lost due to poor health (log)	3.4	3.8	0.4	1.1	0.8	-0.3	-0.6

[1] Significance: *** P<0.01; ** P<0.05; * P<0.1.

[2] Income coffee/(income livestock/100).

Means and Standard Errors are estimated by linear regression. Estimation on the common support. Robust Standard Errors.

Table 3.12. Awareness of Fair Trade (FT) or Utz certification (percentage of interviewed cooperative members who answered positively).

	Utz & FT	Utz	FT	NC
Are you aware of FT certification?	11.69%	25.00%	13.57%	6.97%
Is your own coop FT certified?	11.69%	18.75%	10.05%	1.23%
Are you aware of Utz certification?	7.79%	15.00%	3.02%	2.46%
Is your own coop Utz certified?	7.79%	11.25%	1.51%	0.41%

training was related to Utz or FT. At FT cooperatives, less than 1 out of 7 farmers are aware of the FT certification. For Utz certified cooperatives only 11% knows that their cooperative is Utz certified. In the case of Ndumberi these percentages are respectively 11.69% and 7.79%.

3.3.4 Prices

In theory, better farming practices should lead to better quality, which should enable farmers to receive a higher price for their coffee. Furthermore, certified coffee is associated with higher prices. The price premiums of FT and Utz coffee in Kenya are 3-5% per clean green exported pound of coffee (interview, representative of Taylor Winch, 1-2-2013).

FT farmers (Kiambaa) received higher prices compared to NC farmers in both years and the difference between the two grew significantly over the years (Table 3.8). Other FT certified farmers (Rugi) received lower prices over time (Table 3.11). In the case of Rugi cooperative, no coffee had yet been sold as FT certified at the time of the data-collection in 2013. As such, it is difficult to attribute the observed effect to FT.

Utz certified farmers generally received better prices compared to NC and FT farmers in both years (Table 3.10 and 3.11). This difference between the Utz and other farmers also increased significantly over time. For the comparison with FT we register lower revenues for FT cooperatives compared to both Utz (Table 3.11) and non-certified producers (Table 3.9), but we need to make some reservation regarding the recent nature of FT certification in the latter case.

One of the key benefits associated with certification is that it shortens the supply chain as cooperatives sell directly to international buyers. Two of the cooperatives in our study, Tekangu (Utz certified) and Ndumberi (Utz and FT certified) sold part of their coffee via the direct sales option, also called 'the second window'. In 2011/2012, Tekangu sold 90% of its coffee through the second window. The secretary manager of Tekangu explained that they only sold their low quality coffee through the auction. Ndumberi reported selling roughly 20% of its coffee through direct sales. The main benefit of direct sales, according to the two cooperatives, is that it pays slightly better compared to the general auction. As far as we could establish, the utilisation of the 'second window' was not directly related to FT in the case of Ndumberi cooperative.

3.3.5 Household Income and expenditure

On average, most farmers surveyed earned an important part of their household income through off-farm work and the proportion of income generated from coffee is relatively small (as shown in Table 3.13). A significant difference is that the income of non-certified farmers is higher on average compared to certified farmers. The share of income generated from coffee is smaller for non-certified farmers, compared to their certified colleagues. Looking at the differences over time, we observe a significant difference between FT and conventional farmers at baseline in off-farm earnings (Table 3.9), but these differences disappear at endline and no significant differences over time are reported. The same holds for total income.

An important question is whether the higher prices of certified coffee have a significant positive effect on total household income. Around one third of the total income of the farmers in our survey (between 20 and 46%) is generated with the production of coffee (Table 3.13). Roughly one third of the certified coffee in Kenya (28% for Utz, 30% for FT) is sold as certified coffee (i.e. using the FT or Utz certified label). Taking these two observations together, this means that roughly one ninth of the total income (⅓ × ⅓) is earned from coffee that fetched a certified price. Therefore, it can be concluded that the effect of certified prices (both FT and Utz) on total household income can only be expected to be relatively small.

FT and Utz farmers earn more (and in some cases the same) money from coffee compared to conventional farmers, and Utz farmers earn more (or the same as) from coffee than FT farmers. No significant difference-in-difference between the groups was detected. Earnings from other crops do not contribute substantially to the household income. If we observe significant differences between farmers regarding other crops, we observe that NC farmers report higher income from other crops (Table 3.9 and 3.10). A possible explanation could be that FT and Utz farmers – due to certification – tend to specialise more in coffee than NC farmers, as they expect more benefits from coffee production.

Table 3.13. Income from coffee as percentage of total income.

	Utz and FT	Utz	FT	NC
% income from coffee 2009	21.09	33.62	29.64	20.68
% income from coffee 2013	46.20	43.41	43.86	30.70

FT = Fair Trade certified; Utz = Utz certified; NC = non-certified.

Household expenditure is generally considered a key welfare indicator and an important overall indicator of impact. In few cases some significant differences are observed between the groups. Only in one case do we observe a significant difference over time, caused by a drop in household expenditure by FT farmers, while NC farmers keep the same expenditure level over time (Table 3.8). In another case, both FT and Utz farmers increased expenditures over time, and the significant advantage of Utz over FT was maintained (Table 3.11).

3.3.6 Savings, assets and credit

Whether farmers are able to accumulate capital (money or assets) from past returns, or can access credit, is another important question for impact analysis. Increased financial room for manoeuvre reinforces households' capacity to withstand adverse shocks. Certification did not lead to significantly more accumulation of capital, whether we looked at FT or Utz farmers. We did not find many significant differences between certified and non-certified farmers regarding assets or savings (results for savings not reported in Tables). Non-certified farmers had more livestock in 2013 compared to FT farmers, although the difference over time did not change significantly (Table 3.8). Comparing FT certified and Utz certified farmers in 2013 shows Utz farmers to have more assets, more livestock units and more savings (the latter is not reported in the Table) compared to FT farmers (Table 3.11).

3.3.7 Welfare perceptions

Welfare perceptions regarding experiences during the past five years do not reveal significant differences for any of the groups. Asking about their future expectations regarding the economic situation, we observe more pessimism among non-certified farmers in 2009 compared to Utz and FT farmers (Table 3.9 and 3.10). Over time both Utz and FT farmers became less optimistic about the future economic prospect, shown by the negative values for the difference-in-difference (Table 3.10). In 2013 non-certified farmers are more optimistic than FT farmers, and there is no significant difference between Utz and non-certified farmers anymore. Comparing Utz and FT farmers shows than FT farmers are less optimistic about their future economic outlook compared to Utz farmers in 2013, but no significant differences are observed in the changes over time (Table 3.11).

3.3.8 Indirect effects

The quantitative research also examined several indirect effects of certification, such as spill-over effects, risk attitudes and gender effects. Spill-over effects refer to the implications of engagement in certification for other economic household activities. Coffee farmers are usually involved in multiple activities and the share of income that is generated by coffee sales is not more than a quarter or a third of the total household income on average. For FT certified farmers, the share of income generated by coffee sales increases over time. This may be because certified farmers have more trust in coffee as a reliable and profitable crop due to their membership of a certified cooperative. The higher degree of specialisation in coffee makes FT farmers also more dependent on coffee price variations.

3.3.9 Risk attitudes and investment

Risk aversion and restraints on investments are believed to play an important role in perpetuation of rural poverty. Certification is meant to reduce these behavioural attitudes. However, risk attitudes hardly changed in the cooperatives that were studied. Only in one comparison (Table 3.9) we could observe a significant difference-in-difference: Utz farmers became somewhat less risk averse compared to NC farmers.

Looking at actual investments, we observed significant differences between FT and NC farmers, with respect to investments in new coffee trees. NC farmers started to invest significantly more in new coffee compared to FT farmers (Table 3.9), possibly as a response to increasing coffee prices. However, in other sites we could not observe any direct positive impact of certification on coffee tree renovation.

3.3.10 Gender

Coffee farming is traditionally a men's crop in Kenya, which explains why the majority of the members of the cooperatives in the study area are men. Few women were found to be members of the boards of the cooperatives in the study.[32] Three of the cooperatives (Mikari, Kiama and Rugi) had female board members. At Mikari, for example, the secretary-manager is a woman. No clear relationship was encountered during fieldwork between the certification status (either Utz or FT) of a cooperative and the number of women that were board members. We also looked at the relation between certification and gender. No significant differences were observed between groups in the perceptions and attitudes, either for men or women.

The relationship between certification (both FT and Utz) and health was also studied. We looked at days lost due to health problems and we analysed the treatment sought. No significant differences could be detected between groups and/or over time.

3.4 Institutional implications

Part of the study involved examining the institutional implications of FT and Utz, especially the degree of satisfaction with certification by the cooperative boards and farmers' satisfaction with cooperative performance. In addition, we identified a number of institutional challenges that are relevant for understanding the institutional potential of certification schemes.

---

[32] See Chapter 8 for a more detailed assessment of the role in women in Kenyan coffee cooperatives.

3.4.1 Board-level satisfaction with certification

Board-level satisfaction with FT and Utz certification was mixed. On the one hand, the boards expressed their complacency with the trainings associated with both certification schemes. Besides the trainings in good farming practices (GAP), part of the 'package' of Utz and FT certification includes training for the board regarding issues such as good (financial) management, marketing and the strategic importance of improving production and quality. The boards of certified organisations – without exception – explained that they highly valued these trainings which contributed to better management practices and increased awareness regarding the importance of employing good farming practices. In the specific case of Ndumberi cooperative, the Board explained how their cooperative had benefited from a water tank, metal drying beds and toilets at the factories which they were able to get through the FT social premium.

A key benefit of certification that was cited by the boards of Tekangu and Ndumberi cooperatives is that it improves sales options. Especially being Utz certified was considered to be of key importance due to its demanding nature. In fact, Utz was considered the most demanding of all certification schemes, resulting in a board member of Tekangu describing Utz as 'the mother of all certifications' (FGD Board, Tekangu, 18-1-2013). Once a cooperative has met all conditions for Utz certification, it reportedly becomes easy to get other types of certification, such as FT or Rainforest Alliance. Such multi-certification is considered to be desirable as it increases sales options at the general auction and therefore the chance to get a higher price.[33] Furthermore, board members of Tekangu cooperative also pointed out that certification is key for selling coffee via direct sales. Tekangu tries to sell as much coffee as possible (between 70-90%) via 'the second window' as it gives them slightly higher prices.

The boards of the certified cooperatives were disappointed with the price premiums associated with both FT and Utz. Their initial expectation had been that – once certified – coffee would yield much higher prices. Thus far, however, this expectation has not materialised. According to the boards, the prices they have received for their coffee only marginally increased once they became certified. In the case of Kiambaa cooperative, the Board was especially vocal about its disappointment with the FT price premium. In 2011/2012, the first year that they sold their coffee as certified, the FT price premium they received was only 157 US dollars in total. The board of Tekangu pointed out that the benefits from the slightly higher price of Utz is partly offset by the high costs (400,000 KSh) of the annual Utz audit.

---

[33] See Chapter 4 for a detailed assessment of the impact of multi-certification (in Ethiopia).

3.4.2 Farmers' satisfaction with the cooperative

Organisational consolidation of cooperatives is seen as an important objective of certification. We asked farmers their opinion of the technical services offered by the cooperative and found no differences in most cases. Only when comparing NC and FT farmers in one case at endline we found that NC farmers were more satisfied compared to FT farmers, but no significant effects were found over time (results are not reported in Table 3.8).

We also asked farmers their opinion on commercial and trading capabilities of their cooperatives. Regarding FT farmers, we found contradictory effects at baseline and no significant effects at endline. Comparing Utz and NC farmers showed a significant change in levels of satisfaction with the commercial services offered, which was mainly caused by a change in satisfaction among NC farmers, who became less satisfied about this aspect of their cooperation.

3.4.3 Institutional challenges

According to the (certified) cooperative board members, getting and keeping their members motivated to employ good agricultural practices remains a challenge. This is consistent with the results from the FGDs with farmers in which it was repeatedly asserted that due to the (relatively) low prices, the price fluctuations and the high cost of production 'doing the good agricultural practices is not worth the effort' (FGD farmers, 24-1-2013). The underlying problem is that coffee farming has an image problem as it is not necessarily seen as a profitable business.

A topic that kept recurring during the fieldwork was the issue of youth involvement in coffee farming. A huge problem, encountered at all cooperatives included in our study, is that very few young people are interested in becoming coffee farmers. This is clearly reflected in the average age of the farmers in this study, which is 64 years, with a standard deviation of 15 years. Board members reported very little rejuvenation of their membership. Even at the best performing cooperatives (Ndumberi and Tekangu), board members explained that the youth is not interested in coffee farming. Assuming that the age of the coffee farmers in our study is somewhat representative for Kenyan cooperatives in general, the lack of the interest of the youth means that the future of smallholder coffee farming in Kenya looks rather bleak.

During the FGDs, a number of reasons were put forward as to why young people are not interested in becoming coffee farmers. In summary, young people typically do not perceive coffee farming as a profitable and attractive enterprise due to poor and unstable prices, the high costs of inputs, a lack of regular monthly payments and hard working conditions. Young people were described as having a different mentality compared to their parents' generation and not being patient enough to wait for months between the delivery of the cherry and the payment: 'Young people, they want quick cash and do not want to get dirty' (FGD farmers, 22-1-2013). One of the few young farmers attending the FGDs pointed out that: 'young people have seen their parents living a life in poverty. They want something better for themselves' (FGD farmers, 28-1-2013). One farmer even explained that 'my son told me that coffee farming is like slavery. You work hard and at the end of the day you only see low returns' (FGD farmers, 22-1-2013). Overall, most young people are inclined to look for other jobs which are better paying and offer better working conditions and a continuous income. Consequently farmers explained that they were reluctant to give their land to their sons and daughters out of fear that their coffee trees would be cut.

Another issue that relates to the adoption rate of good agricultural practices is that farmers are paid the same price, irrespective of whether they sell high or low quality coffee to the cooperative. This means that those farmers that do not invest in the quality of their coffee are paid the same price as those making the extra time and money investments. One farmer explained this as follows:

> Here in the factory, all the coffee from different farmers is mixed together whether it is low quality or high quality. Now the farmers who work very hard end up getting disadvantaged because their high quality coffee gets a poor price because of those who bring poor quality (FGD farmers, 24-1-2013).

This situation demoralises farmers and also causes tensions. Several farmers, for example, argued that farmers who fail to adopt good practices should be banned from the factory. Cooperatives, however, cannot force farmers to adopt good practices.

It became clear during the fieldwork that both the cooperatives and the farmers have a tendency to focus primarily on short-term effects of higher prices and price premiums. While Board members and farmers were enthusiastic about FT and Utz certification and the benefits it had brought them, they kept emphasising the fact that it had not brought them significantly higher prices. The potential of certification, both FT and Utz, lies largely in the improvement of quality and production through better farming practices. It thus seems that the existing expectations regarding certification are not always realistic. Not only do the unrealistic expectations have a demoralising effect on farmers once the prices end up lower than anticipated, they divert attention from a key aspect of certification where much gain is to be expected: improving production and quality.

3.5 Challenges at farm level

During the FGDs, farmers were asked to explain and rank the problems they experienced in coffee farming. Five key problems emerged which were broadly similar for all six cooperatives visited in the study:
- *Low prices.* The most important complaint voiced by farmers was that coffee farming yielded little profit due to low prices. Farmers considered any amount above 100

KSh for a kilo of cherry to be a good price. In the past few years, however, they reported only having received a 'good' price for their coffee in 2010. Since 2009, the price per kilo had averaged around 50 KSh. Farmers complained that the low price of coffee has a demoralising effect, resulting in some farmers cutting down trees to plant other crops, neglecting their coffee farms or engaging in other activities such as cattle farming. Especially in Kiambu district, which is located close to Nairobi, farmers were reported to be abandoning or neglecting coffee farming.

- *Price fluctuations.* In the period 2009-2012, farmers reported that prices of cherry per kilogram varied between 20 KSh and 100 KSh. Both certified (FT and Utz) and non-certified farmers experienced such fluctuations. Particularly for FT this is a relevant observation as one of its starting-points is offering farmers protection from price fluctuations by means of a floor price. In Kenya, however, it seems that such a floor price has not been offered. Farmers explained that the price fluctuations contribute to a perception that coffee farming is not a reliable venture to engage in. In addition, they pointed out that the fluctuations undermine their ability to make long-term plans. As a farmer explained, 'how can I make investments in my farm if I don't know what I'll get next year?' (FGD farmers, 28-1-2013). Overall, farmers did not understand how the prices of coffee were established and what caused the high fluctuations.

- *High costs of production.* During all the FGDs, farmers complained about the high costs of inputs (e.g. fungicide, herbicide, and fertiliser), transport costs and labour. According to farmers, these costs had increased over the years, which is confirmed by the survey data. It was argued that the high costs of production contribute to some farmers reducing their use of farming inputs, resulting in lower production and quality. A farmer explained that 'for me the problem is cash. How can I do the inputs if I don't have the cash to buy them and the returns are so low?' (FGD farmers, 25-1-2013). The high costs of inputs are expected to be particularly relevant for certified farmers (both FT and Utz), as employing good agricultural practices is associated with a strong emphasis on using farming inputs. Looking at the quantitative data we observe that NC farmers (Kiama) used less inputs at baseline, but started to use more inputs compared to Utz and FT farmers over time and the difference disappeared.

- *Long payment periods.* Due to the way in which coffee is marketed in Kenya, there is a considerable time lag between the moment in which farmers deliver their coffee to the wetmill and the moment they get paid. The study found considerable differences between the cooperatives, with payment periods ranging from three months to a full year being reported. As coffee is the main cash crop for many farmers, the long payment periods means that they lack a continuous income. Especially in the case of emergency expenses, this can be problematic. The long waiting period was said to reduce the attractiveness of coffee farming – especially for young people – and to be a major cause of coffee hawking (sales to middlemen).

- *Climate change.* According to farmers, the weather is a key factor affecting the production of coffee. Farmers reported increasingly unstable weather conditions and attributed this to climate change. Some of the farmers argued that they had only one 'normal' year in the past five years. The issue of climate change is not only important because it contributes to lower yields and quality, it also undermines the predictability of farmers' income from coffee farming. In addition, climate change is also a relevant issue for this study because it undermines the positive impact of the application of good agricultural practices due to certification.

Another issue that was encountered in three of the six cooperatives that participated in this study is that of farmers were distrusting their board. Farmers from the cooperatives in question suspected the board of their cooperative of abusing their position for personal monetary gain. They suspected, for example, that their boards earned money by delaying payments and taking the interest, 'snatching' the discount gained from buying large quantities of farming inputs and not paying all insurance money in the case of theft. During several FGDs, farmers also raised concerns regarding the lack of real democracy in the cooperative due to the absence of secret ballots and the buying of votes using money or alcohol. While the above issues are certainly relevant as they affect the internal functioning and efficiency of cooperatives, this research could not examine these problems in full depth.[34]

3.6 Challenges at cooperative level

In addition to group interviews with farmers, FGDs were also held with the boards of all six cooperatives. One of the aims of these meetings was to get an idea of the problems faced at the cooperative level. The main issues brought forward during these meetings included:

- *Low and unstable prices.* Similar to the farmers, the cooperative leadership expressed their frustration about the price of coffee which they perceived as artificially low and largely beyond their control. As voiced by one board member: 'we always hear that Kenyan coffee is amongst the best in the world, but still we get paid very little. How is this possible?' (FGD Board, 21-1-2013). Like the farmers, board members do not understand why coffee prices are so low and why there are so many price fluctuations. An explanation for the low prices that was repeatedly brought up was that board members suspect the existence of cartels at the general auction in Nairobi (for more about prices, see Box 3.2). They argued that it is already determined beforehand who buys which coffee at what price. In addition, some Board members suggested that the grading of coffee is rigged, resulting in high quality coffee receiving consistently lower grades. Overall, there was a widespread feeling that people and organisations higher up in the coffee value chain were making lots of money at the expense of smallholder coffee farmers. During several interviews, it was pointed out that the low and unstable prices had resulted in severe tensions between the cooperative board on the one hand and the farmers on the other hand. For example, one board member explained that 'during the Annual General Meeting we encountered a lot of frustration. They [farmers] did not understand how the prices could drop so suddenly and so low. We had to

---

[34] In Chapter 5 and 6 we include studies that focus on cooperative trust and loyalty within coffee cooperatives.

show them everything [grading statement, administrative documents] and still they were not satisfied' (FGD Board, 21-1-2013).

- *Hawking*. Smallholder coffee farmers in Kenya are legally obliged to sell their produce to the cooperative. When they are not selling to the cooperative this is called hawking.[35] At the cooperative-level, hawking is a problem because it reduces the amount of coffee that is sold to the cooperative, leading subsequently to lower total overall revenues. High volumes/revenues are crucial, as Kenyan legislation dictates that cooperatives can only spend a maximum of 20% of their revenues on overhead costs. Consequently, higher revenues mean that the cooperative can invest more in, for example, factory repairs, maintenance and trainings to farmers. In addition, hawking was said to undermine the predictability of revenues which reduces the ability of the cooperative to plan ahead. A board member explained that 'due to hawking, we are missing a lot of coffee. It is hurting us because it affects the cash flow. [...] Because you don't know how much you'll get, you become limited in what you can do' (FGD Board, 21-1-2013). Overall, hawking appeared to be affecting some of the cooperatives more than others.
- *Theft*. All cooperatives experience severe problems related to theft, which was reported to be a common problem in Kenya (Oyuga, 2011). Board members explained that criminals engaged in coffee theft do not hesitate to use violence. In Kiambaa cooperative, for example, there was a big robbery in 2010 in which one armed guard was killed and another one hospitalised for two months. All six cooperatives spend considerable sums of money on security measures (e.g. steel doors, guards), particularly at times when there is a lot of coffee stored in the factories. Without such security measures, it was explained, insurance companies would not pay in the case of theft. Overall, security costs are a major expense for the cooperatives and contribute to higher overhead costs.

3.7 Regional differences

From FGDs it became clear that farmers in Kiambu district are far less focused on coffee farming compared to their colleagues in Nyeri district. As Kiambu district lies very close to Nairobi, farmers in the area have a lot of alternatives to producing coffee. Farmers explained that besides coffee they can easily sell other farm products, such as eggs or milk, to earn an income. In addition, farmers made clear that the proximity to Nairobi meant that there are also opportunities to earn an income outside farming. In Nyeri district on the other hand, local market opportunities appeared to be much more limited. The absence of a large urban area means that farmers in this district have fewer livelihood options available and are more dependent on coffee farming.

---

[35] Hawking is typically caused by farmers' urgent cash needs as it gives quick cash as opposed to the long waiting period associated with selling to the cooperative. In addition, hawking may give farmers a higher price compared to what they would get from the cooperative. In fact, several farmers explained they would like to have the freedom to decide for themselves to whom to sell their coffee. During the fieldwork three types of hawking were mentioned: (1) from farmer to farmer, (2) from farmer to (big) estate, (3) from farmer to miller.

Box 3.2. Price differences between cooperatives.

The price of coffee is determined by numerous factors, many of which lie beyond the cooperatives' control (e.g. changing weather conditions due to climate change, diseases, operations of hedge funds, competition from other coffee producing countries, exchange rate of the dollar). Coffee prices also follow a cycle. There are two key factors, however, that to a certain degree are within cooperatives' control: (1) the quality of coffee, and (2) the size of their overheads.

Regarding the first, there is an abundance of evidence indicating that better quality results in higher coffee prices (see also Section 3.2). This means that cooperatives with many members producing high quality coffee have higher revenues and in principle should be able to pay higher prices to their farmers. The fact that a cooperative has favourable coffee grades, however, does not automatically result in higher prices being paid to farmers. There are many examples of Kenyan cooperatives with relatively good quality coffee that still pay relatively poor prices and of cooperatives with relatively low quality coffee that still pay relatively good prices. This raises the question of how to explain such variations.

Discussions with Solidaridad staff revealed that the overheads of cooperatives are the key factor explaining the above variations. Cooperatives that operate efficiently and are able to reduce overhead costs can pay a larger part of their revenues to farmers, resulting in higher prices. Tekangu cooperative, for example, spends less than 16% of its annual revenues on overheads, which is considerably lower than the legal maximum of 20%. 'We are constantly looking for ways to improve our efficiency, you know, to tighten our belt. Because in the end, we know that the farmer will benefit' (Interview, Board of Tekangu, 28-1-2013).

If they want to increase their income, they have little alternative except to invest in coffee production.

The regional differences are clearly reflected in the survey data (Annex A.1, Table A.2). Farmers in Nyeri district get a higher gross income from coffee compared to farmers in Kiambu district. Furthermore, farmers in Nyeri district spend significantly more on inputs (e.g. fertiliser, spraying) compared to their peers in Kiambu district. This strongly suggests that farmers in Nyeri district are much more involved in employing good agricultural practices. Moreover, spending on farm inputs has increased considerably in Nyeri district between 2009 and 2013 while it has stayed the same in Kiambu district. Finally, the acreage under coffee production has increased considerably in Nyeri district during the period 2009-2013 while the area under coffee production in Kiambu district has stayed the same (Figure 3.10).

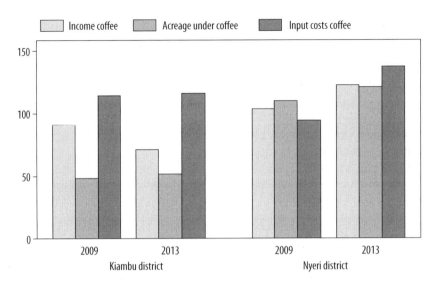

Figure 3.10. Relative price differences between Kiambu and Nyeri districts (normalised indices).

These findings are relevant because they suggest that the returns from certification are highest in areas characterised by high dependence on coffee farming where few alternative livelihood options are available.

3.8 Conclusions

The impact of the price premiums of certified coffee (both FT and Utz) on farmers' income in the six cooperatives surveyed remains fairly limited. Coffee makes up roughly one third to a quarter (between 20% and 46%) of farmers' total income. Furthermore, less than one third of the certified coffee produced in Kenya (28% for Utz, 30% for FT) is sold as certified coffee in Kenya. This means that (roughly) less than one ninth to one twelfth of farmers' income comes from coffee which fetched a certified price (i.e. was sold as certified). We observed significant differences in prices for cherry and dry coffee within years and over time. Certified farmers receive significantly better prices for their coffee, compared to their NC colleagues; Utz farmers get better prices than their FT colleague farmers.

No significant effects were observed in terms of increased production due to certification. Utz farmers were and are selling more dry coffee than FT farmers, but we did not observe significant differences with NC farmers. Although there seems to be a lot of room for improvement, coffee production does not seem to be the most important problem, but rather coffee trade. Certification does not seem to have provoked significant changes in the organisation and structure of the coffee chain.

Most farmers, whether certified or not, maintain a strong specialisation in coffee and some are increasing the acreage under coffee. Differences in acreage under coffee between certified and NC farmers disappear over time.

Farmers selected for certification are usually located in sub-optimal production areas. Consequently, initial gains from certification are usually high, but these tend to disappear once other NC farmers catch up in the process. Most initial gains from trade, therefore, gradually disappear due to spatial externalities. This points to important certification effects in the beginning of the coffee life cycle that tend to even out over time. Utz certified farmers maintain the relative advantage in expenditure levels compared to FT farmers that already existed from the beginning, but differences with NC farmers are mitigated.

The willingness of farmers to invest in coffee farming in Kenya is undermined by (relatively) low prices, price fluctuations, the high costs of production, long payment periods and climate change. Cooperative boards reported that due to these problems it remains a challenge to get and keep their farmers motivated to employ good farming practices.

Farmers expressed their satisfaction with the trainings on good agricultural practices associated with FT and Utz. At the same time, farmers demonstrated a strong tendency to focus primarily on the higher prices associated with certification. This focus can be considered undesirable as it is unrealistic, given the relatively small price premiums of FT and Utz in Kenya, while diverting attention from those aspects of certification where most gain is to be expected: improving production and quality.

Farmers in Kiambu district are far less focused on coffee farming compared to their colleagues in Nyeri district. As Kiambu district lies very close to Nairobi, farmers in the area have a lot of alternatives to producing coffee. Farmers in Nyeri district are more dependent on coffee farming. The absence of a large urban area with a lot of economic activity means that farmers in this district have fewer livelihood options available and are more dependent on coffee farming. If they want to increase their income, they have little alternative except to invest in coffee farming. This suggests that certification has the highest impact in areas characterised by high dependence on coffee farming.

Youth involvement in coffee farming remains problematic. The average age of the farmers in this study was 64 years. Board members reported very little rejuvenation of their membership. Young people do not perceive coffee farming as a profitable and attractive enterprise. Overall, most young people are inclined to look for other jobs which are better paying and offer better working conditions and a continuous income. If the interest of youth in smallholder coffee farmer does not change in the coming years, the future of smallholder coffee farming in Kenya looks rather bleak.

References

Anmer Coffee Company Limited (2010). Monthly Kenya Coffee news, November 2010.

Coffee Research Foundation (2013). Available at: http://www.crf.co.ke/.

Condliffe, K., W. Kebuchi, C. Love and R. Ruparell (2008). Kenya coffee: a cluster analysis. Harvard Business School, USA.

Kenya Coffee Traders Association (KCTA) (2011). The Coffee Quarterly, Issue 17/2011.

Kenya Coffee Traders Association (KCTA) (2012a). Nairobi Coffee Exchange statistics 2000/2001 to 2010/2011 coffee year. Nairobi, Kenya: KCTA.

Kenya Coffee Traders Association (KCTA) (2012b). Kenya Coffee Directory. Nairobi, Kenya: KCTA.

Kenya Coffee Producers and Traders Association (KCPTA) (2013). Available at: http://www.kcpta.co.ke/.

Kenya National Bureau of Statistics (KNBS) (2012). Economic Survey. Nairobi, Kenya: KNBS.

Kimemia, J.K. (2011). Batian coffee: a new coffee variety resistant to coffee berry disease and coffee leaf rust. Ruiru, Kenya: Coffee Research Station.

Kinoti, J. (2005). Opportunities for investment in the coffee sector. Presentation to the USA-Africa Business Summit in Baltimore, June 21-24 2005, Kenya Coffee Board.

Mureithi, L.P. (2008). Coffee in Kenya. Some challenges for decent work. International Labour Office, Geneva, Switzerland.

Mwangi, J. (2011). Government releases Sh1 billion coffee debt waiver. The Star Newspaper, Friday, 16 December 2011.

National Coffee Association USA (NCA USA) (2013). The history of coffee. Available at: http://www.ncausa.org/i4a/pages/index.cfm?pageid=68/.

Oikocredit (2011). Cooperating for development. Amersfoort, the Netherlands: Oikocredit Newsletter 211/2.

Oyuga, C.O. (2011). Identifying and addressing the factors that promote coffee theft in Kenya. Report of the national coffee stakeholders round table meeting held on March 4th, 2011 at the Kenya Comfort Hotel, Nairobi.

USAID (2010). Impact of USAID supported agricultural programs; household income growth and cost-effectiveness for poverty reduction. Washington, DC, USA: USAID.

Annex

A.1. Tables

Table A.1. Summary of the impact of coffee certification, Kenya.

	Kiambu district						Nyeri district					
	FT1 vs. NC[1]			FT2 vs. NC			Utz vs. NC			Utz vs. FT		
	2009	2013	Diff	2009	2013	Diff	2009	2013	Diff	2009	2013	Diff
Income												
Coffee income (×1000 KSh)		>		>		-	>			>		
Coffee income net (×1000 KSh)				>			>	>				
Dry coffee income (×1000 KSh)					<	-	>			>	>	
Cherry coffee income (×1000 KSh)				>			>					
Share of income from coffee (%)		>	+	>			>					
Share of income from coffee versus cattle[2]		>					>		-			
Income other crops (×1000 KSh)				<								
Income Livestock (×1000 KSh)		<										
Nonfarm income (×1000 KSh)												
Nonfarm income net (×1000 KSh)												
Total income (×1000 KSh)	<	<										
Inputs												
Inputcosts coffee (×1000 KSh)	<			>		-	>		-			
Inputcosts other crops (×1000 KSh)	<									<		+
Seedcosts other crops (×1000 KSh)	<		+	<			<		+	<		+
Hired labour coffee (yes/no)		<	-				>					
Costs livestock (×1000 KSh)												
Savings, credit and expenditure												
Credit (×1000 KSh)	<		+							<		
Savings (×1000 KSh)										>		
Expenditure food (×1000 KSh)		>	+									
Expenditure education (×1000 KSh)												
Expenditure energy (×1000 KSh)							>		-	>		
Expenditure transport (×1000 KSh)		<	-	<						>		
Expenditure total (×1000 KSh)										>	>	
Production and prices												
Coffee area (acres)				>		-	>		-	>		
Number of mature coffee trees		<		>			>		-			
Coffee trees per acre				<	>	+	<			<	-	
Coffee yield (kg/acre)	<			>								

Table A.1. Continued.

	Kiambu district						Nyeri district					
	FT1 vs. NC[1]			FT2 vs. NC			Utz vs. NC			Utz vs. FT		
	2009	2013	Diff	2009	2013	Diff	2009	2013	Diff	2009	2013	Diff
Production and prices												
Coffee yield (kg/tree)				>			>					
Coffee sold in cherry form (kg)				>		-	>					
Dry coffee sold (kg)					<	-	>		-	>	>	
Cherry coffee price (KSh/kg)	>	>	+	>	<	-	>	>	+	>	>	+
Dry coffee price (KSh/kg)	>	>	+	<		-		>	+		>	+
Welfare												
Have piped water (yes/no)	>			<			<		+			
Have improved latrine (yes/no)							<					
Animals in stock		<		<							>	
Investment												
Land attached investments (×1000 KSh)												
Made house improvements (yes/no)	<				>	+	<	<		<		-
Investment in new coffee (yes/no)	>			<		-	>			>		
Perceptions												
Economic situation versus 5 years ago (1-3)					<							
Economic situation versus 5 years later (1-3)				>	<	-	>		-	>		
Number of organisations				>	>		>	>		<		
Satisfaction technical assistance (1-5)												
Satisfaction trade assistance (1-5)												
Identification index (1-3)	<		+									
Force index (1-3)						+				<		
Risk, gender & health												
Risk (1-3)				<			<	+				
Gender index (5-25)							>					
Days lost due to poor health (logarithm)				>			>					

[1] FT = Fair Trade certified; NC = non-certified; Utz = Utz certified.
[2] Income coffee/(income livestock/100).
Results from matched difference-in-diference estimation ($P > 0.1$).

Table A.2. Descriptive statistics of studied farms in the Kiambu district.

Kiambu district	Treatment[1]			Control[1]		
	N	Mean	SD	N	Mean	SD
Household (HH) characteristics						
Age of the head	62	69.24	14.73	165	65.88	12.71
Gender of head	62	1.47	0.50	165	1.38	0.49
Marital status of head	62	2.65	1.09	165	2.59	0.98
Highest education level	62	11.00	4.75	166	11.76	4.41
HH size (sum persons)	62	4.52	2.12	167	4.66	2.27
HH size (sum adult equiv.)	62	3.55	1.65	167	3.71	1.85
HH years of education (sum years)	62	32.27	21.25	167	35.17	20.92
Farming experience (yrs)	59	42.25	15.10	157	36.48	17.50
Years lived in locality	58	44.19	13.45	159	42.71	19.68
Accessibility						
Distance to nearest wet mill	62	2.76	2.24	158	2.25	1.76
Distance to wet mill where coffee is delivered	62	1.98	1.25	167	2.21	1.94
Distance to nearest electricity supply	62	0.11	0.29	167	0.09	0.34
Distance to nearest dairy	62	3.05	4.50	167	4.81	5.02
Distance to nearest extension advice	62	3.23	3.26	167	4.20	3.50
Distance to vet service	62	2.75	3.18	167	3.49	3.17
Distance to nearest major market for farm produce	62	4.21	3.48	159	4.56	2.74
Land						
Acreage at HH inception	56	2.30	2.49	158	2.49	2.31
Acreage owned now	57	2.14	2.16	160	2.35	1.84
Number of coffee parcels	62	1.00	0.00	163	1.01	0.11
Number of coffee plots	62	1.10	0.30	163	1.01	0.11
Coffee variety	62	0.79	0.41	167	0.86	0.35
Acreage under coffee	61	0.60	0.61	162	0.87	0.86
Number of mature coffee trees	62	289.77	336.79	160	461.75	433.89
Assets						
Assets owned in 2006 (×1000)	52	42.45	71.73	146	49.55	72.07
Value of assets in 2013 (×1000)	62	225.19	504.43	163	126.46	348.57
Total livestock units in 2013	61	6.97	9.95	162	6.70	7.63
Productivity, input use and sales						
Coffee input cost per acre	53	6.59	16.40	139	6.83	15.98
Kgs of cherry sold	58	371.48	510.42	154	376.83	463.61
Kgs of Mbuni sold	39	34.13	32.60	93	47.87	53.72
Price per kg of cherry	53	50.74	35.98	134	36.74	23.30
Price of kg of mbuni	36	171.83	61.42	80	91.28	78.32

Table A.2. Continued.

Kiambu district	Treatment[1]			Control[1]		
	N	Mean	SD	N	Mean	SD
Income						
Coffee income (reported prices)	62	21.69	37.53	158	13.09	16.29
Income from other crops	61	0.65	3.07	163	1.05	5.08
Income from livestock	61	68.71	129.27	162	93.67	159.56
Share of income from coffee	55	32.11	37.36	145	23.74	35.64
Share of income from coffee versus cattle	33	37.62	58.68	95	19.60	32.51
Perceptions and organisation						
Number of organisations	62	0.24	0.43	163	0.52	0.53
Economic situation versus 5 years ago (1-3)	62	1.37	0.71	160	1.43	0.76
Economic situation versus 5 years later (1-3)	62	1.21	0.52	160	1.29	0.63
Satisfaction technical assistance (1-5)	60	3.12	1.14	161	2.76	1.25
Satisfaction trade assistance (1-5)	60	3.07	1.15	161	2.75	1.17
Identification index	59	2.48	0.62	160	2.48	0.51
Force index	59	2.38	0.53	160	2.12	0.51
Gender and risk						
Gender index male	34	14.35	2.59	97	13.98	3.17
Gender index female	40	14.80	2.00	80	15.11	2.49
Risk	60	2.18	0.47	162	2.14	0.45

[1] Treatment = Ndumberi; control = Kiambaa + Mikari; SD = standard deviation.

Table A.3. Descriptive statistics of studied farms in the Nyeri district.

Nyeri district	Treatment[1]			Control[1]		
	N	Mean	SD	N	Mean	SD
Household (HH) characteristics						
Age of the head	76	60.46	13.38	176	61.40	14.00
Gender of head	76	1.21	0.41	177	1.29	0.46
Marital status of head	76	2.33	0.77	176	2.52	0.91
Highest education level	77	10.74	3.77	187	9.92	4.09
HH size (sum persons)	77	4.13	1.98	187	3.90	1.82
HH size (sum adult equiv.)	77	3.12	1.48	187	2.95	1.36
HH years of education (sum years)	77	28.44	17.31	187	26.33	17.37
Farming experience (yrs)	77	36.34	19.36	182	36.08	17.01
Years lived in locality	77	42.43	20.60	182	36.97	17.64
Accessibility						
Distance to nearest wet mill	76	2.03	1.02	183	1.66	1.12
Distance to wet mill where coffee is delivered	77	1.79	1.55	187	1.27	1.12
Distance to nearest electricity supply	77	0.55	0.90	187	0.46	0.72
Distance to nearest dairy	77	2.29	3.92	187	1.19	1.95
Distance to nearest extension advice	77	2.52	3.76	187	3.17	3.02
Distance to vet service	77	2.00	1.72	187	2.30	2.12
Distance to nearest major market for farm produce	76	4.93	2.99	184	4.16	3.85
Land						
Acreage at HH inception	76	2.00	1.71	183	2.08	1.86
Acreage owned now	76	1.87	1.74	183	1.76	1.39
Number of coffee parcels	77	1.01	0.11	185	1.02	0.13
Number of coffee plots	77	1.01	0.11	185	1.02	0.13
Coffee variety	77	0.78	0.42	187	0.83	0.38
Acreage under coffee	76	0.70	0.65	183	0.69	0.66
Number of mature coffee trees	77	203.32	139.34	185	217.02	165.66
Assets						
Assets owned in 2006 (×1000)	73	35.33	39.17	177	38.84	51.01
Value of assets in 2013 (×1000)	76	68.94	108.92	185	100.94	233.91
Total livestock units in 2013	77	10.03	8.34	185	8.33	8.13
Productivity, input use and sales						
Coffee input cost per acre	64	18.87	26.75	166	14.54	21.47
Kgs of cherry sold	77	652.86	841.38	179	604.50	648.43
Kgs of Mbuni sold	65	65.05	70.43	147	48.39	48.40
Price per kg of cherry	74	87.86	30.80	170	54.51	22.87
Price of kg of mbuni	65	106.55	40.49	141	84.24	29.51

Table A.3. Continued.

Nyeri district	Treatment[1]			Control[1]		
	N	Mean	SD	N	Mean	SD
Income						
Coffee income (reported prices)	74	49.54	50.55	182	35.10	43.67
Income from other crops	76	0.55	3.82	180	1.38	5.89
Income from livestock	77	41.58	124.72	186	34.12	72.92
Share of income from coffee	71	38.33	31.15	173	29.21	27.77
Share of income from coffee versus cattle	33	267.40	483.99	93	129.27	195.31
Perceptions and organisation						
Number of organisations	76	0.16	0.54	184	0.13	0.33
Economic situation versus 5 years ago (1-3)	77	1.34	0.64	185	1.34	0.61
Economic situation versus 5 years later (1-3)	77	1.29	0.58	184	1.26	0.54
Satisfaction technical assistance (1-5)	77	3.30	1.17	183	3.25	1.18
Satisfaction trade assistance (1-5)	77	3.29	1.28	183	3.19	1.22
Identification index	77	2.41	0.56	182	2.31	0.66
Force index	77	2.22	0.53	182	2.30	0.59
Gender and risk						
Gender index male	42	14.21	2.96	112	13.89	2.53
Gender index female	45	14.36	3.02	86	15.15	2.64
Risk	77	2.25	0.38	184	2.18	0.33

[1] Treatment = Tekangu; control = Rugi + Kiama; SD = standard deviation.

Table A.4. General information on Kiambu and Nyeri districts

	Kiambu district	Nyeri district	Kenya[1]
Population	1,623,282	693,558	821,491
Surface area (km^2)	2,543	3,337	12,368
Density (people per km^2)	638	208	66
Poverty rate, based on KIHBS (%)[2]	27.2	32.7	47.2
Share of urban population (%)	60.8	24.5	29.9
Health and education outcomes			
Fully-immunised <1 yr (%, 2010/2011)	64.8	46.3	64.0
Malaria (as % of all 1st outpatient visits)	19.0	3.2	27.7
Tuberculosis in every 10,000 people (2009/2010)	46	32	39.0
HIV+ ante-natal care clients (%, 2010)	4.8	4.4	5.9
Population with primary education (%)	58.5	61.4	66.6
Population with secondary education (%)	17.3	19.8	12.7
Access to infrastructure			
Improved water (% households 2009)	78.1	69.3	66.5
Improved sanitation (% households 2009)	99.6	99.6	87.8
Electricity (% households 2009)	53.0	26.3	22.7
Paved roads (as % of total roads)	16.0	8.9	9.4
Good/fair roads (as % of total roads)	44.8	40.7	43.5
Service coverage			
Delivered in a health centre	68.9	84.0	37.5
Qualified medical assistant during birth	68.4	84.0	37.6
Had all vaccinations	90.0	85.1	75.0
Adequate height for age	69.3	44.8	59.8
Can read and write	87.4	92.9	66.4
Attending school, 15-18 years	70.1	72.8	70.9

[1] All entries in the 'Kenya' column show county averages.

[2] County poverty rates are derived by dividing the total number of poor people in each county in 2005/2006 by the total population in each county.

Table A.5. Probit models after matching

Variable	Utz vs. non-Utz certified		
	Coef.	SE	Significance
Kiambu district			
Sex	0.169	0.272	0.535
Highest level of education	-0.005	0.017	0.789
Farming experience (years)	-0.003	0.012	0.811
Years household lived in locality	-0.003	0.010	0.783
No. of persons/household	0.014	0.045	0.755
Land owned at the start	0.059	0.072	0.416
Distance from homestead to nearest dairy	-0.036	0.025	0.149
Total asset value(3 years ago)	0.000	0.000	0.787
Distance from homestead to nearest extension	-0.003	0.045	0.944
Distance from homestead to nearest vet	-0.036	0.052	0.492
Distance from homestead to nearest wet-mill	-0.014	0.075	0.851
Distance from homestead to nearest market	0.076	0.052	0.144
Constant	-0.044	0.663	0.947

No. of observations = 134
LR chi^2 (12) = 6.25
Prob. > chi^2 = 0.9031
Pseudo (R^2) = 0.0341

Variable	Coef.	SE	Significance
Nyeri district			
Sex	-0.202	0.341	0.554
Highest level of education	-0.010	0.027	0.719
Farming experience (years)	0.004	0.019	0.835
Years household lived in locality	0.002	0.019	0.931
No. of persons / household	0.038	0.069	0.583
Land owned at the start	-0.033	0.055	0.554
Distance from homestead to nearest dairy	0.032	0.042	0.453
Total asset value(3 years ago)	0.000	0.000	0.708
Distance from homestead to nearest extension	-0.055	0.035	0.116
Distance from homestead to nearest vet	-0.025	0.072	0.729
Distance from homestead to nearest wet-mill	0.105	0.126	0.403
Distance from homestead to nearest market	-0.018	0.046	0.69
Constant	0.410	0.788	0.603

No. of observations = 128
LR chi^2 (12) = 4.98
Prob > chi^2 = 0.9587
Pseudo (R^2) = 0.0289

A.2. Figures

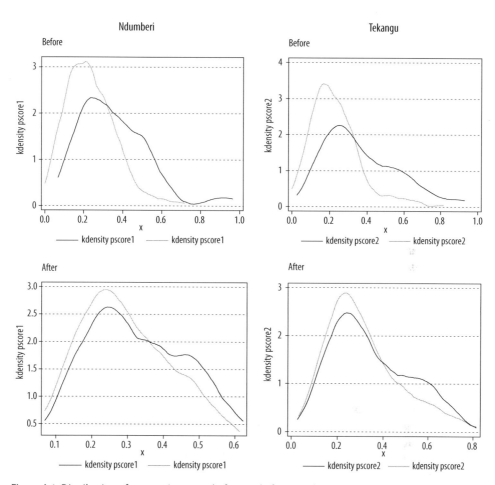

Figure A.1. Distribution of propensity scores before and after matching

Chapter 4

Impact of multiple certification on smallholder coffee farmers' livelihoods: evidence from southern Ethiopia

Amsaya Anteneh Woubie, Roldan Muradian and Ruerd Ruben
For correspondence: r.ruben@maw.ru.nl; amsayanteneh@gmail.com

4.1 Introduction

Coffee is – next to petroleum – one of the most valuable agricultural commodities traded at international markets (Arslan and Reicher, 2010; Rodriquez, 2012). Today, coffee remains one of the most important sources of export income for East African nations (i.e. Ethiopia, Uganda, Kenya, and Tanzania). Ethiopia is known to be the birthplace and the primary centre of biodiversity of Arabica coffee (Daviron and Ponte, 2005; Labouisse *et al.*, 2008). The main production systems in Ethiopia are forest coffee in the traditional way, semi-forest coffee, garden coffee, and plantation coffee owned by the state (Labouisse *et al.*, 2008; Stellmacher and Grote, 2011). Considering the country's suitable altitude, rainfall, temperature, and fertile soil, the potential for coffee production in Ethiopia is very high.

Ethiopia contributes around 5% to the world coffee production (Arslan and Reicher, 2010) and represents more than 30% of the total regional coffee supply in Sub-Saharan Africa, being the 5th largest global producer of Arabica coffee (ICO, 2011) after Brazil, Vietnam, Indonesia and Colombia. Coffee, besides its cultural importance, has an important place in the Ethiopian economy since it provides 35% of total export earnings of the country (CSA, 2008). Ethiopian coffee production is characterised by two distinct features, namely: (1) it is dominated by smallholder farmers, while plantation production plays a minimum role; and (2) Ethiopia is the origin of the worldwide coffee Arabica gene-pool (Stellmacher and Grote, 2011).

About 95% of coffee in Ethiopia is produced by over one million smallholder coffee farmers living on subsistence farms that are smaller than half a hectare of land (Gemech and Struthers, 2007); the remaining 5% of coffee is produced at large-scale plantations. About quarter of the Ethiopian population is directly or indirectly involved into the coffee value chain (Bastin and Matteucci, 2007). The livelihoods of these smallholder coffee farmers are based on rather insecure low-input low-output agricultural production systems which make them particularly vulnerable to poverty, since their wellbeing is mainly dependent on income from coffee. On the other hand, coffee is a worldwide traded cash crop with new markets emerging, and many coffee-dependent developing countries, such as Ethiopia, are struggling with suitable marketing arrangements for their coffee. While coffee is an important income source for developing countries, coffee prices are highly volatile and crises are common (Cashin *et al.*, 2002). The international nature of coffee marketing and sales directly exposes smallholder coffee producers in developing countries to strong international price fluctuations.

The coffee price crises that happened regularly in the period between 1990-2004 had enormous economic and social impacts on smallholder coffee grower farmers around the globe (Méndez *et al.*, 2010). Since the coffee price is largely determined by international exchange markets in New York and London (Kodama, 2009), coffee producing countries are price-takers in the world market, and are therefore prone to external shocks in coffee prices over which they have little influence or control. Due to this feature, coffee producing countries will continue to be highly vulnerable to natural cycles that are endemic in the production of primary agricultural commodities like coffee. Since the coffee price is largely determined at international exchange markets, smallholder coffee farmers have been among the hardest hit by coffee price volatility. While coffee trade is big business, local Ethiopian smallholder coffee farmers receive only a fraction of the retail price and continue to be engaged in marginal subsistence farming.

In an effort to identify ways out of the periodic crisis and to confront the coffee price crisis, high expectations were placed on the role of various 'sustainable' and 'responsible' coffee certification initiatives (Méndez *et al.*, 2010; Wollni and Zeller, 2007) as alternative options for smallholder coffee farmers in coffee producing regions of the world. Due to growing demands for healthier and more socially- and environmentally-friendly coffee in larger consumer countries, coffee certification in cooperatives gradually gained wide recognition and significance worldwide (Jena *et al.*, 2012; Petit, 2007; Stellmacher and Grote, 2011). The main principle of certification is to provide smallholder coffee farmers with new opportunities to improve their wellbeing and it is argued that labelling can be a suitable strategy for providing smallholder coffee farmers with access to markets that allow them to generate higher and more stable cash income from coffee sales.

The main idea behind certification is that consumers are motivated to pay a price premium for products that meet certain precisely defined and assured quality standards (Grote *et al.*, 2007; Wissel *et al.*, 2010). In today's consumer markets, being able to label a product as 'organic' or 'Fair Trade' and to protect the label from counterfeiting is considered a valuable marketing advantage. The price premiums are intended to be used for promoting socio-economic change and/or environmental sustainability in the production areas. In this context, voluntary product certification standards such as Fair Trade are promoted as critical devices to make smallholder farmers in developing countries less susceptible to volatile 'free' world market prices and to enhance their market integration in order to contribute to improvements in their socio-economic situation.

Some of the most common certification types that are found in Ethiopia are: organic, Fair Trade, Forest Stewardship Council, Utz certified, Rainforest Alliance, Bird Friendly, as well as several combinations of these certifications, such as the double certified organic and Fair Trade (Volkmann, 2008). Each certification regime is based on different standards and principles, defined with a set of criteria and indicators. Various certifications are expected to offer a combination of benefits to smallholder coffee farmers, including a higher price and more stable income, increased market access, and technical assistance, thus serving as multiple pathways for supporting the livelihoods of coffee producing households (Ruben and Fort, 2011). In turn, smallholder coffee farmers are required to meet certain required production and management standards. Furthermore, their respective organisations (in this case: primary coffee cooperatives) are also subject to periodic inspections by standards organisations, since most certification is undertaken through cooperatives.

As the number of certification initiatives in coffee increased, and consumers in the north became more and more aware of different certification types regarding issues of quality, taste, health, and environment, it became more important for them and for national governments, cooperative organisations, and international donor agencies that support the coffee cooperations to investigate and accurately document the impact of these alternative forms of certification on smallholder coffee farmers' livelihoods.

Despite the expansion of coffee cooperative certification and the growing importance of certification for the improvement of livelihoods of smallholder coffee farmers in coffee producing areas of Ethiopia, there is still a lack of empirical evidence that can quantify and substantiate the welfare impact of certification in general, and the implications of double and triple certification in particular for smallholder coffee farmers' livelihoods. Moreover, understanding of the mediating role of coffee cooperatives on rural livelihoods in Ethiopia is limited.

The principal objective of this field study was to empirically estimate the impact of double (Fair Trade/organic) and triple (Fair Trade/organic/Utz) certifications on various well-being indicators of smallholder coffee farmers at household level in Sidama Zone, Southern Ethiopia, using a propensity score matching (PSM) method to guarantee a balanced comparison. By analysing the welfare impact of double and triple certification, we aim to contribute to a better understanding of the potential role of different certification regimes and to provide valuable insights regarding their mutual interaction. The study will be useful to generate empirical evidence on whether double and triple certification has rural livelihood development impacts on smallholder coffee producer farmers in the study area.

The remainder of this chapter is structured as follows: Section 4.2 starts with a concise description of the structure of coffee production and exchange in Ethiopia, followed by a short comparison with findings regarding multi-certification impact elsewhere in the world in Section 4.3. In Section 4.4 we discuss the sources of data and methods for data analysis applied in this study. Section 4.5 outlines the statistical approach for comparing the characteristics of smallholder coffee farmers that belong to the treatment and control groups, highlighting major differences between coffee farmers that belong to different certification categories. Section 4.6 analyses the main differences between treatment and control groups for the selected outcome indicators. Section 4.7 discusses major study findings and suggests some policy implications.

4.2 Coffee production and exchange in Ethiopia

As compared to other regions such as Latin America, the use of environmental, socio-economic, and/or health-related certification standards in agriculture is a relatively new and recent phenomenon in Ethiopia (Jena *et al.*, 2012). However, in recent years, attention has been given to the certification of agricultural products in general and non-timber forest products in particular by international certification agencies, standard bodies, governmental and non-governmental development organisations, and private companies supplying specialty markets (Jena *et al.*, 2012; Stellmacher and Grote, 2011). The certification of forest coffee in Ethiopia started in 2002 with the aim of conserving the forests and providing the smallholder farmers with better livelihood prospects. The coffee certification is mainly undertaken within the coffee cooperative structure (Stellmacher and Grote, 2011), and smallholder coffee farmers could participate in certification through their primary cooperatives. In Ethiopia, certification focuses mainly on coffee since coffee is: (1) the main export crop of the country's economy and the main income source for millions of smallholder coffee farmers that live in poverty; and (2) it is a resource with high potential to be marketed as a specialty gourmet product on the world's major coffee markets.

Normally, the Ethiopian coffee marketing chain follows two alternative pathways. The first options is through the Ethiopia Commodity Exchange (ECX), which was established in April 2008 with the objectives of implementing a national agricultural marketing information system that connects all regions and provides relevant and timely market information to various market actors, in order to establish and strengthen vertical and horizontal linkages among producers, cooperatives, wholesalers, processors and exporters through an organised trading platform. The second marketing option is a direct export pathway through the cooperative unions (Meijerink *et al.*, 2010). Certified coffee is expected to be sold only through the coffee marketing cooperative unions and is directly exported to different countries in the world, even while cooperative unions are not able to buy all of the certified coffee from individual coffee farmers (Kodama, 2009). Since 2001 cooperative unions have been legally allowed to bypass the national coffee auction system and since 2009 they can bypass the ECX, and sell directly to international exporters (FDRE, 2008; Jena *et al.*, 2012; McCarthy, 2001; Petit, 2007; Stellmacher and Grote, 2007).

To improve the overall effectiveness of cooperative performance in the country, the current government of Ethiopia (People's Revolutionary Democratic Front) promotes restructuring of the whole cooperative sector, including the coffee sub-sector, and has established coffee cooperative unions (second-layer cooperative organisations) as umbrella organisations since the 1990s (Getnet and Anullo, 2012; Jena *et al.*, 2012). The main aim of establishing coffee cooperative unions is to provide protection, resources and expertise to the primary coffee cooperatives, so that they can overcome coffee export problems and capture increased revenue from coffee sales. Currently, 10 coffee cooperative unions function in the country, and Sidama Farmers' Coffee Cooperative Union – our case study – is the second largest union in Ethiopia.

4.3 Impact of multi-certification

Although various empirical studies have been carried out in previous years to assess the impact of product certification on smallholder coffee farmers' livelihoods, these studies usually lack reliable baseline studies to be used as a benchmark. Most previous studies also present biases in their methodology with respect to farmer selection. Furthermore, many certification studies that were conducted focus on the effect of a single certification regime (mainly Fair Trade). Generally, given the importance of evaluating claims that participation in certification brings advantages to producers, the literature on certification impact analyses is surprisingly scarce.

Earlier empirical studies (Dörr, 2009; Kodama, 2009; Milford, 2004; Philpott *et al.*, 2007; Ronchi, 2002) showed that certification could improve returns to smallholder coffee farmers. Several studies (Jena *et al.*, 2012; Ruben and Fort, 2011; Valkila, 2009; Valkila and Nygren, 2009) indicate, however, that the increase in income due to certification is usually quite modest. To the best of our knowledge, no systematic research is available on the impact of double and triple certification on farm-households' livelihood. We therefore seek to understand and measure this impact with the aim of better understanding the mutual interactions between certifications systems and processes. This study is therefore designed to fill this information and knowledge gap by conducting an empirical investigation at farm-household level using comprehensive survey data from Sidama Zone, Southern Ethiopia. We compare smallholder coffee farmers certified only by Fair Trade (single) with otherwise similar farmers that are recognised as Fair Trade/organic (double) or Fair Trade/organic/ Utz (triple) certified. Certification is expected to significantly contribute to improved livelihoods of smallholder coffee farmers by enhancing their income through premium payments and by stabilising welfare through minimum prices. We hypothesise that double and triple certification has an additional effect on the livelihoods of smallholder coffee farmers over and above the impact of single certification.

Multi-certification refers to a situation where cooperatives adhere to several – partly overlapping – production standards for coffee. Since standards include some similar criteria, efforts are made to synchronise compliance monitoring. Access to a certification and the use of certification seals are important tools to access markets that value sustainable production practices. Regrettably, different standards require specific instruments to demonstrate compliance with their respective requirements. In some cases, an organisation must implement a number of instruments – many of them in parallel – to demonstrate compliance with the same (environmental or social) principles of different standards. In addition, in some cases, certifying institutions require the implementation of various instruments for the same standard. All of this hinders the efforts of smallholder organisations to become certified in order to access high-demand markets.

Most coffee companies and organisations market coffees with two, three or more certifications, so field production, profit, processing and marketing needs to meet various standards and norms, whose compliance is monitored by several different agencies, each with its own formats and standard interpretation criteria. Farmers' cooperatives increasingly rely on multiple certification for the following reasons (Schreiber and Costilla Mora, 2011; Sustaineo, 2013):
- More than half of the certified or verified coffee produced according to the administration of the schemes is not sold as such due to limited market demand.
- Farmers prefer to reduce and spread risks and therefore engage simultaneously with different certification schemes.
- Marginal costs of compliance tend to reduce if farmers only need to take few additional measures to become eligible for an additional certificate.
- Different certification schemes might offer specific advantages and benefits in terms of production technologies, training and quality.

Multiple certification requires concerted efforts on the part of several standards organisations. Efforts are made to harmonise joint compliance with the following international standards: (1) IFOAM (International Federation of Organic Agriculture Movements) Guidance Manual for Smallholder Group Certification; (2) Internal Control Systems (Utz certified); (3) Standard for Group Certification (Rainforest Alliance – Sustainable Agriculture Network); and (4) Common Requirements for Producer Group Certification (International Social and Environmental Accreditation and Labelling – ISEAL). In addition, the guidelines for the evaluation of the equivalence of organic producer group certification schemes applied in developing countries (European Commission), recommendations of the National Organic Standard Board (US Department of Agriculture), clarifying document regarding the Fair Trade Standards for Smallholder Organisations (Fair Trade labelling Organisation) and C.A.F.E. Practices smallholder supplement (from Starbucks) are considered.

4.4 Data and approach

To evaluate the impact of double and triple certification on the livelihoods of smallholder coffee farmers that are members of local cooperatives, household survey data was collected from a random sample of coffee farmers in southern Ethiopia through face-to-face interviews. The survey was conducted from June 2010 to January 2011 in five districts (Dale, Wonsho, Shebdino, AletaWondo, and AletaChuko) of the Sidama Zone, one of the major coffee growing zones in the Southern region of the country. The study area is located 270 km south from the capital, Addis Ababa.

To select our sample, we followed a multi-stage random sampling method. Out of the 45 primary coffee cooperatives composing Sidama Farmers' Cooperative Union[36], we selected ten co-ops, based on performance indicators. The members' sample was drawn randomly from the registration lists of the selected primary cooperatives. The total survey sample consists of 700 co-op member smallholder coffee farmer households. The sample was designed to include three different groups of respondents: (1) smallholder coffee farmers certified only by Fair Trade (FT) (single certified); (2) coffee farmers certified under FT/organic (double certified); and (3) coffee farmers certified under FT/organic/Utz (triple certified). Household-level data was collected through an identical questionnaire for farmers under single, double, and triple certification regimes.

We first present the descriptive statistics of our sample to give an overall picture of the surveyed smallholder coffee farmers that belong to different certification groups. We selected 10 primary coffee marketing cooperatives out of 45 coffee cooperatives under the Sidama Union that were (1) single certified (Fura, DebonaWiecho, Megara and Ganie Cooperatives), (2) double certified (Fero, Telamo, HalonaGelma, and Gerbicho Lela Cooperatives) and (3) triple certified (Gedibonasheicha and Bokasso Cooperatives). We subsequently divided the smallholder cooperative member coffee farmers into three groups: (1) only FT certified (single certified), (2) FT/organic certified (double certified), and (3) FT/organic/Utz certified (triple certified). In this study FT certified (single) coffee farmer households are used as a control group. Table 4.1 provides information on the number of cases and sample sizes per certification type.

The survey format covered a large number of issues, such as household characteristics, production and marketing of coffee, social capital, farmers' perception of the cooperative performance, types of marketing channels, savings and credit, degree of participation in coffee marketing cooperatives and the status of various certification schemes. In order to complement quantitative data with qualitative information, in-depth interviews were also held with various relevant cooperative stakeholders at district, zonal, regional, and federal levels, as well as with coffee farmers in the field. Additional expert interviews were conducted with staff members of the Sidama Union and co-op experts in the capital city of Addis Ababa.

---

[36] The union is a second level cooperative organisation established by more than one primary cooperative organisation with similar objectives.

Table 4.1. Number of cases and sample size by certification type of coffee cooperatives under the Sidama Union.

Certification type	Number of cases	Sample size (n)	Percentage
Fair Trade/organic	4 cooperatives	280	40
Fair Trade/organic/Utz	2 cooperatives	140	20
Fair Trade only	4 cooperatives	280	40
Total	10 cooperatives	700	100

4.5 Measuring the impact of double and triple certification on coffee farmers' livelihood

Our objective is to empirically assess the impact of double and triple certification on smallholder coffee farmers' livelihoods in the study area, using a number of selected outcome variables. Usually, the main empirical challenge for conducting an impact evaluation study of this kind resides in the ability to answer the question: 'What would have happened to households participating in double and triple certifications if they had not participated?' Given this type of hypothetical situation, it is not empirically possible to observe the counterfactual. Just taking the mean outcome of non-participants as a control group to conduct impact analysis is likely to generate selection bias (Bourguignon, 1999; Ruben and Fort, 2011; White and Bamberger, 2008). The selection bias makes the observed control group an inappropriate counterfactual.

In any non-randomised sample usually there are two main potential sources of selection bias, i.e. observable and unobservable characteristics biases. Participating households might differ from non-participants in observable aspects such as wealth and educational level, which might influence the household's decision to join the cooperative or participate in certification (Fischer and Qaim, 2014). Furthermore, participating households might differ from non-participating households in unobservable aspects such as motivation, risk preference and entrepreneurial spirit (Bernard *et al.*, 2008; Heckman *et al.*, 1997). This might also influence household's decisions for joining a programme or become co-op member.

To overcome the above selection problem, PSM is commonly used (Heckman *et al.*, 1997; Jalan and Ravallion, 2003; Rosenbaum and Rubin, 1983; Rubin, 1974; Rubin and Thomas, 1996). PSM identifies a counterfactual that controls for all observable factors within the treatment group.

A two-stage propensity score matching method was used to overcome biases and it enables us to measure the impact of double and triple certification on coffee farmers' livelihoods by comparing the mean difference of (matched) double and triple certified coffee households with single certified households having similar propensity scores. To do so, we first need to estimate each treatment group household's 'propensity score' or likelihood of joining certification, using a probit model where the dependent variable is the certification status as the selection variable conditional on basic characteristics of both the treatment and the control group. The propensity score of each coffee farmer measures their tendency to participate in double and triple certification. The magnitude of a propensity score lies between 0 and 1; the larger the score, the more likely it is that the coffee farmer would join the certification programme.

After estimating the propensity score, the second step is to compose balanced groups based on their estimated propensity scores. Coffee farmers in each group should have similar propensity scores. Both groups can then be compared with respect to the performance based on several matching methods.[37] In this particular study, we used the kernel matching method proposed by Heckman *et al.* (1997) because it is a widely-used method for estimating results in this type of analysis. In kernel matching, each treated unit is matched with a weighted average of all control units with weights that are inversely proportional to the distance between the propensity scores of treated and controls (Getnet and Anullo, 2012). Based on the matched sample, we compute measures of double and triple certification impact on the participating coffee farmers.

In this study, impacts of both types of certification on participating coffee farmers are measured in terms of household coffee income, average price, productivity, access to credit, savings, and accessing technical assistance. The average treatment effect on the treated (ATT) measures the average difference between the (treated) units and their corresponding non-treated (control) match. Once each treated unit is matched with a control unit, the difference between the outcome of the treated unit and the outcome of the control unit is compared. The mean difference in performance between the matched treated observations follows a t-test for statistical significance. If the difference is positive and statistically significant, then the treatment is yielding its expected impact.

4.6 Results

We first describe the characteristics of coffee farmers in the double and triple certification groups (Table 4.2). The livelihood of local coffee farmers in the study area is based on household-based subsistence agriculture, mainly focusing on the production of coffee. According to our survey result, farmers cultivate extremely small plots of agricultural land. On average, coffee households own 0.5 hectares of land (which reflects the dramatic land scarcity in the study area) – mainly used for the cultivation of coffee. Coffee is the main cash crop for many households living in and around the study area. Most interviewed cooperative members stated that they obtain

---

[37] Different methods of matching have been proposed in the estimation process of the ATT in the literature (Heckman *et al.*, 1997; Rosenbaum and Rubin, 1983; Smith, 1997). The most widely used are: nearest-neighbour matching, radius matching, kernel matching, and stratification matching.

Table 4.2. Description of variables and summary statistics.

Variables	Fair Trade/organic (double)			Fair Trade/organic/Utz (triple)		
	Certified	Control[1]	P-value	Certified	Control[1]	P-value[2]
Age of the household head (yrs)	49.37	50.79	0.259	46.56	50.79	0.007**
Educational level of the household head (level 0-6)	1.92	1.85	0.538	2.31	1.85	0.002**
Family size (#)	7.71	7.42	0.181	7.64	7.42	0.441
Years of coffee farming (yrs)	29.05	30.25	0.263	27.28	30.25	0.024*
Proportion of land allocated to coffee (%)	0.45	0.44	0.398	0.49	0.44	0.024*
Amount of coffee produced (kg)	868.54	992.34	0.234	1427.98	992.34	0.002**
Access to credit (1 = yes)	0.02	0.04	0.219	0.03	0.04	0.578
Savings (1=yes)	0.12	0.16	0.182	0.16	0.16	0.926
Access to technical assistance (1 = yes)	0.39	0.36	0.542	0.41	0.36	0.287
Wealth status (1-2 score)	1.65	1.67	0.792	1.94	1.67	0.000***

[1] Single Fair Trade certified farmers were used as control.

[2] *** significant at 1% level; ** significant at 5% level; * significant at 10% level.

most of their cash income from coffee sales. The descriptive result also show that the educational level of the cooperative members is generally low. The ethnic and religious composition of the study area follows the country-wide heterogeneity in Ethiopia. [38]

The comparison of coffee farm households between certification groups (Table 4.2) reveals some differences that need to be taken into account for the impact analysis. Control group coffee farmers (with single certification) are somewhat younger and less educated when compared with FT/organic/Utz (triple certified) farmers. In terms of wealth status, there is also a statistically significant difference between farmers categorised under single certification and triple certification, showing that the latter are wealthier than farmers certified by FT only. Statistically significant differences are also observed between single certified and triple certified coffee farmers in terms of land allocation for coffee production. The mean area of land for coffee production in the triple certified group is (0.49 hectares) is somewhat larger than the average area size for single certified farmers. However, we did not find statistically significant differences between the two groups in terms of family size, access to credit, access to technical assistance, and savings. This might be due to the fact that most coffee co-ops only scarcely provide some of these services to their members.

---

[38] The interviewed cooperative members are dispersed among several ethnicities: 97.1% belonged to the Sidama people, 1.3% to the Amhara, 0.7% to Guragie, 0.6% to Oromo, while 0.3% identified themselves as belonging to other ethnic groups. In terms of religion, 85% of the interviewed cooperative members are Protestant, 3.5% are Catholic, 2.7% are Muslim, 2.5% are Ethiopian Orthodox Christian, and the remaining 6.3% are categorised as other.

4.6.1 Awareness of certification

Table 4.3 reports on the percentage of respondents that were aware of being certified. All certified cooperative member respondents were asked whether they knew about their cooperative's certification. We found that there was still a very low level of awareness on certification schemes and how certification premiums are allocated, and much confusion prevails amongst members of certified coffee cooperatives about what certification means. Serious questions can be raised regarding the widespread lack of a clear understanding of Fair Trade among cooperative members.

About 98.6% of the farmers interviewed did not have any knowledge of the certification of their cooperative. It seems that certification is not actively promoted nor understood by those who are certified. When we compare for each certification the level of awareness separately, 15% of farmers understood FT/organic/Utz certification somewhat better than Fair Trade only.

From our field interviews we can conclude that certification in general was better understood by the executive committee members of primary coffee cooperatives, and fully understood by the staff and board members of the second-level coffee cooperative (Sidama Union) in the study area. These findings show the existence of general deficiencies in the information transfer and promotional capacity regarding certification. Similarly, we also asked the same respondents about the existence of certification premiums. Even though the FT premium is supposed to be one of the most important benefits for smallholder coffee farmers from the FT certification, farmers received limited information about FT premium use. Out of all respondents, 86.8% coffee farmers did not know about the existence of the certification premium. In the field we observed that the certified cooperatives in the study area invested most of the premium in elementary school construction, the provision of electricity for rural communities, and the construction of a coffee warehouse. From our study and field observation we found clear concerns related to accountability, lack of transparency, misunderstanding and miscommunication between coffee cooperative members, primary coffee cooperatives and the union.

Table 4.3. Percentage of respondents from cooperatives with awareness on certification.

Label	Cooperatives		
	Single certification (Fair Trade)	Double certification (Fair Trade/organic)	Triple certification (Fair Trade/organic/Utz)
Fair Trade	1.4	4.2	6.0
Organic	-	2.5	18.0
Utz certified	-	-	15.0

4.6.2 Matching results

In this sub-section, we report the empirical results of our study. We first conducted the matching analysis in order to guarantee un-biased samples. Tables 4.4 and 4.5 provide the results of the probit estimates of the double and triple certified farms, and Figure 4.1 and 4.2 outline the corresponding propensity score distributions.

To analyse the data we mainly refer to the results of the kernel estimation method. Based on the propensity score matching procedure explained above, we made a comparison between (1) single and double certified; and (2) single and triple certified cooperative member smallholder coffee farmers. Table 4.6 presents the difference between single and double certification and Table 4.7 presents the difference between single and triple certified coffee farmers' wellbeing. Each comparison analyses significant differences in the defined impact indicators included in the study (coffee income, average price, productivity, access to credit, savings, and access to technical assistance).

According to the results of the kernel estimation method in Table 4.6, we did not find statistically significant differences between single and double certified coffee farmers in terms of productivity, access to credit, access to technical assistance and savings. On the other hand, statistically significant differences were observed in coffee revenue and average price between the single and double certified coffee farmers after matching. In this case, double certified coffee farmers receive a better price and higher coffee revenue than single certified coffee farmers in the study area. Although not statistically significant, the results of the kernel matching estimation for coffee farmers

Table 4.4. Probit estimates and marginal effects of participation in double-certification (Fair Trade and organic).

Variables	Binary probit model			
	Probit estimates		Marginal effects	
	Coef.	P-value[1]	Coef.	P-value[1]
Age (years)	-0.00	0.730	-0.001	0.730
Sex (0 = female, 1 = male)	0.32	0.174	0.126	0.174
Religion (0 = otherwise, 1 = Protestant)	-0.07	0.003**	-0.029	0.003**
Years of coffee farming (years)	-0.00	0.674	-0.001	0.674
Education household head (level 0-6)	-0.02	0.066*	-0.008	0.066*
Total family size (number)	0.03	0.189	0.011	0.189
Land allocated to coffee (ha)	-0.10	0.524	-0.039	0.524
Constant	-0.08	0.821		0.821

[1] *** significant at 1% level; ** significant at 5% level; * significant at 10% level.

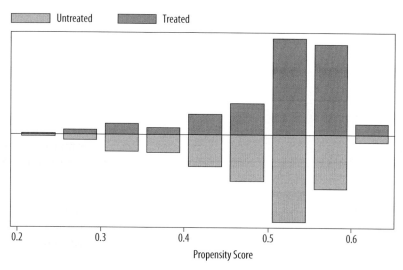

Figure 4.1. Propensity score distribution for double certification (Fair Trade + organic).

Table 4.5. Probit estimates and marginal effects of participation in triple-certification (Fair Trade, organic and Utz).

Variables	Binary probit model			
	Probit estimates		Marginal effects	
	Coef.	P-value[1]	Coef.	P-value[1]
Age (years)	-0.01	0.534	-0.002	0.534
Sex (0 = female, 1 = male)	0.14	0.598	0.050	0.598
Religion (0 = otherwise, 1 = Protestant)	-0.13	0.001**	-0.045	0.001**
Years of coffee farming (years)	-0.00	0.788	-0.001	0.788
Education household head (level 0-6)	0.06	0.296	0.022	0.296
Total family size (number)	-0.01	0.685	-0.004	0.685
Land allocated to coffee (ha)	0.46	0.011*	0.163	0.011*
Constant	-0.25	0.542		0.542

[1] *** significant at 1% level; ** significant at 5% level; * significant at 10% level.

under the category of double certification point to a negative effect on savings. This negative effect seems to be driven by the significantly lower savings of double certified farmers as compared to single certified farmers. This might be related to the higher investment requirements of double certification.

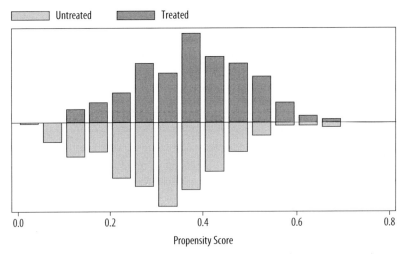

Figure 4.2. Propensity score distribution for triple certification (Fair Trade + organic + Utz).

Table 4.6. Comparison of Fair Trade/organic (double) versus only Fair Trade certified coffee farmers using various matching methods.[1]

Outcome variable	Ps-match kernel			Ps-match neighbour (5)			Radius		
	Diff.	SE	T-stat	Diff.	SE	T-stat	Diff.	SE	T-stat
Coffee revenue (ETB)	636.09	534.78	1.21	367.95	429.33	0.86	235.87	317.38	0.74
Average price (ETB/kg)	0.36	0.14	2.68*	0.38	0.12	3.14**	0.41	0.10	4.32**
Productivity (kg/ha)	151.44	138.90	0.37	217.36	108.77	2.00*	240.29	84.52	2.84*
Access to credit (1 = yes)	0.00	0.02	0.28	-0.01	0.02	-0.77	-0.02	0.01	-2.03
Savings (1 = yes)	-0.05	0.04	-1.16	-0.03	0.04	0.84	-0.02	0.03	-0.70
Access to technical assistance (1 = yes)	-0.02	0.06	0.32	0.04	0.05	0.80	0.03	0.03	0.80

[1] *** significant at 1% level; ** significant at 5% level; * significant at 10% level; SE = standard error.

Table 4.7 presents the mean differences between single certified and triple certified farmers. We did not find a statistically significant difference between single and triple certified coffee producer farmers in the study area in terms of livelihood-related variables such as credit. This is not surprising, given the fact that Fair Trade contracts often did not include pre-financing facilities for producers. Similar results are also observed in relation to savings and access to technical assistance. Although not statistically significant, the results of the matching estimation for coffee farmers under the category of single and triple certification reveals a negative effect on access to credit and savings. This negative effect seems to be driven by the significantly

Table 4.7. Comparison of Fair Trade/Organic/Utz (triple) versus only Fair Trade certified coffee farmers using various matching methods.[1]

Outcome variable	Ps-match kernel			Ps-match neighbour (5)			Radius		
	Diff.	SE	T-stat	Diff.	SE	T-stat	Diff.	SE	T-stat
Coffee revenue (ETB)	2081.46	753.78	2.76*	1424.77	626.57	2.27*	2491.68	523.22	4.76***
Average price (ETB/kg)	0.71	0.14	5.20***	0.73	0.04	3.16**	0.77	0.08	9.70***
Productivity (kg/ha)	516.14	166.69	3.10**	670.30	141.47	4.74***	795.53	120.26	6.61***
Access to credit (1 = yes)	-0.02	0.03	-0.82	-0.00	0.02	-0.13	-0.01	0.02	-0.72
Savings (1 = yes)	-0.01	0.06	-0.12	-0.04	0.04	-0.85	0.00	0.03	0.11
Access to technical assistance (1 = yes)	0.05	0.07	0.69	0.05	0.06	0.90	0.05	0.04	1.24

[1] *** significant at 1% level; ** significant at 5% level; * significant at 10% level; SE = standard error

lower credit access and savings of triple certified coffee farmers as compared to single certified farmers.

On the other hand, and most interestingly, there is a statistically significant difference between the triple certified and single certified coffee farmers after matching in terms of coffee performance criteria. Triple certified farmers earned better coffee revenues, got better average prices, and reached a higher productivity. In this case, price and productivity benefits seem to be the main mechanism through which certification effects are realised. These differences are strong enough to represent a clear welfare effect on the member coffee farm-households. In both cases we did not find, however, significant differences between single against double and triple certified coffee farmers in terms of other livelihood-related indicators such as access to credit. This is not surprising, given the fact that coffee cooperatives with limited financial resources were not able to extend credit to their members in the study area.

4.7 Discussion and implications

This chapter analysed the impacts of double and triple certification on the well-being of smallholder coffee farmers in southern Ethiopia, paying special attention to effects on coffee revenue, coffee price, productivity, access to credit, saving, and access to technical assistance. Our results provide new empirical evidence about the additive effects of double and triple certifications on key livelihood indicators. In this final section, we discuss the following major findings of the study: (1) cooperative member coffee farmers' level of knowledge of certification is poor and limited; (2) double and particularly triple certification generate significant effects on coffee prices, yield and revenues; (3) a combination of certification regimes does not have a statistically significant effect on other livelihood variables (credit, savings, technical assistance); and (4) additional effects of multiple certifications on coffee farmers welfare might be gained, i.e. more certification labels enhance potential gross effect.[39]

The livelihoods of smallholder coffee farmers in Ethiopia are based on insecure, low-input low-output agricultural production systems, which make them particularly vulnerable to poverty. Certification of their main export crop, coffee, through cooperative structures is argued to be one of the strategies for providing small-scale coffee farmers better access to markets that allow them to generate higher and more stable cash incomes. Although certification is a new and a recent phenomenon in Ethiopia, various types of coffee certifications such as Fair Trade, organic and Utz certified have been implemented since 2002.

Although certification schemes were relatively well understood by executive committee members of primary coffee cooperatives and fully understood by staff and board members at the Union level, the awareness of members of certified cooperatives about the functioning and purpose of certification is quite limited. When asked about certification standards, most coffee farmers could not answer. This finding raises the question of communication and inclusiveness of the members in their respective coffee cooperatives, which are crucial in the success of any certification standard. This finding suggests that coffee marketing cooperatives have not been able to convey information about certification to their members effectively (Ruben and Heras, 2012). This might influence member coffee farmers' efforts to meet the standards required by certifying organisations. Our findings also show general deficiencies in information transfer and lack of promotional capacity in certification and related activities at local level. Generally, it seems that certification is not actively promoted or understood by those who are certified. In addition, cooperatives lack transparency with respect to their internal control systems and the distribution of premiums along the supply chain. This implies that coffee farmers are not strongly involved in the knowledge exchange that is required to enhance record keeping and higher quality standards maintenance, which could lead to lack of accountability, transparency and communication between members, primary cooperatives and the union regarding certification. Furthermore, the issue of farmers' limited knowledge of certification raises doubts about the ability of certifications to empower significantly marginalised small producers (Valkila and Nygren, 2009).

In a similar vein, Stellmacher and Grote (2011) conducted empirical research on forest coffee certification in Ethiopia and also found a lack of understanding regarding certification by those who are certified. Murray *et al.* (2006) and Jena *et al.* (2012) register similar results among members of coffee cooperatives in Ethiopia, which suggests that lack of awareness about certification standards and procedures is a generalised phenomenon among certified coffee farmers in this country.

---

[39] Note we did not analyse the costs of multiple certification, so net effects could not be determined. In general, annual certification range between USD 5,000 and USD 8,000 for each standard and are divided by the number of farmers according the delivered supplies. Some economies of scale can be reached with certification through the cooperative union.

The existing literature on the impacts of certification has focused primarily on the economic benefits farmers receive from participating in these schemes. No study has been done so far regarding the effect of multiple certifications on smallholders' livelihood. Using propensity score matching technique, in this study, we estimated the impact of double and triple certifications on several coffee farmers' livelihood indictors. In line with other studies (Bacon, 2005; Barham and Weber 2011; Barham *et al.*, 2011; Baumann *et al.*, 2012; Becchetti and Constantino, 2008; Méndez *et al.*, 2010; Murray *et al.*, 2003; Raynolds, 2002; Ruben and Fort, 2011; Valkila, 2009), our empirical results provide clear evidence of an impact of certification involvement on income. Income effects are also additive. According to our results, double-certified coffee farmers receive better price and higher income than single certified farmers; and triple certified farmers receive better price and higher income than double-certified farmers in the study area.

Price and productivity seem to be the main mechanisms through which the effects of certification are realised. The price premium offered to producers by certification schemes could provide incentives and investment opportunities to enhance productivity (Beuchelt and Zeller, 2011; Rueda and Lambin 2013). However, the relationship between price, productivity and income is not always straightforward. For instance, Méndez *et al.* (2010) compared Fair Trade/organic certified growers with conventional ones across several Central American countries and Mexico and found evidence of a price premium but limited impact on incomes and other livelihood measures.

Credit provision is a key issue for coffee farmers since the various forms of upgrading, such as productivity, product quality and complying with standards require investments (Dunn *et al.*, 2006). However, we did not find statistically significant differences between the considered groups regarding access to credit. Furthermore, the surveyed respondents stated that they have not obtained credit from their respective cooperatives. This is not surprising, given the fact that coffee cooperatives in the study area have limited financial resources and currently are not able to extend credit to their members (Rueda and Lambin, 2013). Furthermore, in-depth group discussions with coffee farmers revealed that the only institution providing financial services to them are government-supported regional microfinance organisations. Yet, this financial service is very limited and not available to all coffee farmers who need credit. On the other hand, when coffee producers face financial constraints, they normally obtain loans from private coffee merchants, who request coffee growers to pay back the loan with coffee during the harvesting period. This practice puts farmers at a disadvantage position since they are compelled to sell their coffee at prices set by private buyers, which are usually lower than the prevailing market price. The lack of certification effects on savings can also be explained by the fact that saving is uncommon as a practice in the study area. The effect of multiple certifications on members' access to technical assistance is also not statistically significant. However, in general, we found that the provision of technical assistance is minimal among the studied coffee cooperatives.

Unlike many Latin American countries, coffee certification is a recent development in Ethiopia. Since there is still a considerable lack of empirical studies around this subject, further research is needed to improve the information on practical performance, efficiency and effectiveness of certification interventions and related activities, so as to gain new insights about the potential role of multiple certifications in improving the livelihoods of small scale coffee farmers in Ethiopia.

Certification of Ethiopian coffee cooperatives alone is unlikely to bring about significant poverty alleviation among cooperative members. Along the promotion of certification, more attention should be given to increase the technical, financial and human capacities of primary cooperatives to make them stronger and more effective partners in the value chain. The strength of producer cooperatives' internal organisation – their member identity, leadership, and organisational capacity – is central to certification success (Raynolds *et al.*, 2004). Furthermore, in order to further increase the effectiveness of certification in improving smallholder livelihoods, we recommend to harmonise certification standards and to optimise the certification system in terms of control systems, communication of the requirements, and management of costs and benefits.

References

Arslan, A. and C.P. Reicher (2010). *The effects of the coffee trade marking initiative and Starbucks publicity on export prices of Ethiopian Coffee*. Working Paper No. 1606. Kiel, germany: Kiel Institute for the World Economy.

Bacon, C. (2005). Confronting the coffee crisis: 'can Fair Trade, organic, and specialty coffees reduce small-scale farmer vulnerability in Northern Nicaragua'? *World Development* 33: 497-511.

Barham, B.L. and J.G. Weber (2011). The economic sustainability of certified coffee: recent evidence from Mexico and Peru. *World Development* 40(6): 1269-1279.

Barham, B.L., M. Callenes, J. Lewis, S. Gitter and J. Weber (2011). Fair Trade/organic coffee, rural livelihoods, and the 'agrarian question': southern Mexican coffee families in transition. *World Development* 39(1): 134-145.

Bastin, A. and N. Matteucci (2007). Financing coffee farmers in Ethiopia: challenges and opportunities. *Savings and Development* 31(3): 251-282.

Baumann, F., M. Oschinski and N. Stahler (2012). On the effects of Fair Trade on the welfare of the poor. *Journal of International Development* 24: S159-S172.

Becchetti, L. and M. Constantino (2008). The effects of Fair Trade on affiliated producers: an impact analysis on Kenyan farmers. *World Development* 36(5): 823-842.

Bernard, T., A. Taffesse and E. Gabre-Madhin (2008). Impact of cooperatives on smallholders commercialization behavior: evidence from Ethiopia. *Agricultural Economics* 39: 147-161.

Beuchelt, T.D. and M. Zeller (2011). Profits and poverty: 'certification's troubled link for Nicaragua's organic and Fair-Trade coffee producers, *Ecological Economics* 70(7): 1316-1324.

Bourguignon, F. (1999). *The mystery of the vanishing benefits*. World Bank Research Paper No. 2153. Washington, DC, USA: The World Bank.

Cashin, P., C.J. McDermott and A. Scott (2002). Booms and slumps in world commodity prices. *Journal of Development Economics* 69(1): 277-296.

Central Statistical Authority (CSA) (2008). Ethiopian third round population census. Addis Ababa, Ethiopia: CSA.

Daviron, B., and Ponte, S. (2005). *The Coffee Paradox: Global Markets, Commodity Trade and the Elusive Promise for Development*. London, UK: Zed Books.

Dörr, A.C. (2009). Economic analysis of certification in the Brazilian fruit chain. Göttingen: Cuvillier Publisher.

Dunn, E., J. Sebstad, L. Batzdorff and H. Parsons (2006). Lessons learned on MSE upgrading in value chains: a synthesis paper. *MicroREPORT#71*.

Federal Democratic Republic of Ethiopia (FDRE) (2008). Building on progress: a plan for accelerated and sustained development to end poverty. Available at: http://tinyurl.com/pg9tmu7.

Fischer, E. and M. Qaim (2014). Smallholder farmers and collective action: what determines the intensity of participation? *Journal of Agricultural Economics* 65(3): 683-702.

Gemech, F. and J. Struthers (2007). Coffee price volatility in Ethiopia: effects of market reform program. *Journal of International Development* 11(42): 1131-1142.

Getnet, K. and T. Anullo (2012). Agricultural cooperatives and rural livelihoods: Evidence from Ethiopia. *Annals of Public and Cooperative Economics* 83(2): 181-198.

Grote, U., A.K. Basu and N. Chau (eds.) (2007). *New frontiers in environmental and social labeling*. Heidelberg, Germany: Physica Publisher.

Heckman, J.J., H. Ichimura and P.E. Todd (1997). Matching as an econometric evaluation estimator: evidence from evaluating a job training programme. *Review of Economic Studies* 64(4): 605-654.

International Coffee Organization (ICO) (2011). *ICO Indicator Prices*. Available at: http://www.ico.org/prices/p2.htm.

Jalan, J. and M. Ravallion (2003). Estimating benefit incidence for an anti-poverty program using propensity score matching. *Journal of Business and Economic Statistics* 21(1): 19-30.

Jena, P., T. Stellmacher and U. Grote (2012). The impact of coffee certification on small-scale producers' livelihoods: evidence from Ethiopia. Available at: http://tinyurl.com/kwal37d.

Kodama, Y. (2009). The effects of Fair Trade on coffee producers: a case study of Ethiopian coffee cooperatives. In: S. Ege, H. Aspen, B. Teferra and B. Shiferaw (eds.) *16th International Conference of Ethiopian Studies*. Trondheim, Norway: NTNU-trykk, pp. 297-299.

Labouisse, J., Bellachew, B., Kotecha, S. and Bertrand, B. (2008). Current status of coffee (*Coffea arabica* L.) genetic resources in Ethiopia: implications for conservation. *Genetic Resources and Crop Evolution* 55(7): 1079-1093.

McCarthy, S. (2001). *The history of agricultural cooperative development in Ethiopia. Cooperative business today*. Addis Ababa, Ethiopia: Voca-Ethiopia.

Meijerink, G.W., D. Alemu, J. Mheen-Sluijer and J.H.M. van der Wijnands (2010). *Institutional innovation in African markets: can commodity exchanges address sustainability issues?* Contribution paper 19th EAAE Seminar, Capri, Italy, June-July 2010. Available at: http://tinyurl.com/p95523p.

Méndez, V., C. Bacon, M. Olson, S. Petchers, D. Herrador, C. Carranza, L. Trujillo, C. Guadarrama-Zugasti, A. Cordon and A. Mendoza (2010). Effects of Fair Trade and organic certifications on small-scale coffee farmer households in Central America and Mexico. *Renewable Agriculture and Food Systems* 25(3): 236-251.

Milford, A. (2004). *Coffee, co-operatives and competition: the impact of Fair Trade*. Bergen, Norway: Chr. Michelsen Institute.

Murray, D., L.T. Raynolds and P.L. Taylor (2003). *One cup at a time: poverty alleviation and fair trade coffee in Latin America*. Fort Collins, CO, USA: Fair Trade Research Group, Colorado State University.

Petit, N. (2007). Ethiopia's coffee sector: a bitter or better future? *Journal of Agrarian Change* 7(2): 225-263.

Philpott, S., P. Bichier, R. Rice and R. Greenberg (2007). Field-testing ecological and economic benefits of coffee certification programs. *Conservation Biology* 21(4): 975-985.

Raynolds, L.T. (2002). *Poverty alleviation through participation in Fair Trade coffee networks: existing research and critical issues*. Background paper prepared for project funded by the Community and Resource Development Program, New York, NY, USA. Available at: http://tinyurl.com/nratxrm.

Raynolds, L.T., D. Murray, and P.L. Taylor (2004). Fair Trade coffee: building producer capacity via global networks. *Journal of International Development* 16: 1109-1121.

Rodriquez, B.R. (2012). Institutions in the Mexican coffee sector-changes and responses. Wageningen, the Netherlands: Wageningen University.

Ronchi, L. (2002). *The impact of Fair trade on producers and their organizations: a case study with coocafé in Costa Rica*. Brighton, UK: University of Sussex.

Rosenbaum, P.R. and D.B. Rubin (1983). The central role of the propensity score in observational studies for causal effects. *Biometrika* 70: 41-55.

Ruben, R. and J. Heras. (2012). Social capital, governances and performance of Ethiopian coffee cooperatives. *Annals of Public and Cooperative Economics* 83(4): 463-484.

Ruben, R. and R. Fort (2011). The impact of Fair Trade certification for coffee farmers in Peru. *World Development* 40(3): 570-582.

Rubin, D.B. and N. Thomas (1996). Matching using estimated propensity scores: relating theory to practice. *Biometrics* 52(1): 249-264.

Rubin, D.B. (1974). Estimating causal effects of treatments in randomized and nonrandomized studies. *Journal of Educational Psychology* 66: 688-701.

Rueda, X. and E. Lambin (2013). Responding to globalization: impacts of certification on Colombian small-scale coffee growers. *Ecology and Society* 18(3): 21.

Schreiber, F. and C. Costilla Mora (2011). Tools for multiple certification in coffee producing groups. Lima: Scan Procedure Manual.

Smith, H. (1997). Matching with multiple controls to estimate treatment effects in observational studies. *Sociological Methodology* 27: 325-353.

Stellmacher, G. and U. Grote (2011). Forest coffee certification in Ethiopia: economic boon or ecological bane? Working Paper Series 76. Bonn, Germany: Zentrum für Entwicklungsforschung, University of Bonn.

Sustaineo (2013). Improving smallholder livelihoods: effectiveness of certification in coffee, cocoa and cotton. Hamburg, Germany: Sustaineo.

Valkila, J. (2009). Fair Trade organic coffee production in Nicaragua—sustainable development or a poverty trap? *Ecological Economics* 68(12): 3018-3025.

Valkila, J. and A. Nygren (2009). Impacts of fair trade certification on coffee farmers, cooperatives, and laborers in Nicaragua. *Agriculture and Human Values* 27(3): 321-333.

Volkmann, J. (2008). *Assessment of certification options for wild forest coffee in Ethiopia*. CoCE Project Report Sub-project 5.4. Available at: http://tinyurl.com/pzou4pc.

White, H. and M. Bamberger (2008). Impact evaluation in official development agencies. Special issue on impact evaluation. *IDS Bulletin* 39(1): 1-11.

Wissel, S., A. Berghöfer, R. Jordan, S. Oldfield and T. Stellmacher (2010). Certification and labeling. In: TEEB – The Economics of Ecosystems and Biodiversity for Local and Regional Policy Makers. United Nations Environment Programme, pp. 161-171.

Wollni, M. and M. Zeller (2007). Do farmers benefit from participating in specialty markets and cooperatives? The case of coffee marketing in Costa Rica. *Agricultural Economics* 37(2): 243-248.

Chapter 5

Maintaining sustainable livelihoods: effects of Utz certification on market access, risk reduction and livelihood strategies of Kenyan coffee farmers

Mirjam Schoonhoven-Speijer and Ruerd Ruben
For correspondence: mha.schoonhoven@gmail.com

5.1 Introduction

Since the turn of the century, a renewed focus on agriculture and rural development has become visible. For 500 million rural households, representing an estimated 1.5 to 2 billion people worldwide, agriculture remains the main opportunity to find their way out of poverty (Hazell *et al.*, 2010; World Bank, 2007). In order to make development through agriculture happen, farmers need to be able to market their produce at local or global markets. These represent opportunities for income generation, professionalisation and diversification (Ruben *et al.*, 2006). However, risks such as price uncertainties and the requirements and high standards of international markets might raise new barriers for small-scale producers to find suitable outlets (Fafchamps, 2004; Shiferaw *et al.*, 2008; World Bank, 2011).

Bridging the gap between local economic development and global value chain integration asks for the establishment of new institutional and organisational networks. Whereas Fair Trade (FT), launched some forty years ago, was based on voluntary standards promoting equitable market access for smallholder coffee cooperatives, newer initiatives such as Utz certified (Utz) emphasise private initiatives with market-conform conditions that support farmer's income through dynamic efficiency gains (Raynolds *et al.*, 2007; Ruben and Zuniga, 2011). Large commodity companies often favour private standards, because voluntary standards may lead to production inefficiencies (Ruben and Zuniga, 2011). Critics emphasise, however, that a market-based approach might be too much focused on providing access to export markets and too little on reducing vulnerability (Vorley *et al.*, 2012).

Ruerd Ruben and Paul Hoebink (eds.) **Coffee certification in East Africa**
DOI 10.3920/978-90-8686-805-6_5, © Wageningen Academic Publishers 2015

This chapter focuses on the latter issue: whether farmers included in Utz certification schemes not only benefit in terms of higher production and income, but also in terms of reduced vulnerability and enhanced resilience. With this focus we intend to contribute to several strands of research and knowledge. Many earlier studies assessing the impact of standards only focused on outputs (e.g. higher prices, training provided) rather than on outcomes (e.g. higher incomes, new skills acquired) or livelihood impacts (changes in material wealth, social well-being and empowerment) (Nelson and Pound, 2009). Therefore, we add to the knowledge concerning outcome effects such as attitudes towards the cooperative, and impact effects concerning risk reduction of certified farmers. Additionally, most earlier studies examine the effects of Fair Trade, while less substantial research is done on new (private) standards such as Utz certification (Ruben and Zuniga, 2011).

Theoretically we make connections between the sustainable livelihoods (SL) framework (Chambers and Conway, 1992) and value chain theory (Kaplinsky and Morris, 2001). The SL framework provides insight into the assets, capabilities and activities of households that contribute to a sustainable living. The advantage of the SL framework is that it is based on a multi-dimensional definition of poverty and well-being. It focuses, however, too much at the household level, and provides less insights in linkages at local, regional or international level (Scoones, 2009). To overcome this problem, we connect the SL framework with broader processes of globalisation and international trade by integrating it with a value chain perspective. Value chain theory pays attention to the distribution of value-added and risk amongst parties involved in the supply chain. We focus on how Utz certification influences the benefits to farmers participating in producer organisations through the enforcement of contracts. We thus also contribute to debates concerning inclusion in value chains, by examining how farmers manage risks in formal markets (Seville *et al.*, 2011).

The field research was conducted among coffee farmers in central Kenya, who are organised in cooperatives. We selected two Utz certified cooperatives, and compared them with two neighbouring cooperatives that were not involved in any certification scheme, but were otherwise similar in terms of farm-household and cooperative characteristics to the certified farmers.

5.2 Theoretical framework and hypotheses

5.2.1 Livelihoods and institutions

A livelihood is the means of gaining and securing a living through the use of assets, capabilities and activities. Assets, the capital base from which different productive streams are derived, are closely related to capabilities, the opportunities and abilities that a person has to generate valuable outcomes (Chambers and Conway, 1992). Together, assets and capabilities shape the opportunity set of activities for the livelihood strategies of a household (Ellis, 1998). Activities include, for instance, growing coffee and/or keeping livestock. The ability to follow a certain livelihood strategy is also influenced by the context of a household. The agro-ecology conditions determine which crops farmers can cultivate, whereas political conditions influence how easy it is for farmers to engage with cooperatives.

Our research focuses on the link between context and livelihoods, as shaped by institutions. Institutions are defined as 'the rules of the game' that define incentives and sanctions affecting people's behaviour (Dorward *et al.*, 2005). Institutions thus mediate the ability to carry out strategies and achieve certain outcomes (Scoones and Wolmer, 2003). Institutions can also create barriers or restrictions and provide opportunities or gateways to sustainable livelihoods. Consequently, the mediating capacities of institutions determines *why* households make certain choices to use a combination of resources for pursuing specific strategies. Since the SL framework does not fully recognise these relationships, we additionally draw on theories of risk perception and risk behaviour to explain why certain choices are made. Hereafter, we discuss how specific institutional rules – enforced by producer organisations and Utz certification – influence (perceived) risks and mediate livelihood choices.

5.2.2 Market constraints and shocks

For small-scale farmers, the choice to be involved into certain markets contains a continuous tension between the risky advantages of market participation and the conservation of a non-market basis for survival (Ellis, 1998; World Bank, 2001). The markets in which smallholders are engaged are often imperfect and incomplete, and deficiencies such as the absence of regulatory institutions are especially profound in rural areas (Dorward *et al.*, 2005). Farmers' insecurity is further increased by other types of shocks, such as climate variations, vulnerable social-economic status and bad politics at the state level (Dercon, 2008). Thus, smallholder farmers tend to pursue dual objectives: not only to maximise income and consumption, but also to manage and reduce risks and avoid vulnerability (Ellis, 1998).

Risk refers to the possibility that something unfavourable might occur (Smith *et al.*, 2000). People's behaviour is not only influenced by the measurable, objective risks that they face, but also, or even more, by their subjective perceptions of risks and the possible consequences of different uncertain events (Doss *et al.*, 2008). The combination of experienced shocks and risk perceptions leads to choices that farmers make. These include choices for income-generating activities and choices for insurance through savings or network-based risk-sharing arrangements (Fafchamps, 2003). Being persistently prone to a variety of shocks might lead to chronic poverty, since the priority might become more and more towards minimising vulnerability to shocks and thus avoiding investments that might yield higher returns in the future. People then might become trapped below a critical threshold of wealth that is necessary to get out of poverty (Barrett, 2005).

Institutions, such as producer organisations (POs) and certification standards, can have a positive or mitigating influence on risk attitudes, as they have the ability to make market systems more inclusive and integrated by reducing transaction costs and enforcing contracts (Rodrik, 2000; World Bank, 2001). In practice they are linked together, since Utz certification is often provided through established producer organisations.

5.2.3 Producer organisations and certification: market access and vulnerability

Being member of a PO can improve the efficiency of agricultural marketing (Bijman and Wollni, 2008). Collective marketing of the harvest reduces transaction costs of individual farmers and improves their marketing power by providing abilities to negotiate for better prices (Dorward *et al.*, 2005). Sales are likely to become more stable, leading to a more stable income stream through mutual insurance of otherwise uninsured risks (Key and Runsten, 1999). Due to low managerial capacity, however, also involuntarily costs might occur, such as a delay of payment and/or insufficient provision of technical and commercial assistance (Milford, 2004). Other governance issues that can occur are elite capture, legal restrictions and exclusion of the poor (World Bank, 2001; Mude, 2006). POs thus need strong internal governance and an established asset base to make sure that these involuntary costs are kept to a minimum (Barham and Chitemi, 2009).

The strength of internal governance depends on several underlying dynamic forces, most importantly: collective action and trust. Collective actions implies that group resources, knowledge and efforts are combined to reach a goal shared by everyone (Place *et al.*, 2004). Trust is a condition that facilitates collective action; it has instrumental value in reducing risks and transaction costs of relationships, strengthening bonds between individuals and facilitating information exchange (Murphy, 2002; Williamson, 2000). Especially when formal institutions are failing to meet local information or market needs, the exchange of knowledge through trust is important for meeting cooperation and collective action. Trust is therefore considered as the most relevant factor for enabling voluntary cooperative action (Ostrom, 2003).

For the successful functioning of cooperatives through trust and collective action, member's active participation in the cooperative is of key importance. Problems arise when not all members participate in the creation of benefits, but free-ride on the work of others without contributing to the provisions the PO is offering (Milford, 2004). Free-riding may encourage the under-production of the cooperative's commodity (Ostrom, 2003). Another problem is the cost of control (Milford, 2004). Since costs to control the management are shared, the incentive for an individual farmer might not be high enough to participate actively in situations in which the management underperforms, or shows to be corrupt (Milford, 2004).

Receiving Utz certification should lead to several improvements in cooperative management and practices, from which farmers are expected to benefit. These comprise the strengthening of farmer organisations in terms of good governance, and increased efficiency for the provision of technical as well as commercial services (Tegemeo institute, 2009). The greater accessibility of farmers to these services contributes to higher productivity, higher producer prices and higher enterprise and farm incomes. Utz certified adds to the resilience of farmers by enforcing contracts which provide security on prices and the provision of extension services (Ruben *et al.*, 2006). Utz certified contracts reduce monitoring costs and are especially preferred in markets with high-quality demand, such as speciality coffee. For farmers, such contractual arrangement reduce price uncertainty. Saenz and Ruben (2004) showed that the existence of a contract can reduce uncertainty to the producer, thus enabling investments in land improvements and better crop management. Product quality is further reinforced by institutional variables like technical assistance and delivery frequency.

5.2.4 Hypotheses

Based on the before-outlined theoretical framework, we formulated three hypotheses to assess the effects of Utz certification on the livelihood of coffee farmers in Kenya. We argue that Utz certification can reduce vulnerability in several direct and indirect ways. The direct mechanism relies on strengthening the services that producer organisations offer. An important guarantee for asset accumulation required to upgrade the quality and quantity of coffee is the support that farmers receive from their cooperative organisation (Ruben, 2008). These interventions directly lead to harvests of higher quantity (yield) and better quality, for which farmers can receive a higher price (Hypothesis 1). This subsequently leads to the indirect effect that farmers may perceive their cooperative as a more reliable partner (Hypothesis 2). Reliability is operationalised in terms of mutual trust and loyalty. In the presence of trust, farmers can realise transactions with the confidence that other farmers will also do what they are supposed to do (Blandon *et al.*, 2009). This is expected to reduce farmers' vulnerability to behavioural uncertainty. Consequently, free-riding behaviour will be reduced and members-farmers are expected to maintain more loyalty towards the cooperative and refrain from side sales. Trust and loyalty enable individual risks to be partially shared (Fafchamps, 2003). Collective action advantages permit smallholders to better withstand years of adverse production (Carter, 1987). A good functioning cooperative thus assures the basis for further individual improvements (Ruben, 2008). The impact of market-related shocks is reduced, allowing farmers to cope better with non-market related risks and shocks (Hypothesis 3).

5.3 Materials and methods

Four Kenyan coffee cooperatives have been selected for field research: two cooperatives that received Utz certification (treatment groups) and two cooperatives not participating in any certification program (control groups). Solidaridad, the non-governmental organisation (NGO) funding Utz certification programs, was instrumental in the choice of the following treatment groups: Rianjagi Cooperative, situated in the Embu district, and Kangunu Cooperative, located in the Mathioya district. We searched for control cooperatives located close to the treatment groups to ensure similar agro-ecological circumstances and a comparable socio-economic context. In addition, we preferred cooperatives with likewise characteristics in terms of the number of wet mills, membership size and governance structures. This would allow for a with/without appraisal, whereby differences in behaviour and responses between the treatment and control group provide a counterfactual to the results reached by the target group (Ruben, 2008).

The control group selected for Rianjagi Cooperative in the Embu district is Kithungururu. Both Kithungururu and the Utz cooperative split from the same larger cooperative (Kapingazi) in 1997. The control group chosen for Kangunu, a single factory cooperative, is Kamagogo, part of the four wet mill cooperatives Kiru in Mathioya district.[40] Table 5.1 shows main figures on coffee production, sales and coffee prices of all four cooperatives for the 2009-2010 season.

5.3.1 Methods

We relied on a mixed methods approach (Creswell, 2003) to get adequate insights in market access, vulnerability and risk perception of farmers, using a combination of participatory risk mapping, household surveys, risk gaming and in-depth interviews. A mixed methods approach allows for the triangulation of data and offers more complete insights in the research issues. Participatory risk mapping (PRM, developed by Smith et al., 2000) is used to get insights in the experienced and perceived risks among cooperative members at individual, household and cooperative level (for more information, see Pratt and Loizos, 2003; Quinn et al., 2003; Smith et al., 2000; Tschakert, 2007). Data gathered through risk mapping shows the relative importance of several

Table 5.1. Overview of production and payments of four cooperatives (2009-2010 season).[1]

Cooperative	Number of members	Production (×1000 kgs)	Kgs per member	Sales (×1000 KSh)	Payment (×1000 KSh)	Payment (KSh/kg)	Payment (% of sales)
Embu district							
Rianjagi (Utz)	1,502	857	571.00	50,324	38,154	50.00	75.82
Kithungururu	1,811	643	355.40	39,755	31,444	47.00	85.28
Mathioya district							
Kangunu (Utz)	1,360	723	529.07	47,327	40,219	55.65	84.98
Kamagogo	756	339	448.67	9,920	9,208	40.10	92.82

[1] Data received from cooperatives, February 2011.

[40] It was not possible to compare Kangunu with another single factory cooperative in the district, since only one other coffee cooperative with a single wet mill existed. This wet mill reached a much lower coffee production and met different growing conditions since it was located at another altitude level.

problems as perceived by individual people. A PRM meeting with participation of 10 people was performed in every cooperative, taking into account the variation among cooperatives. Sampling was done in a stratified random way to include farmers from different areas of the cooperative. During group discussions a series of different risk events were identified, ranked ordered in terms of their severity, and it was discussed how participants address or solve these risks.

A field survey was conducted to gather most household level data, which was done through single visit farm-household interviews. Survey questions were based on literature and a questionnaire used earlier by Tegemeo Institute and the Centre for International Development Nijmegen (CIDIN) (Kamau et al., 2010). All statements were translated from English to locally used languages (Ki-embu or Kikuyu). Respondents were mainly the household head[41] or the spouse. Data collection covered coffee production and marketing activities for the 2010 coffee year, i.e. the period from September 2009 to August 2010. We used a stratified systematic sample approach drawing from the population census of each cooperative (Thomas et al., 1998). The sample was divided in geographical strata either based on villages (Utz) or election areas (non-Utz). The total number of surveys completed was 218: 56 each for Rianjagi (Utz), Kithungururu and Kangunu (Utz) Cooperatives, and 50 for Kamagogo Cooperative.

In addition, a risk game was performed by 50 to 56 people per cooperative, using the format of a Choose Lottery experiment. Such behavioural field experiments examine the attitudes towards risks. Participants are presented with a series of lottery options and are asked to select one from a list which varies high and low pay-outs (Annex A.1). Depending on how risk-averse the participant are, they trade off expected return for less variability (Cardenas and Carpenter, 2008). We used as a stake the price a farmer might receive for the harvest of one coffee tree in the coming year – roughly resembling a two days income – creating the necessary incentive for participants for taking the game seriously (Cardenas and Carpenter, 2008). The choices that were presented to the participants ranged from fully risk-averse to risk-neutral.

At the end of the research, a semi-structured questionnaire was used to interview six to eight farmers per cooperative. Semi-structured interviews are especially valuable to answer 'why' or 'how' research questions, since answers to such questions are often too complex to include into predefined survey options (Thomas et al., 1998). The topics that were explored in-depth in the interviews refer to the attitudes towards the cooperative, and issues related to risk perception and risk management. Since a large part of the interview emphasises risk attitudes and choices related to risks, the selection of farmers was based on those who participated earlier in the risk game. A sample was selected that included farmers ranging from extreme risk averse to almost risk neutral.

---

[41] A farm household is defined as 'family members who stay within the household for a period of at least one month for the last twelve months. Together the household members have a shared income and shared expenditures', see Kamau, M., L.O. Mose, R. Forte and R. Ruben (2010).

5.3.2 Data analysis

Data was collected between January 2011 and May 2011, and processed in the field as much as possible. Quantitative data were analysed by performing independent sample t-tests, factor analysis and multiple regression. Validity and reliability of the data was ensured by performing tests such as Cronbach's Alpha and Chow tests. To examine the comparability of treatment and control groups we calculated the probability of being in the treatment or control group for several variables which are independent from the impact of certification. Table 5.2 shows that for the Embu region there are differences in age of household head, the land owned and distance to the market. For the Mathioya region differences occurred in terms of age of household head, and distance to the market. These differences are relatively small and in the case of distance to the market almost insurmountable due to the study design. Therefore, we can conclude that our samples are to a great extent comparable. To extend the validity of the analysis, we control for between groups differences in statistical analyses and triangulation of outcomes with other data will be used in qualitative analyses.

Table 5.2. Probability of becoming Utz certified (Model 1 – logistic regression).[1]

	Embu				Mathioya			
	Mean	SE	Exp(B)	Sign.[2]	Mean	SE	Exp(B)	Sign.[2]
Constant	-7.220	3.747	0.001	**	-12.993	7.671	0.000	**
Gender household head (HH) (% male)	0.459	0.707	1.583		0.503	0.726	1.653	
Age HH (years)	0.292	0.133	1.339	**	0.342	0.255	1.408	*
Age[2] HH	-0.003	0.001	0.997	**	-0.003	0.002	0.997	
Education HH (yrs)	0.008	0.059	1.008		0.028	0.085	1.028	
Household size (number)	0.153	0.140	1.166		-0.112	0.165	0.894	
Land owned by HH (acres; log)	-0.603	0.335	0.547	**	0.374	0.429	1.453	
Value assets (KSh; log)	-0.045	0.225	0.956		-0.109	0.277	0.897	
Distance to the market (km)	-0.176	0.097	0.839	**	0.935	0.214	2.547	***
Chi[2]	14.420	**			39.136	***		
Nagelkerke pseudo R[2]	0.177				0.492			
Chow test	27.000	***			26.030	***		

[1] Dependent variable: Utz certification (y/n).
[2] Significance level: * = α<0.10; ** = α<0.05; *** = α<0.01.

5.4 Results

We will discuss three categories of impact from the Utz certified label: (1) direct effects including production and productivity outcomes; (2) behavioural effects related to trust and loyalty towards the cooperative; and (3) effects on risk attitudes concerning coffee marketing and other shocks. The before-outlined hypotheses are tested using a series of dependent variables: yield, trust in the cooperative, loyalty to the cooperative, performance of the cooperative, risk index of all risk event and a risk index related to coffee production and exchange (see Annex A.2 for an elaboration of these indexes).

We use different model specifications. The first regression model run is a logistic regression where the possibility of being Utz certified is tested against independent variables that are thought not to be influenced by membership of a cooperative. Secondly, an ordinary least square (OLS) regression model is used to get more insight in the effects of Utz certification on the coffee yield of farmers. This is followed by a two stage least squares (2SLS) regression model that analyses the effects of trust, loyalty and risk occurrence on each other. A 2SLS approach is used since loyalty and trust are endogenous variables for the base model explaining risk occurrence (Wooldridge, 2008).

5.4.1 Farm and household characteristics

Key descriptive characteristics concerning coffee production for all four cooperatives are reported in Table 5.3. For Embu region, differences in inputs between Utz certified farmers and the control group farmers are rather minimal. Farmers only differ in the number of young coffee trees, which is significantly higher for Utz certified farmers. The technical information received by farmers is significantly more for Rianjagi (Utz) than for Kithunguruu farmers: 96% of the former farmers received training during the last four years, against only 49% of the control-group farmers. In addition, Rianjagi farmers are more satisfied with the technical assistance they received, scoring significantly higher on the technical assistance index. The averages of the monetary benefit index do, however, hardly differ from each other (see Annex A.2 for an elaboration of both indexes). Farmers are thus equally satisfied with the price they received for their crop.

The outputs realised with the above-described inputs and technical assistance show that in Embu region, Kithungururu (non-Utz) farmers reach a higher coffee harvest than Rianjagi (Utz-certified) farmers in absolute terms. The harvest per tree of Kithungururu farmers is also slightly and significantly higher. This difference in output results in a higher absolute revenue stream and a higher profit level from coffee for Kithungururu (non-Utz) farmers. There are three possible explanations. In the first place, it appeared from interviews that Utz certified farmers did appreciate the technical assistance they received, but this does not yet pay off in a higher harvest compared to the control group. The underlying differences with respect to the number of young not yet fruit-bearing trees might be part of the explanation. Investments

Table 5.3. Descriptive characteristics of coffee production and risk attitudes.

	Embu district					Mathioya district				
	Rianjagi (Utz)		Kithungururu			Kangunu (Utz)		Kamagogo		
	Mean	SD	Mean	SD	Sign.[1]	Mean	SD	Mean	SD	Sign.[1]
Input										
No of young trees (0-3 yrs)	20.23	53.99	5.22	23.36	**	7.98	22.98	6.63	17.48	
No of mature trees (>3 yrs)	304.37	223.22	361.00	324.40		251.07	115.74	227.39	300.30	
Workforce in farm household (no)	2.00	1.08	1.90	0.92		2.02	1.18	1.88	0.88	
Hired labour (%)	0.67	0.47	0.63	0.49		0.83	0.38	0.70	0.47	*
Use of fertiliser (%)	0.94	0.24	0.84	0.37	**	0.98	0.15	0.93	0.26	
Total inputs costs (×1000 KSh)	5.44	5.08	5.29	4.75		8.53	6.44	5.51	3.92	***
Technical assistance										
Attended training (%)	0.96	0.19	0.49	0.51	***	1.00	0.00	0.86	0.35	***
Technical assistance (index)	0.40	0.53	-0.92	1.23	***	0.54	0.23	0.02	0.96	***
Monetary benefits (index)	-0.04	1.02	0.15	0.96		0.25	0.76	-0.41	1.16	***
Output										
Total harvest (kg)	809.67	827.79	1,171.48	1,057.70	**	1,541.21	1,123.72	1,022.40	1,496.58	**
Coffee/mature tree (kg)	3.32	4.13	4.45	4.67	*	6.42	4.03	5.40	7.19	
Coffee revenue (×1000 KSh)	40.48	41.39	55.06	49.71	*	85.77	62.54	41.00	60.01	***
Profit per tree (×1000 KSh)	0.14	0.19	0.19	0.21		0.32	0.22	0.18	0.28	***
Perception of turnover[2]	2.35	0.89	2.49	0.87		2.33	0.93	1.86	0.95	**
Attitudes										
Performance of cooperative	0.132	1.048	0.188	0.793		0.147	0.855	-0.527	1.193	***
Trust in cooperative	0.106	1.000	0.149	0.892		-0.107	0.972	-0.225	1.192	
Trust in members	-0.161	0.937	-0.585	1.020	**	0.141	0.976	0.645	0.773	***
Loyalty	0.336	0.689	-0.338	1.150	***	0.176	0.979	0.029	1.004	
Corruption[3]	3.077	1.557	2.184	1.302	***	2.452	1.400	3.419	1.651	***
Risk index (all events)	0.076	1.091	0.447	1.152	*	-0.563	0.352	0.163	0.990	***
Risk index (coffee shocks)	0.150	1.047	-0.246	0.673	**	-0.485	0.234	0.573	1.354	***
Outcome risk game[4]	2.889	1.183	3.789	1.273	**	3.737	1.327	2.905	1.758	*

[1] * = α< 0.10; ** = α< 0.05; *** = α< 0.01.

[2] Perception of turnover: 1 = loss, 2 = equal, 3 = profit.

[3] Based on a Likert-scale score on the statement: 'There occurs a lot of corruption in the cooperative to which I sell my coffee'.

[4] Number of participants risk game: Rianjagi (n=18), Kithungururu (n=19), Kangunu (n=19), Kamagogo (n=21).

of fertiliser and labour in these trees not yet deliver results in terms of harvest and revenue. In the second place, Rianjagi cooperative was certified in 2007, and the survey was done over the 2009-2010 season. It might thus be too early for already obtaining the effects of certification in terms of improved harvest. Thirdly, unobserved effects might play a role; for instance, more effective investments in the provision of inputs by certain cooperatives.

For Mathioya region, differences between the certified and non-certified cooperative are more profound. The average amount of money spent on inputs is significantly higher for Utz certified farmers. Farmers of both cooperatives also differ significantly with respect to the assistance they receive from their cooperative: The Utz certified farmers received significantly more training, are more satisfied with the technical assistance received, and with their associated monetary benefits. The significantly higher outputs realised by Kangunu (Utz) farmers combined with technical assistance shows that the certification program seems to have a strong positive effect on the coffee productivity of its farmers. Kangunu farmers harvest, on average, 500 kg more berries than Kamagogo farmers. This translates into almost one kg of coffee more per tree, and a quarter higher profit rate per coffee tree. Higher input costs of Kangunu farmers are thus paying off in a higher profit. Interviews confirm that certified farmers were mainly positive about their cooperative efforts to stimulate good practices in coffee production, especially through training and higher coffee payments. Coffee prices encourage farmers very much to put more efforts into their coffee.

5.4.2 Trust and loyalty

Trust was measured with a set of eight statements based on a Likert scale. Factor analyses showed that these items are associated with two dimensions of social trust; one for trust in the cooperative as a whole (trust in coop), and the second representing the trust that farmers have in the coffee growing practices of other cooperative members (trust in members). Loyalty is defined as the willingness of farmers for selling coffee only to the cooperative and thus refrain from side sales. It was measured with 5 items which were combined into one factor.

Table 5.3 shows the descriptives of these dependent variables and main explanatory variables. Farmers in the Embu region do not differ in their opinion on the performance of the cooperative; both are equally satisfied with the way the cooperative performs in terms of efficiency and profits. Rianjagi farmers (Utz) have more trust in the coffee production of the members of their cooperative than Kithungururu farmers. Farmers explained during interviews that improvements in coffee practices due to Utz certification increased their trust in the performance of other farmers. Rianjagi farmers also score higher on the proxy for loyalty to the cooperative, which implies that they are less inclined to sell to another party than Kithungururu farmers. Rianjagi (Utz) farmers do, however, perceive more corruption in their cooperative than non-Utz certified farmers do. The cost of controlling the management seems problematic for Rianjagi farmers. Farmers were especially pointing at the secretary manager and the bookkeeper[42] who are in charge of the cooperative funds. Kithungururu (non-Utz) farmers, however, praised their current management committee, which is an improvement in comparison with their former committees.

Cooperative performance outcomes of the two cooperatives in Mathioya region are slightly different. Members of Kangunu (Utz) cooperative consider the performance of their cooperative higher and corruption lower compared to their non-certified counterpart. The trust in the cooperative does not significantly differ between both cooperatives, while trust between members of the cooperative is higher for Kamagogo (non-Utz) members than Kangunu farmers. At Kangunu, free-riding seems to occur more frequently, and farmers showed some critique to their cooperative members, especially to the ones delivering coffee of lower quality and inferior quantity. These farmers are thought to reduce prices for other farmers that deliver coffee of higher quality, thus occasioning a typical free-riders problem. In Kamagogo cooperative, most farmers appear to be on the same side. They understand from each other that they can become demoralised by low prices that are received for their coffee, and feel that most farmers do their utmost best given the limited resources they have to reinvest in their coffee.

We relied on an OLS regression to explain the underlying determinants of trust and loyalty that farmers exhibit towards their cooperative. Table 5.4 presents the results of the OLS-regression with the proxies for loyalty (model 2A) and trust (model 2B) as dependent variables. For Embu region, household characteristics are of little influence on trust and loyalty of farmers towards their cooperative. Wealth of the household, in terms of the asset value, and the size of the coffee harvest, are of significant influence on trust in the cooperative. This can be explained by the fact that a higher yield is supported by the services that farmers received from the cooperative. Technical assistance only influences loyalty, while monetary benefits appear in both models: higher perceived monetary benefits lead to higher levels of trust and loyalty. This is in line with the findings of Saenz and Ruben (2004), who concluded that loyalty is influenced by non-price factors such as technical assistance, as well as price factors. It also confirms the importance of the price that farmers receive for their coffee. Whether farmers were Utz certified – controlling for all the above effects – has no significant effect for trust, but it appears to be relevant for loyalty. Other variables, such as trust in cooperative members and technical assistance, are however of greater importance for enhancing trust.

These differences between loyalty and trust in the cooperative might be due to the focus of Utz certification programs. Their main focus is on improving coffee practices of farmers through technical assistance, and far less through improvements in farm and cooperative management (Raynolds et al., 2007). Technical assistance is indeed

---

[42] While executing the research, we also noticed ourselves that the bookkeeper and secretary manager were suspicious about how we were proceeding with our research, and tried to control the way in which the research was executed.

Table 5.4. Trust in cooperative and loyalty towards cooperative (Model 2 – OLS regression).

| | Embu district | | | | | | Mathioya district | | | | | |
| | Model 2A trust | | | Model 2B loyalty | | | Model 2A trust | | | Model 2B loyalty | | |
	Mean	SE	Sign.[1]	Mean	SE	Sign.[1]	Mean	SE	Sign.[1]	Mean	SE	Sign.[1]
Constant	0.610	0.819		-0.082	0.892		1.562	1.153	*	1.202	1.218	
Household (HH) characteristics												
Gender HH head (1=male)	-0.202	0.255		0.118	0.278		-0.143	0.267		-0.243	0.271	
Age HH head (yrs)	0.013	0.006	**	0.008	0.007		-0.013	0.009		-0.006	0.010	
Max education HH (yrs)	-0.022	0.024		-0.019	0.026		-0.032	0.028		0.033	0.030	
Total value assets in KSh (log)	-0.150	0.081	**	-0.047	0.088		0.094	0.112		-0.086	0.117	
Total coffee harvest in kg (log)	0.200	0.098	**	0.105	0.107		-0.194	0.148	*	-0.015	0.158	
Cooperative characteristics												
Technical assistance (index)	-0.051	0.089		0.195	0.097	**	0.368	0.163	**	0.054	0.173	
Monetary benefits (index)	0.286	0.083	***	0.115	0.090	*	0.254	0.118	**	0.066	0.125	
Trust in coop. members (index)	0.230	0.088	***	0.180	0.095	**	0.317	0.129	***	0.228	0.137	**
Corruption	-0.183	0.059	***	-0.201	0.064	***	-0.197	0.070	***	-0.074	0.074	
Utz certified (1 = yes)	0.193	0.211		0.551	0.229	***	-0.121	0.261		0.132	0.278	
Adj. R²	0.326			0.313			0.246			-0.024		
F-value	5.799	***		4.793	***		3.736	***		0.802		

[1] Significance: * = α<0.10; ** = α<0.05; *** = α<0.01.

influencing farmer's loyalty towards the cooperative for delivering their coffee production. Major managerial improvements have, however, not occurred: it even seems that levels of corruption have increased since Utz certification was obtained.

For Mathioya region, trust in the cooperative is not explained by household characteristics except for the total coffee harvest, which is inversely related to trust: farmers with a lower harvest have higher levels of trust in their cooperative, possibly because they expect future support for upgrading their production. Technical assistance and monetary benefits are both positively significant for trust in the cooperative, as does trust in other members. Lastly, corruption has the expected negative influence. In both models, there appears to be no significant difference in trust for Utz certified or non-certified farmers. The model for loyalty in Mathioya has a very low explained variance; only trust in the cooperative members is contributing to loyalty. The loyalty that farmers express is thus for a major part mediated by the trust they have in their fellow members.

5.4.3 Indirect effects: risk reduction

We expect that trust and loyalty towards the cooperative influence the risk perception of members of a cooperative. This hypothesis is examined by the use of a two stage least square (2SLS) regression, since the model might involve endogeneity (Wooldridge, 2008). We seek to explain the risk perception of farmers related to, among others, the trust and loyalty of farmers towards their cooperative. Trust and loyalty are, however, endogenous in this model; they are explanatory variables, but are jointly determined with our dependent variable because we use the same control variables in both models. We therefore need to control for the correlation of the variables trust and loyalty with the error term of the model. The variables used for risk perception are based on participatory risk mapping outcomes (Smith *et al.*, 2000). We interviewed farmers on the incidence and severity of several types of risks, which resulted in two indexes: one for the perception of risks specifically related to coffee, and another index explaining general risk perception of farmers (including coffee risks).

Descriptives of these variables were presented in Table 5.3. On average, in Enbu region farmers of Kithungururu (non-Utz) scored higher on the general risk index compared to Rianjagi (Utz) farmers. In other words, they are more concerned about the incidence and severity of a range of possible future shocks. If we focus, however, on risks concerning coffee, Utz certified farmers score higher than non-certified farmers. Rianjagi farmers are thus stronger concerned about (coffee) market constraints, but significantly less about other shocks. These outcomes are confirmed by the results from the risk game, since the game was framed in such a way that it related to coffee farming. This is not in line with our hypothesis that Utz certified farmers are likely to be less risk averse.

In Mathioya region, the control group (Kamagogo) experiences more concerns about coffee shocks, as well as on other shocks not directly related to coffee. Here, Utz certified farmers are less risk averse concerning coffee risks, as well as on other issues, and these risk perception differences were confirmed during the risk game. This might be explained by the theory on asset poverty thresholds (Barrett, 2005), that points to a minimum required level of assets before being able to withstand shocks that could lead to fallbacks into poverty. It seems that Kamagogo farmers are 'below the threshold' of assets and capabilities that is required to grow toward a high productive steady-state. Instead, they are struggling with choosing between allocating resources towards consumption or making investments in the production of coffee. For Kangunu farmers, Utz certification appears to work as a type of cargo net being in place, which helps them to find ways out of poverty, and overcome structural limitations related to market constraints.

A closer analysis of variables explaining the score of farmers on both risk indexes is shown in Table 5.5 for Embu region. Regarding household characteristics, the most important indicators are the age of the household head, and the combined value of assets and livestock. Farmers with a higher level of physical and/or human assets

Table 5.5. Explaining risk perceptions, Embu district (Model 3 – 2SLS regression).

	Model 3A: all risks			Model 3B: all risks			Model 3C: coffee risks			Model 3D: coffee risks		
	Mean	SE	Sign.[1]	Mean	SE	Sign.[1]	Mean	SE	Sign.[1]	Mean	SE	Sign.[1]
Constant	3.142	0.952	***	2.729	0.994	***	1.382	0.691	**	1.111	0.787	*
Household (HH) characteristics												
Gender HH head (1=male)	0.212	0.323		0.362	0.329		0.236	0.234		0.403	0.261	*
Age HH head (yrs)	-0.011	0.008	*	-0.013	0.008	*	-0.009	0.006	*	-0.013	0.007	**
Max education HH (yrs)	-0.030	0.031		-0.023	0.031		-0.026	0.022		-0.015	0.025	
Total asset value (KSh, log)	-0.253	0.101	***	-0.204	0.103	**	-0.116	0.073	*	-0.060	0.081	
Total coffee harvest (kg, log)	0.106	0.128		0.051	0.129		0.035	0.093		-0.048	0.102	
Cooperative characteristics												
Trust in cooperative (index)	-0.396	0.114	***				-0.447	0.083	***			
Loyalty to cooperative (index)				-0.285	0.114	***				-0.184	0.091	**
Utz certified (1 = yes)	-0.433	0.210	**	-0.241	0.230		0.317	0.152	**	0.436	0.182	***
Adj. R²	0.193			0.144			0.309			0.129		
SEE	1.009			1.039			0.733			0.823		
F-value	4.378	***		3.381	***		7.339	***		3.091	***	

[1] Significance: * = α<0.10; ** = α<0.05; *** = α<0.01.

are less worried about upcoming shocks, and assets are important for the degree of security experienced. Assets thus help farmers to cope with and recover from shocks (Hulme and Sheperd, 2003).

Variables at the cooperative level are of major importance for both risk indexes. The level of trust in the cooperative and loyalty towards the cooperative are both negatively significant in all models. Higher levels of trust in the cooperative lead to a less negative perception of future shocks, and the same holds for stronger loyalty towards the cooperative. Risk sharing within the cooperative is thus an important way of reducing (behavioural) risks related to the cooperative, as well as vulnerability to other household shocks. This finding is fully in line with earlier research on risk conducted by Carter (1987) and Fafchamps (2003).

The influence of Utz certification is, however, not confirming our expectations. The influence of Utz certification appears with a negative significant sign in model 3A, indicating that Utz certified farmers are less risk averse when it concerns general risks. Utz certified shows, however, a positive parameter in model specification 3C and 3D, pointing to the fact that Utz certified farmers are more risk averse when it concerns risks within coffee. A possible explanation might be that certified farmers, for instance due to the corruption at managerial level, invest less of their returns in coffee, but instead prefer to spread their risks by investing in other income-generating activities.

Table 5.6 shows the results for Mathioya region. A remarkable difference with the model explaining risk aversion in Embu is that household characteristics show more influence, while wealth in terms of asset value and coffee harvests are not significantly influencing risk behaviour. Age and education are both positively significant, implying that perceptions on risk occurrence and severity are higher for older farmers with a higher level of education. We expected a higher level of education, and therefore a higher level of capabilities in the households, to lead to lower levels of vulnerability. Paying school fees might, however, be a risk in itself. Dercon (2008) argues that not finishing school is often done as a coping strategy, but leads to a reduction of capabilities in the future. Otherwise, education of older farmers might be outdated with respect to current improved agricultural practices.

The proxies for trust in the cooperative and loyalty towards the cooperative are consistently negatively significant, meaning that higher trust in the cooperative and greater loyalty towards the cooperative lead to lower risk occurrence and severity. This confirms our earlier findings for Embu region. The producer organisation is thus an important factor for reducing risks of small-scale coffee farmers. In addition, being Utz certified is now for all models negatively significant. Utz certified farmers thus experience fewer risks and shocks than their non-certified counterparts, while controlling for other household and cooperative characteristics. These findings are in line with our original hypothesis, but contrary to the findings for Embu region (Rianjagi, Utz). Consequently, context matters in registering the effects of coffee certification.

Table 5.6. Explaining risk perceptions, Mathioya district (Model 4 – 2SLS regression).

	Model 4A: all risks			Model 4B: all risks			Model 4C: coffee risks			Model 4D: coffee risks		
	Mean	SE	Sign.[1]	Mean	SE	Sign.[1]	Mean	SE	Sign.[1]	Mean	SE	Sign.[1]
Constant	0.013	0.696		0.347	0.784		-0.464	0.880		0.049	1.055	
Gender HH head (1 = male)	-0.120	0.164		-0.133	0.186		-0.001	0.207		-0.018	0.249	
Age HH head (yrs)	0.015	0.006	***	0.017	0.007	***	0.011	0.008	*	0.014	0.009	*
Max education HH (yrs)	0.028	0.018	*	0.048	0.020	***	0.014	0.022		0.044	0.027	**
Total asset value (KSh, log)	-0.039	0.071		-0.107	0.079	*	0.034	0.090		-0.072	0.107	
Total coffee harvest (kg, log)	-0.101	0.093		-0.090	0.105		-0.030	0.118		-0.014	0.141	
Trust in cooperative (index)	-0.340	0.065	***				-0.533	0.082	***			
Loyalty to cooperative (index)				-0.177	0.079	**				-0.258	0.107	***
Utz certified (1 = yes)	-0.642	0.149	***	-0.668	0.168	***	-0.998	0.188	***	-1.042	0.226	***
Adj. R²	0.427			0.269			0.489			0.264		
SEE	0.626			0.707			0.792			0.951		
F-value	9.940	***		5.423	***		12.470	***		5.297	***	

[1] Significance: * = α<0.10; ** = α<0.05; *** = α<0.01.

5.5 Discussion

Vulnerability reduction is an essential condition if small-scale farmers are to gain from effective income stabilisation strategies. We argued that Utz certification reduces vulnerability through the cooperative of which coffee farmers are a member, in several direct and indirect ways. Table 5.7 shows our initial hypotheses and the registered results in each of the two study region.

Hypothesis 1, which predicts that Utz certification leads to a higher harvest, was rejected for the Utz certified cooperative in Embu. Whereas Utz certified farmers in Embu did receive better technical assistance than their counterparts, and this assistance was indeed a significant influence on their production, it did not result in better prices. The hypothesis was confirmed for the Mathioya region, where Kangunu cooperative (Utz) coffee yields were significantly higher, reinforced by good technical assistance, an adequate system of input provision and a high coffee price are main conditions for stimulating a higher harvest (Barham and Weber, 2012; Ruben, 2008). Farmers agreed that higher prices were especially stimulating for producing coffee of high quality and quantity.

Concerning Hypothesis 2, we can conclude that for the Embu region, Utz certification positively influences the loyalty of farmers towards their cooperative. However, certified farmers did not differ from their counterparts in trust towards the cooperatives; they sometimes even experience higher levels of corruption. Certified farmers were thus facing difficulties with controlling their management, which is a common aspect of many cooperatives (Milford, 2004). However, certified farmers do show stronger trust in the fact that their fellow cooperative members produce coffee of high quality and sufficient quantity (scale). These differences between loyalty and trust in the cooperative might be explained by the focus of Utz certification programs. Its main orientation is towards improving coffee practices of farmers through technical assistance, and less attention is given to structural improvements in cooperative

Table 5.7. Overview of hypotheses and outcomes.

Utz certified compared to non-certified farmers	Embu	Mathioya
1. Have a higher harvest, because	–	+
a. they receive better extension services	+	+
b. and receive higher prices for their coffee	–	+
2. Start to see their organisation as a reliable partner, because	±	±
a. they have more trust in their cooperative	–	–
b. and are more loyal towards their cooperative	+	+
3. Are less risk-averse	±	+

+ = confirmed, – =rejected, ± = partly confirmed.

management (Raynolds *et al.*, 2007). In Mathioya region, similar outcomes are found. Utz certified farmers are more loyal towards their cooperative, but no differences with regard to the levels of trust in the cooperative are registered. The explanation for the latter is slightly different than for Embu region: farmers show lower levels of trust in their cooperative members, which is thought to be caused by free-riding. Farmers who performed better thus faced a lower average price for their coffee. Certified farmers could thus not achieve economic optimal production. Still, they received satisfactory prices for their coffee, which were higher than those for the control cooperative.

With respect to Hypothesis 3, loyalty and trust towards the cooperative were both important in explaining the risk perception of farmers: higher levels of trust and loyalty lead to a substantial reduction of risk aversion. Utz certification in Embu, however, shows a partially positive influence on risk perceptions. Overall, risk aversion is lower among Utz certified farmers, but risk aversion related to coffee shocks is higher for Utz certified farmers, and especially if we control for trust towards the cooperative. This might be explained by the lower confidence that Utz certified farmers in Embu maintain towards their management. It is also in line with theory; trust has an instrumental value in helping to reduce risks and transaction costs of market relationships (Williamson, 2000).

Results for the Mathioya region are in accordance with our hypothesis: Utz certified farmers are generally less risk averse than non-certified farmers, and this holds for coffee shocks, as well as for shocks in general. Likewise, loyalty and trust towards the cooperative show a positive influence on risk reduction. This confirms our theory that producer organisations have an important risk sharing function (Carter, 1987; Fafchamps, 2004), and that certification has possibilities to contribute to this by enhancing farmer's trust and loyalty towards their cooperative.

Our results moreover indicate that the conditions under which cooperatives operate are important for a successful implementation of certification schemes in cooperatives. We confirmed that the combination of technical assistance and higher prices that Utz certification intends to offer to farmers is indeed important, and these benefits could further enhance loyalty and trust towards the cooperative. On the other hand, Utz certification might also be negatively influencing trust, if certification is causing corruption amongst the management (as in the Embu case), or when it appears to initiate free-riding (as in Mathioya region). Reaping the fruits of higher yields and better coffee quality thus also depends on transparency and efficiency of the management of producer organisations, as well as on a well-functioning input supply and output-marketing system. Some of the studied certified cooperatives, especially in Embu, scored less convincingly on these factors. We can nevertheless conclude that Utz certification – if applied under the right conditions – can indeed play an important role in the successful inclusion of smallholders in value chains.

5.6 Outlook: new insights and remaining questions

Our field research findings emphasise the importance of understanding the influences of institutions on rural livelihoods. Institutions are acknowledged in the livelihoods framework as important factors influencing livelihood outcomes. Our theoretical framework provides better insights into how local livelihoods are linked to (inter) national markets through, for instance, producer organisations and Utz certification. A good understanding of the influence of the global economy on local economies and related economic choices is increasingly important due to the renewed focus of development policy and practice on sustainable agriculture and responsible trade.

We applied these theories on the case of Utz certification schemes in Kenya. Most earlier research on certification focuses on Fair Trade schemes, while little research has been conducted so far on private standards (Ruben and Zuniga, 2011). In addition, studies that focus on evaluating the impact of certification mainly report on outputs and outcome levels (Nelson and Pound, 2009). In addition, we examined the prospects for vulnerability reduction both within and outside markets as a key element of supply chain integration. Our findings show that the successful reduction of market imperfections, due to Utz certification, can reduce vulnerability to other non-market shocks as well. However, our findings are still location-specific and more research is needed to closely examine the conditions under which these effects materialise.

Producer organisations and certification schemes are important institutions mediating the access of farmers to international market outlets. Our study confirms that producer organisations are indeed important for reducing market vulnerability (Blandon *et al.*, 2009; Milford, 2004). On the other hand, we also found some evidence for the fact that producer organisations might constrain equitable access to market due to corruption and free-riding (Barham and Weber, 2012; Mude, 2006). Utz certification schemes appear to be particularly successful if they offer a complete package of technical assistance, higher prices (due to better quality), and regular input supply, which needs to be provided by an efficient and transparent cooperative management structure. Input supply appeared to be the least successfully organised, even though input delivery systems are very important for boosting production (Mude, 2006). Our findings show that this is especially a problem for poorer farmers, who do not have the means to buy inputs elsewhere if the supply system of their cooperative fails. This demonstrates the risks of inclusion in value chains with higher quality standards. Farmers face the risk of being locked into unprofitable production activities if market constraints are severe, which may lead to risk-averse choices and condemns them of being trapped in chronic poverty. More in-depth research is therefore needed regarding farmers' choice-making processes towards technological intensification, as well as options for reducing the dependence of (poorer) farmers on support systems such as producers organisations and certification schemes.

Our study still leaves open several questions on other strands of theory and research. Regarding livelihood strategies, we mainly examined risk perceptions, and did not study effects on income diversification strategies thoroughly. For analysing the effects of certification schemes on the inclusion in value chains, it would be interesting to compare several options of vulnerability reduction inside and outside coffee. We mainly focused on the production side of the household, and less on consumption patterns. A recurring theme in our findings was, for instance, the preference farmers that have for 'lump sum pay-out', because they can use this larger amount for specific investments, such as education fees or house upgrading. More research needs to be done on these relations.

A final issue we want to emphasise is that Utz certified is still a relatively 'young' label. At the time of research, the certified cooperatives in Mathioya and Embu had been certified for respectively 5 and 4 years. Research done a few years from now may notice a stronger internalisation of certification schemes, which could lead to other outcomes. It might then also be possible to perform longitudinal research and examine changes over time. Such longitudinal research could give better insight into longer-term effects of certification schemes, and whether shifts in livelihood strategies are indeed sustainable over a longer time period.

References

Barham, B.L. and J.G. Weber (2012). The economic sustainability of certified coffee: recent evidence from Mexico and Peru. *World Development* 40(6): 1269-1279.

Barham, J. and C. Chitemi (2008). Collective action initiatives to improve marketing performance: lessons from farmer's groups in Tanzania. *Food Policy* 34: 53-59.

Barrett, C.B. (2005). Rural poverty dynamics: development policy implications. *Agricultural Economics* 32(1): 45-60.

Bijman, J. and M. Wollni (2008). *Producer organizations and vertical coordination: an economic organization theory perspective*. International conference on cooperative studies. Köln: ICCS.

Blandon, J., S. Henson and J. Cranfield (2009). Small-scale farmer participation in new agri-food supply chains: case of the supermarket supply chain for fruit and vegetables in Honduras. *Journal of International Development* 21: 971-984.

Cardenas, J.C. and J. Carpenter (2008). Behavioural development economics: lessons from field labs in the developing world. *Journal of Development Studies* 44(3): 311-338.

Carter, M.R. (1987). Risk sharing and incentives in the decollectivization of agriculture. *Oxford Economic Papers* 39: 577-595.

Chambers, R. and G.R. Conway (1992). Sustainable rural livelihoods: practical concepts for the 21st century. *IDS Discussion Paper* 296.

Creswell, J.W. (2003). *Research design: qualitative, quantitative and mixed methods approaches*. Thousand Oaks, CA, USA: Sage Publications, Inc.

Dercon, S. (2008). Fate and fear: risk and its consequences in Africa. *Journal of African Economies* 17(2): 97-127.

Dorward, A., J. Kydd, J. Morrison and C. Poulton (2005). Institutions, markets and economic co-ordination: linking development policy to theory and praxis. *Development and Change* 36(1): 1-25.

Doss, C., J. McPeak and C.B. Barrett(2008). Interpersonal, intertemporal and spatial variation in risk perceptions: evidence from East Africa. *World Development* 36(8): 1453-1468.

Ellis, F. (1998). *Peasant economics: farm households and agrarian development.* Cambridge, UK: Cambridge University Press.

Fafchamps, M. (2003). *Rural poverty, risk and development.* Cheltenham, UK: Edward Elgar Publishing Ltd.

Fafchamps, M. (2004). *Market institutions in sub-Saharan Africa: theory and evidence.* Cambridge, MA, USA: MIT Press.

Hazell, P., C. Poulton, S. Wiggins and A. Dorward (2010). The future of small farms: trajectories and policy priorities. *World Development* 38(10): 1349-1361.

Hulme, D. and A. Sheperd (2003). Conceptualizing chronic poverty. *World Development* 31(3): 403-423.

Kamau, M., L.O. Mose, R. Fort and R. Ruben (2010). *The impact of certification on smallholder farmers in Kenya: the case of Utz certification programme in coffee.* Nairobi, Kenya: Tegemeo Institute, Egerton University.

Kaplinsky, R. and M. Morris (2001). *Handbook for value chain research.* Ottawa, Canada: IDRC.

Key, N. and D. Runsten (1999). Contract farming, smallholders, and rural development in Latin America: the organization of agroprocessing firms and the scale of outgrower production. *World Development* 27(2): 381-401.

Milford, A. (2004). *Coffee, cooperatives and competition: the impact of Fair Trade.* Bergen, Norway: Chr. Michelsen Institute.

Mude, A.G. (2006). *Weaknesses in institutional organization: explaining the dismal performance of Kenya's coffee cooperatives.* Contributed paper International Association of Agricultural Economists Conference, Gold Coast, August 2006.

Murphy, J.T. (2002). Networks, trust and innovation in Tanzania's manufacturing sector. *World Development* 30(4): 591-619.

Nelson, V. and B. Pound (2009). *The last ten years: a comprehensive review of the literature on the impact of fairtrade.* Greenwich, UK: Natural Resources Institute, NRI.

Ostrom, E. (2003). How types of goods and property rights jointly affect collective action. *Journal of Theoretical Politics* 15(3): 239-270.

Place, F., G. Kariuki, J. Wangila, P. Kristjanson, A. Makauki and J. Ndubi (2004). Assessing the factors underlying differences in achievements of farmer groups: methodological issues and empirical findings from the highlands of Central Kenya. *Agricultural Systems* 82: 257-272.

Pratt, B. and P. Loizos (2003). *Choosing research methods: data collection for development.* Oxford, UK: Oxfam.

Quinn, C. H., M. Huby, H. Kiwasila and J.C. Lovett (2003). Local perceptions of risk to livelihood in semi-arid Tanzania. *Journal of Environmental Management* 68: 111-119.

Raynolds, L.T., D. Murray and A. Heller (2007). Regulating sustainability in the coffee sector: a comparative analysis of third-party environmental and social certification initiatives. *Agriculture and Human Values* 24: 147-163.

Rodrik, D. (2000). Institutions for high-quality growth: what they are and how to acquire them. *Studies in Comparative International Development* 35(3): 3-31.

Ruben, R. (ed.) (2008). *The impact of Fair Trade.* Wageningen, the Netherlands: Wageningen Academic Publishers.

Ruben, R., M. Slingerland and H. Nijhoff (2006). Agro-food chains and networks for development: issues, approaches and strategies. Dordrecht, the Netherlands: Springer.

Ruben, R. and G. Zuniga (2011). How standards compete: comparative impact of coffee certification schemes in Northern Nicaragua. *Supply Chain Management* 16(2): 98-109.

Saenz, F. and R. Ruben (2004). Export contracts for non-traditional products: chayote from Costa Rica. *Journal on Chain and Network Science* 4(2): 139-150.

Scoones, I. (2009). Livelihoods perspectives and rural development. *Journal of Peasant Studies* 36(1).

Scoones, I. and W. Wolmer (2003). Introduction: livelihoods in crisis – challenges for rural development in southern Africa. *IDS Bulletin* 34(3): 1-14.

Seville, D., A. Buxton, and B. Vorley (2011). *Under what conditions are value chains effective tools for pro-poor development?* London, UK: IIED/Sustainable Food Lab.

Shiferaw, B., G. Obare, and G. Muricho (2008). Rural market imperfections and the role of institutions in collective action to improve markets for the poor. *Natural Resources Forum* 32(1): 25-38.

Smith, K., C.B. Barrett and P.W. Box (2000). Participatory risk mapping for targeting research and assistance: with an example from East African pastoralists. *World Development* 28(11): 1945-1959.

Tegemeo Institute (2009). *Impact assessment of fair and responsible trade in coffee – Kenya household survey.* Nairobi, Kenya: Egerton University.

Thomas, A., J. Chataway and M. Wuyts (1998). *Finding out fast: investigative skills for policy and development.* London, UK: SAGE publications.

Tschakert, P. (2007). Views from the vulnerable: understanding climatic and other stressors in the Sahel. *Global Environmental Change* 17: 381-396.

Vorley, B., E. del Pozo-Vergnes, C. Gribnau, B. Ghose and D. Muñoz (*2012*). Feature: making markets work for smallholders? Capacity and agency. *Capacity.org* 44.

Williamson, O. E. (2000). The new institutional economics: taking stock, looking ahead. *Journal of Economic Literature* 38(3): 595-613.

Wooldridge, J.M. (2008). Instrumental variables and two stage least squares. In: J.M. Wooldridge (ed.) *Introductory econometrics: a modern approach.* Mason, IL, USA: South-Western Cengage Learning.

World Bank (2001). *Building institutions for markets.* World Development Report 2002. Washington, DC, USA: World Bank.

World Bank (2007). *Agriculture for development.* World Development Report 2008. Washington, DC, USA: World Bank.

World Bank (2011). *Africa development indicators 2011.* Washington, DC, USA: World Bank.

Annex

A.1. Tables

Table A.1. Risk categories[1]

Choices	Option 1 = green (p=50%) KSh/10 kg coffee	Option 2 = red (p=50%) KSh/10 kg coffee	Risk aversion class	Expected value KSh/10 kg coffee
1	100	100	Extreme	100
2	190	90	Severe	140
3	240	80	Intermediate	160
4	300	60	Moderate	180
5	380	20	Slight-neutral	200
6	400	0	Neutral-negative	200

[1] Based on the worksheet developed by Barr (2003); values used are framed to the local Kenyan context of coffee farmers.

A.2. Operationalisation of indexes in factor analysis

The two indexes, 'technical assistance' and 'monetary benefits' are based on one principal component analysis; the index scores reflect the two components forthcoming from the analysis. The Cronbach's alpha (CA) of the combined index is 0.670.

- Index of technical assistance' contains the following statements (scores on Likert 1-5 scale):
  - I attended a training program through your cooperative (yes/no);
  - I learned better coffee practices;
  - I am provided with sufficient technical assistance;
  - I am provided with sufficient knowledge to improve the quality of my coffee.
- Index of monetary benefits is based on the following statements (scores on Likert 1-5 scale):
  - I received higher coffee prices;
  - my coffee productivity increased;
  - my household income increased;
  - I am provided with sufficient fertilisers and pesticides.

All other indexes are generated with the use of principal component analysis, thereby converting a set of possibly correlated variables into a set of values of linearly uncorrelated variables (principal components). The variables are based on statements using a 5-point Likert scale, unless stated otherwise. We use the following indexes:

- 'Trust in the cooperative' has a CA of 0.795 and is based on the following statements:
  - I trust the management committee of the cooperative;
  - I trust the rules of my cooperative;
  - I trust the information provided by my cooperative;
  - I trust the staff members of the cooperative;
  - I am sure that the cooperative will sell my coffee at a good price.
- 'Trust in the cooperative's members' has a CA of 0.637 and is based on the following statements:
  - I trust the members of my cooperative;
  - I trust that the members of my cooperative do everything they can to produce coffee of high quality and quantity;
  - I trust that members only bring coffee to the factory that they grew themselves.
- 'Loyalty' has a CA of 0.626 and is based on the following statements:
  - I intend to continue the relationship with the cooperative;
  - it is most likely that I leave when better opportunities appear;
  - if an individual buyer offers me a 10% better price than the cooperative, I will sell to him; I am more interested in the price of my coffee than on the relation with my cooperative;
  - I sell to temporary buyers that might not buy again from me.

- 'Performance' has a CA of 0.809 and is based on the following statements:
  - the cooperative is an efficient organisation; the cooperative is a profitable organisation;
  - the cooperative is an organisation that reacts efficiently in the face of events;
  - I am very satisfied with the cooperative's overall performance.
- 'Coffee risks' has a CA of 0.738 and is based on the following risk components:
  - poor coffee payment; delay of payment of coffee;
  - lack of inputs for coffee;
  - lack of knowledge and agricultural skills (coffee);
  - lack of good leadership of the cooperative;
  - lack of transparency at the cooperative.
- 'All-risks' has a CA of 0.682 and is based on all coffee risks, as well as the following risk components:
  - lack of money; inability to pay school fees for children;
  - lack of jobs for educated youth; food shortages;
  - lack of water for domestic use;
  - lack of farm inputs;
  - lack of knowledge and agricultural skills on farming;
  - lack of markets and low prices for farm produce.

Chapter 6

Blessing of the bean or curse of the cooperative? – willingness to invest and trust of farmers in coffee cooperatives of Ethiopia

Christine Plaisier
For correspondence: c.plaisier@maw.ru.nl

6.1 Introduction

Given the dominant role of agriculture in the Ethiopian economy, it is of key importance to develop the agricultural sector for achieving economic growth (World Bank, 2005, 2007). Most poor people live in rural areas and are smallholders depending on agriculture for their livelihood. These smallholder farmers in Ethiopia are facing high transaction costs, lack of market information, poor infrastructure, and weak capital markets (Wolday and Gebre-Madhin, 2003). In order to overcome these constraints, the government of Ethiopia considered agricultural marketing cooperatives as one of the main pillars of development and as key institutions in its Agricultural Development Led Industrialisation Strategy for unlocking Ethiopia's agricultural growth potential. The government tries to reduce poverty by providing a better institutional environment for integrating smallholders into international markets (FDRE, 2005).[43] This is based on the idea that for integration into increasingly commercial and global chains for agricultural products, one of the most effective ways for poor smallholder farmers is to engage actively into the market through cooperative organisation and collective action (Hellin *et al.*, 2009). Given the difficulties that individual farmers face, some of them seek to form or join a cooperative to enhance their bargaining position in competitive agricultural markets (Blokland and Gouet, 2007).

This chapter focuses on coffee cooperatives. Coffee is the major export crop and coffee marketing cooperatives are the best-known and the largest cooperatives in Ethiopia. Moreover, Ethiopia is the perceived birthplace of the coffee bean and cooperatives

---

[43] This strategy is followed by the *Agricultural cooperatives sector development strategy 2012-2016* in which agricultural cooperatives are assigned a key role as facilitators of rural social-economic development (FDRE, 2012).

are seen as the backbone of the Ethiopian agricultural policy. Cooperatives are social institutions that exist for mutual support purposes, as well as firms aiming at profit maximisation (Francesconi, 2008). This study intends to improve our understanding of the role played by cooperative organisations in changing farmers' behavioural with regard to trust, risk attitudes and willingness to invest. Differences were made in the mechanisms of horizontal cooperative action in the context of weak and strong performing cooperatives. Fieldwork for data collection took place in the period of January-April 2010. Three different research methods were used: (1) a total of 232 surveys were undertaken among member households of four selected cooperatives; (2) three behavioural experiments were conducted in each cooperative concerning trust, risk attitude and likelihood of investments; and (3) case studies took place through a series of in-depth interviews with cooperative members.

This chapter is structured as follows: in Section 6.2. we outline the theoretical framework underlying the research on cooperative behaviour; this is followed in Section 6.3 with a short description of the local context where field research took place. In Section 6.4 we discuss the analytical methods for operationalisation of the key concept and in Section 6.5 the empirical approach for field data collection is outlined. Section 6.6 presents the descriptive results of the field work, while in Section 6.7 we present the estimates of interactions between trust, loyalty and collective action parameters. Section 6.8 concludes with policy implications and suggestions for further analysis.

6.2 Theoretical framework

This research relates the performance of the cooperative to the engagement of its members, mediated by the level of trust and willingness to invest. To do so, the study addresses the following research questions[44]:
1. To what extent does the performance of the cooperative influence members' engagement, willingness to invest and trust?
2. How does trust influence willingness to invest and engagement?
3. How are members' engagement with the cooperative and their willingness to invest related to each other?

We first elaborate the theoretical concepts used in the study (Section 6.4) and hereafter outline the analytical strategy for their empirical operationalisation (Section 6.5).

6.2.1 Trust

Several studies stress the importance of trust in a cooperative context – both trust between members and trust of members in leadership (James and Sykuta, 2005). Valentinov (2004) states that internal coordination and resource allocation in cooperatives are primarily determined by the quality of interpersonal relations between

---

[44] We present a summary of the research and only selected results. For more detailed account of the research design, methodology, perceived relations and results (Plaisier, 2010).

members. According to Ostrom (2003), trust is the core link between networks and collective action and the most relevant factor to provide voluntary cooperative action. One would expect that if a group of people have a common interest they will naturally get together and fight for the common goal. Olson (1971) explains in his seminal study 'Logic of the Collective Action' that this is however generally not the case. One of the problems of collective action refers to the danger of free-riding behaviour: an individual might receive benefit from the collective good without assuming the necessary individual costs. Trust is therefore very important since it assures that other persons will not take advantage even if they might derive economic benefits, thus enabling self-enforcement of collective action. Even if it pays to commit free-riding or ignore the rules in a contract, less people will be inclined to do so it in the presence of mutual trust (Putnam, 1993).

Six (2007) outlines the downward or upward spiralling processes of trust and their internal feedbacks. Individual's initial beliefs will or will not be confirmed through the impact of their actions on other persons. If confirmed, the beliefs will appear as self-fulfilling prophesies. Prior beliefs about causation affect the intake of information about the event observed (Six, 2007). Trust-building is thus based on positive feedbacks which imply the possibility not only of upward spiralling processes, but also of the risk of downward spiralling processes. Based on this theory, this downward and upward spiralling processes can be applied to the cooperative's performance and the role of trust. A good performing cooperative leads to more trust (here downward spiral) and more trust leads to a better performance (upward spiral). For the scope of this research it is unfortunately not possible to detect both relations, and we therefore focus on the downward spiralling process. The hypothesis is that a good performing cooperative leads to higher levels of trust.

6.2.2 Willingness to invest

Theoretically, cooperatives offer many advantages to smallholders, such as quality control, increased prices, economies of scale, and sustainable long-term relationships with foreign buyers, improved bargaining power, and the benefits of realising larger and more stable business. Cooperatives also provide access to information and enable participation in niche markets for their members (Anteneh, 2009). As a result of these advantages, risks and uncertainty are reduced and access to credit is improved, which enables producers to make long-term investments. Such long-term investments are considered to be of key relevance for poverty alleviation strategies that focus on changes in risk behaviour as a pre-condition for reducing asset poverty (Ruben et al., 2009). Two of the structural causes of rural poverty are the high risks that farmers face and the limited (profitable) investment opportunities they have. Poor households are not able to withstand the losses which might result from taking risky decisions and they have little access to credit to make long-term investments in order to overcome their vulnerable position (Barrett, 2005). Because of the importance of investments and the crucial role cooperatives could play in this regard, the research focuses on the willingness to invest among farmers affiliated with cooperatives. It therefore elaborates on the relation between performance of the cooperative and willingness to invest and on the underlying factors influencing willingness to invest.

Investments can be at individual level (e.g. planting more coffee trees on the private plot) or at collective level (e.g. building of a school in the community or improving roads or coffee processing facilities). This distinction is of particular importance when working in a cooperative. Collective goods are critical for a cooperative because members join not only for their individual benefits but also for the benefit of their community and the collective good. In order to be able to perform better, collective investment in the cooperative are required. This type of investment asks for engagement with the cooperative. Engagement with the cooperative is not limited to financial investments (like the re-investment of dividend in the cooperative) but also includes investment in time and efforts for participation in and creating loyalty to the cooperative (e.g. delivery of produce).

This is related to the issue of trust. The relationship between trust in the cooperative and willingness to invest in a cooperative is explained by Paldam and Svendsen (2000). They state that if members trust in and are loyal to a cooperative, they will agree to set aside as much as they can afford in order to face possible (financial) shortages. Conversely, if farmers have a low level of trust in a cooperative, they are not likely to invest in collective goods for the benefit of the cooperative. In this research this presumed relationship between willingness to invest and different levels of trust is further investigated.

6.2.3 Time horizon, risk attitude and income

From literature and empirical research, it appears that factors which drive investment decisions are, among others, the attitude towards risk, the time preference (time horizon) and the composition of income. Smallholder farmers are generally risk averse and face constant difficulties in buffering various risks forthcoming by from adverse health, climatic and socioeconomic shocks (Holden et al., 1998). When future returns are uncertain, risk-averse decision makers will favour projects with shorter payback periods and will be less willing to invest in projects with longer-term benefits (Bluffstone and Yesuf, 2008). Another important issue with regard to willingness to invest is the so-called time-horizon or time preference of smallholders (Borgen, 2004). It is typically argued that poor people, particularly those facing food shortages, have a higher rate of time preference than their wealthier counterparts because they are more concerned about their present needs than they are about saving for the future (Murphree, 1993). Composition of the income of farmer households is the third important element influencing willingness to invest. Nonfarm activities can be an important source of cash income, which can potentially improve farm productivity if it is used to finance farm input purchase or longer-term capital investments. Nonfarm activities can also provide income during periods outside harvest time, thus helping to reduce the variance of overall household income in cases of imperfect correlation between farm and nonfarm sources of income. In addition, nonfarm income can be helpful to mitigate risk and improve food security by allowing the household to buy food in cases of production shortfall, thus smoothing income inter-annually (Reardon *et al.*, 1994). These three factors are taken into account for analysing farmers' attitude towards investments.

In this research we try to understand behavioural aspects with respect to trust and willingness to invest in order to get better insight in the mechanisms of horizontal cooperative action which contribute to the performance of a cooperative. Moreover, our empirical research can further the understanding of how to enhance the potential contribution of coffee cooperatives for improving the livelihoods of smallholder member farmers in the research area. The level of trust is expected to be lower in weak-performing cooperatives compared to strong-performing ones. Because of the presumed relationship between trust and in-depth investments, it is also expected that in a low trust environment individual farmers are less engaged with their cooperative, and thus are less willing to invest in collective goods. We expect a positive influence of cooperatives' performance on farmers' engagement, their willingness to invest and trust. Trust in turn, is expected to have a positive relation with cooperative engagement and willingness to invest. These relationships are controlled for differences in time-horizon, risk-attitudes, income level and several intrinsic individual and farm-household characteristics.

6.3 Research context

Successful performance of marketing cooperatives is a necessary condition for the survival of cooperatives, since there is competition from other firms in the market. Cooperatives are member-based organisations, but incentives to become or stay member depend on the performance of the cooperative. A number of studies conducted on Ethiopian coffee marketing cooperatives indicate, however, that the performance results of these cooperatives have been varied and mixed (Oxfam, 2008). In some cases, there is an exclusion of the poor, low members' engagement, scarce loyalty of members and a lack of trust. These studies indicate that some cooperatives are performing well, while others show disappointing results for various reasons. According to Bernard and Spielman (2008) and Francesconi (2008), distrust is one of the main reasons why cooperatives in Ethiopia hardly have impact on sales to the market. Our research has taken place in the context of a comparison of weak and strongly performing coffee cooperatives, which are selected according to economic criteria maintained by the cooperative union to which they belong.

The choice for Ethiopia as research area is made for the dominant role of coffee in the agriculture and the importance and presence of many coffee cooperatives (CIA, 2009; World Bank, 2005). Sidama Union, located in the Southern region of Ethiopia, is chosen because coffee is main source of income in this region, the affiliated cooperatives are relatively easily accessible and vary strongly in performance from very weak to very strong.

Coffee cooperatives in Ethiopia have a two-tiered structure. Farmers deliver the red beans to the primary cooperatives, which process and store them, and later sell them to a cooperative union. The union is in charge of further processing, grading and international commercialisation. The point of departure of the present study was the observation that the level of economic performance and management among primary cooperatives belonging to the Sidama coffee union varies considerably locally, which poses serious challenges to the governance and performance of the union. Such variation occurs despite the fact that all primary cooperatives societies are located in the same region and are composed by farmers with similar cultural and socio-economic background.

In the Sidama region, primary cooperatives operate under the umbrella of the Sidama Coffee Farmers Cooperative Union (SCFCU). SCFCU represents 45 cooperatives with over 87,000 farmers and is the second largest coffee producing cooperative union in Ethiopia. The two strongest and the two weakest performing Sidama primary cooperatives were selected. The selection was based on different economic (e.g. coffee production, deliveries) and non-economic indicators (e.g. good governance) collected during interviews with officials and board members at cooperative, district and regional levels. The coffee cooperatives studied in this research are situated in four different districts (Wonsho, Shebedino, Dale and Aleta Chuko). The primary cooperatives are all established in 1976. All cooperatives produce organic coffee and three cooperatives are Fair Trade certified. The cooperatives Telamo (n=56) and Fero (n=57) were identified as strong performing units. Kege (n=60) and Dongora Kabado (n=59) were defined as weak performing units. Since we focus on the attitudes of coffee farmers towards (collective) investments and their levels of trust, research took place at different levels: both the household and the individual farmer level.

6.4 Operationalisation of main concepts

6.4.1 Trust

Several studies emphasise the importance of differentiating trust at different levels, dimensions and objects (Gambetta, 2000; James and Sykuta, 2005; Mistzal 1996; Platteau, 1994; Uslaner, 2002). Trust is generally operationalised in three different dimensions: the general, social and institutional level. Generalised trust refers to the belief that most people, irrespective of their individual or group characteristics or objectives, can be trusted. This dimension of trust applies to the trust that people have in others in any given society (Dakhli and De Clercq, 2004). This is commonly investigated by asking the generic question (Knack and Keefer, 1997: 1256): 'Generally speaking, would you say that most people can be trusted or that you can't be too careful in dealing with people?' Social trust means confidence in the people we know. According to Newton (2001) it is crucial to divide political and social forms of trust, whereby the latter means trust in family, friends, community-members and neighbours. Dakhli and De Clercq (2004) consider institutional trust as the trust that people have in institutions and organisations. Institutional trust means trust in the cooperative, in its board and in its members. Since institutional trust not only concerns persons, this dimension of trust is also measured in terms of rules of the cooperative the information and services provided by the cooperative. Social and institutional trust can be measured in survey questions with a Likert scale with levels of ranging from 1 (not at all) to 5 (very much). An index of institutional and social trust is then constructed. In addition to the survey method, trust can also be measured in the so called trust game (Section 6.5).

6.4.2 Willingness to invest

With regard to investments, several decisions have to be made. The first is whether to invest (yes or no). If there is sufficient willingness to invest, the second decision is whether to invest in individual and/or collective goods. Both types of investments – individual and collective – can be important for improving a persons' situation, but a cooperative needs investments of its individual members in order to survive, to function and to perform well (e.g. Anteneh, 2009; Heras, 2009). The first open question included in the survey to find out whether people prefer investments or consumption is: 'If you would win x Birr, how would you spend the amount?' In addition, the statement 'I will not make any investment because you never know what will happen. It's better to use and enjoy what you have right now' is added. Another open question is asked about preferences for different kinds of investments and whether individual (e.g. purchasing land, house improvements, children's education, clothes, etc.) or collective goods (e.g. construction of school, water provision, infrastructure, cooperative assets, etc.) are preferred. Several statements are also presented with regard to individual or collective investments; for example: 'Whatever happens, you should first invest in your family' and 'I would never invest in the community because no one invests in the community'. In addition to the open question and the statements, respondents are asked for their preferences for five specific investment categories, of which some are individual and other are collective types of investments.

6.4.3 Cooperative engagement

Members of the cooperative can be engaged with their cooperative in different ways. One could invest with money, but also with time, efforts and participation. Engagement with the cooperative is therefore operationalised through several concepts: (1) loyalty, (2) participation, (3) commitment, and (4) financial investment. Loyalty refers to economic transaction of members through the delivery and sale of their coffee crop through the cooperative. Respondents are therefore asked to whom they sell their coffee and if they would sell their coffee to another party if a certain amount of payment is offered. Open statements like 'I would sell more if...' are presented in addition. Another way of engagement is participation in the cooperative affairs. This means the attendance of the general assembly and participation in voting for board and committee members. Here also statements are presented to assess members participation and willingness to participate, like: 'I would participate more if...'. To measure commitment, several statements are presented, like 'I am very committed to the cooperative', 'I intend to continue the relationship with the cooperative' and 'It is most likely that I leave the cooperative when better opportunities elsewhere appear'. Financial investments, the fourth dimension, can be done by re-investing part of the dividend in the cooperative (instead of dividing it among the members) and by buying additional shares of the cooperative in order to create more cooperative assets. In addition, some open questions are presented about the ways that dividend can be spent, how the cooperative should divide the dividend and about the willingness to buy additional shares. Several statements, like 'I would never invest in the cooperative because it won't benefit me' and 'Dividend should be re-invested in the cooperative' are asked in addition. Finally, engagement with the cooperative is also measured in the so called VCM game. This game is conducted to identify the behavioural likelihood of members' investments into the cooperative (Section 6.5).

6.4.4 Time horizon, risk attitude, income

The variables time horizon, risk attitude and income(-composition) are chosen as major control variables. Time-horizon is measured in the survey with a so called time preference question: 'Would you prefer to receive 100 Birr today' or 'Would you prefer to receive x Birr in one year'. Analysis of the answers reveals a turning point (the mean amount of the switch from today to one year later). The second key variable of risk attitude is measured with statements in the survey and through the so called risk game (Section 6.5). Six statements are therefore presented: (1) 'Every day I get more convinced that who does not risk, does not earn'; (2)'In order to make some money, I am willing to risk and lose'; (3) 'I only invest when I am certain that I have a good investment'; (4) 'Investing in new crops is very risky, I had rather not do it'; (5) 'I prefer to invest in something safe' and (6) 'I would borrow money if I was convinced that investing in a business would give me good profits.' Income composition is measured in the survey through questions regarding several income resources and their average percentage contribution to household income.

6.5 Research methods

For data collection, we relied on field interviews, survey data and behavioural experiments (gaming). We outline each of these approaches and discuss their usefulness for addressing the research questions.

6.5.1 Interviews

For the field survey, the survey sample was estimated using the method suggested by Poate and Daplyn (1993). This resulted in a minimum number of 60 surveys per cooperative (240 in total). Eventually, 232 surveys were undertaken among member households of the four selected cooperatives.[45] Both male and female members participated.[46] The survey took between 1.5 and 2 hours per farmer household and was held in the local language *Sidamic*.[47] Non-response was very low because the completed surveys were immediately checked to deal with errors and non-response. The survey consisted of 42 questions, primarily structured closed and open-ended questions and a preference ranking with regard to investments.

6.5.2 Experiments

Participants for the experiments were randomly selected from the survey sample. Three different experiments were done in the four selected cooperatives with 16 participants in each experiment. The experiments were used to gather information about three topics: trust, risk and investment in the cooperative. Trust and risk attitude were also measured in the survey but the experiments allow us to measure the existing norms of trust and reciprocity more precisely than only through survey questions (Cardenas and Carpenter, 2008). Possible contradictions in stated and actual behaviour can thus be detected by using both the survey and the games.

The three games were played at all four cooperatives with 16 participants in each game. The same persons of a cooperative participated in each game. Results from the two strong and the two weak cooperatives were combined and thus 32 observations were collected for each type. The games were played with real money and amounts were adapted to local standards. The appropriate size of fees (starting amount of 10 Birr in each game) was determined in the field and fees were paid out immediately. Every game took about 2.5 hours (including the explanation) and the games were played with two enumerators. The games were played anonymously, but a registration system with simple signs (e.g. sun, moon) allowed tracing decisions back to specific people, so behaviour of a participant in the game could be compared to information from that participant in the survey.

The trust game was played by pairs of individuals and each pair was made up of a player 1 and a player 2. Each player received an amount of 10 Ethiopian Birr and the experiment consisted of two stages. In the first stage, player 1 decided whether (s)he wished to transfer part (or all) of the amount received to player 2 and if so, how much. The researcher tripled this amount so that sending money was socially efficient, because player 2 was then asked to decide whether (s)he wanted to return part (or all) of the money (s)he received from player 1. This amount was not tripled. Second mover behaviour measures trustworthiness and reciprocity, while first mover behaviour measures trust in the other player, which is also a member of the cooperative.

---

[45] Within probability sampling, the simple random sampling approach was chosen.

[46] 163 Male members (85 in weak and 78 in strong cooperatives) and 69 female members (34 in weak and 35 in strong cooperativess).

[47] Four trained local enumerators were hired.

Experiments to construct risk preferences have a long tradition in development literature, which started with Binswanger (1980) and has been largely motivated by the proposition that impatience and risk aversion might explain why poor people remain poor. In the game setting, the participants were presented with a series of hypothetical gambling options with outcomes of equal chance. Participants played the game with dies and could win on average one and a half day of wages. All players received 10 Birr and were asked with what amount they wanted to play the game with. The answer was written down before starting the actual game with the die. This in order to avoid influence of other players on the decision of an individual player. All numbers of the die (1-6) had a specific outcome. When the die rolled at 1 for example, the player lost the entire amount he bet. However, when the die rolled at 6, the amount bet was tripled. It appeared that the game was first hard to understand for most farmers so extra attention was paid to the explanation and when necessary the game was played first by enumerators.

The third game played is the public goods game, the so called Voluntary Contribution Mechanism (VCM) game (Isaac *et al.*, 1984). This game allows players to contribute to a public good, which has the incentive structure of a prisoner's dilemma (Cardenas and Carpenter, 2008). In this game the same 16 farmers participated. Participants were given an amount of 10 Birr in an envelope and they were given the choice to place the amount (or part of it) on the private account that would only benefit the decision-maker itself or in the public account that would benefit everyone in the group (the cooperative). The principle of the game is that when all players send the whole amount of 10 Birr to the cooperative account, all players will be better off in the end; they would then receive the maximum amount. Each player received two envelopes. One with 10 Birr and one empty envelope. The player then could put the amount for the public account of the cooperative in this empty envelope. When taking the decision, the farmers were given privacy. When all players made a decision, the envelopes meant for the public account were collected in one big envelope which stood for the cooperatives' account. The players waited outside while the researcher reported the amount each player sent to the cooperative and the total amount contributed to the cooperative. This total amount of the cooperative account was then tripled by the researcher and equally divided among all (16) players.

The quantitative data were analysed by performing a wide range of statistical tests, notably the independent sample t-test, multiple regression, principal component and factor analysis. Moreover, certain tests were performed to ensure the validity and reliability of the data, such as the Cronbach's alpha, Chow and Durbin Watson tests. Regression analysis was used to indicate whether a specific correlation is significant (at a 95% confidence interval). See Figure 6.1 for the methodological scheme.

6.5.3 Interviews

Next to the games and interviews, four in-depth case studies in each cooperative were conducted and the information necessary was gathered through in-depth and semi-

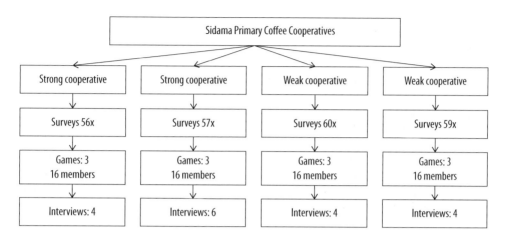

Figure 6.1. Methodological outline of the field research.

structured interviews. For this, purposive sampling took place and 16 interviews were held in total. Interviews were focused on obtaining more qualitative and in-depth knowledge about cooperative dynamics and perceived membership relationships.

6.5.4 Descriptive statistics

Individual characteristics of respondents of the two types of cooperatives are broadly similar concerning gender, civil status, ethnicity and education (Annex). There is, however, a significant difference in age: farmers of strongly performing cooperatives are much younger. There are also several differences with respect to household characteristics: households of strongly performing cooperatives are relatively younger and somewhat larger in size. There are no significant differences in land ownership, number of (coffee) trees and size of the coffee harvest (red cherry). With regard to household machinery assets and income (farm and non-farm), farmers of strongly performing cooperative have significant higher scores. Figures show that farmers, both of strong and weak cooperatives, do not differ much in average years of membership (24 years).

There are, however, some differences in coffee sales to the cooperative. It appears that members of weak cooperative often sell their coffee to other parties and deliver less to their own cooperative. From the interviews it appears that several reasons motivate these side sales. The weaker cooperatives have a lower management capacity (cooperative workers, processing sites, transportation) and they therefore refuse sometimes to purchase the red cherries of their members. In addition, incentives for farmers are lower because for many years there received no dividend payments, and the cooperative offers almost no services and limited information to members and therefore a low level of trust in management prevails (as expressed at least 6 times in the open interviews).

All members surveyed were asked for their perception on the performance of their cooperative (1 = very weak; 5 = very strong), their degree of satisfaction (1 = strongly disagree to 5 = strongly agree) and the presence or absence of perceived problems (1 = yes; 0 = no). Results show (Table 6.1) that the original division between weakly and strongly performing cooperatives (based on cooperative records) is in line with members' opinions.

Members of strong cooperatives also rate the performance of their cooperative very high and this differs significantly from members of weak cooperatives. In weak cooperatives significantly more problems (like no dividend payments and delayed payment, corruption and limited capacity to purchase coffee from the members) have to be faced. Farmers were also asked for the satisfaction with their cooperative and significant differences between weak and strong cooperatives are confirmed.

6.6 Results

Results are presented of the measurement outcomes of each of the three main analytical concepts and the estimations used for testing the presumed relations:
- trust in Ethiopian coffee cooperatives and its relation with cooperative performance;
- willingness to invest in Ethiopian cooperatives and its relation with cooperative performance;
- engagement with Ethiopian cooperatives and its relation with cooperative performance.

6.6.1 Trust

Trust is measured both in the survey and in the trust game. In Table 6.2 significant differences in trust between cooperative types are presented based on survey data. General trust is low, and the mean (where yes = 1) is 0.06 in weak and 0.21 in strong cooperatives which differ significantly from each other. Social trust has a mean value of 3.1 and the mean of institutional trust is 3.5 (using a 1-5 Likert scale). Results of trust

Table 6.1. Cooperative performance: perceptions, problems and degree of satisfaction.

Variables	N		Mean		Standard deviation		Sign.[1]
	Weak	Strong	Weak	Strong	Weak	Strong	
Perception performance	119	113	2.20	4.35	0.693	0.839	***
Problems in cooperative	119	113	0.71	0.23	0.454	0.423	***
Satisfaction cooperative	119	113	2.96	3.83	0.924	0.895	***

[1] *** significant at 1%.

Table 6.2. Outcomes from trust data survey.

Variables trust survey	N		Mean		Standard deviation		Sign.[1]
	Weak	Strong	Weak	Strong	Weak	Strong	
General trust (0-1)	119	113	0.06	0.21	0.236	0.411	***
Social trust (1-5)	119	113	2.969	3.248	0.884	0.871	**
Institutional trust (1-5)	119	113	3.088	3.881	0.632	0.591	***

[1] ** significant at 5%; *** significant at 1%.

outcomes all show significant differences in the level of trust. Members of strongly performing cooperative have significantly more general, social and institutional trust. Reasons for the level of trust are found in the performance, the organisation and capability of the management and experiences in the past. As one farmer of a weak cooperative said: 'People gave up to trust'.

Results from trust statements in the survey are confirmed by outcomes of the trust game (Table 6.3). Although the mean amount out of 10 Birr sent to the other player is 2.84 Birr in the weak and 3.34 Birr in the strong cooperatives, the difference is not significant. The amount player 2 returned to player 1 is, however, significantly different between the two cooperatives: 2.50 Birr is returned in weak cooperatives compared to 3.44 Birr in the strong ones. The amount expected from the other player is always higher in the strong cooperatives, albeit not significant different. There are no significant correlations between the trust variables from the survey and the game.

Table 6.3. Outcomes from trust game.

Variables trust game	N		Mean		Standard deviation		Sign.[1]
	Weak	Strong	Weak	Strong	Weak	Strong	
Amount sent to other as player 1	32	32	2.84	3.34	1.483	1.771	
Amount expected from player 1	32	32	4.06	4.72	2.271	2.750	
Amount received from player 1 (×3)	32	32	8.53	10.03	4.450	5.313	
Amount returned to 1 as player 2	32	32	2.50	3.44	1.545	2.526	*
Amount expected from player 2	32	32	5.66	6.00	3.107	4.370	
Total amount game	32	32	15.69	24.17	4.395	15.60	**

[1] * significant at 10%; ** significant at 5%.

Regression analysis of the trust game outcome show significant influences from the variables age and household assets (Table 6.4). Younger members which have more household assets send a larger amount to the other player. It must be added here that members of the strong cooperatives are significantly younger and richer in terms of household assets. It is therefore not possible to state on the basis of this game that members of strong cooperatives give more because they have more trust.

Although there is no uniform level of trust in all cooperatives, almost all interviewees (10) agree that trust is very important for the cooperative to function well. Trust is necessary for the development of the cooperative (3) and leads to more participation (5), or as one respondent expressed: 'No trust, no coffee' and another farmer of Kege stated: 'This cooperative still exists due to trust of the members'.

Table 6.4. Institutional trust (OLS regression). Production function of institutional trust by cooperative performance.

Variables	Weak			Strong		
	Coeff	SE	Sign.[1]	Coeff	SE	Sign.[1]
Individual and household						
Gender	-0.363	0.151	**	-0.251	0.471	**
Age household head	-0.011	0.008		-0.016	0.006	**
Education household head	-0.031	0.021		-0.037	0.018	**
Household size	-0.057	0.035		0.017	0.024	
Household age	0.000	0.016		0.004	0.011	
Household employment	-0.744	0.412	*	0.420	0.360	
Asset endowments						
Livestock assets index	-0.034	0.031		0.026	0.029	
Household assets index	-0.016	0.100		0.104	0.060	*
Machinery assets index	0.258	0.146	*	-0.038	0.087	
Production						
Total land (ha)	-0.070	0.087		0.013	0.053	
Total trees (no)	0.005	0.000		-0.005	0.000	**
Coffee trees (no)	-0.005	0.000		0.005	0.000	
Coffee harvest (kg)	0.000	0.000	*	0.005	0.000	*
Cooperative						
Performance cooperative	-0.033	0.071		0.255	0.082	***
Satisfaction performance	0.235	0.062	***	0.209	0.062	***
Constant	4.127	0.670	***	2.638	0.471	***
F-test	3.332		***	5.801		***
Adjusted R^2	0.229			0.393		
Durbin-Watson	2.071			1.957		

[1] * significant at 10%; ** significant at 5%; *** significant at 1%; SE = standard error.

Regression analyses were conducted to identify models with predictors for trust.[48] The model consists of four categories of independent variables: (1) individual and household characteristics; (2) household assets; (3) (coffee) production, and (4) cooperative behaviour (perception, satisfaction). The model for institutional trust is presented in Table 6.4.

Weak and strong cooperative have different predictors for institutional trust. Most important variables for trust in the weak cooperatives are gender (negative), household employment (negative), machinery assets, coffee harvest and satisfaction with performance. Most significant is the positive relation with satisfaction: more satisfaction with the performance of the cooperative goes along with more institutional trust. This function explains 23% of the trust level measured in weak cooperatives and 39% in the strong cooperatives. Gender, age and education of the household head, household assets, total number of trees and coffee harvest are important predicting variables for trust in the strong cooperatives. With regard to the relation with the cooperative performance, perception of the performance and satisfaction with that performance have a strong and positive significant relation with institutional trust in both situations.

6.6.2 Willingness to invest

We start presenting the results of preferences for consumption or investments. The latter is afterwards divided into preferences for individual or collective investments. The first question with regard to willingness to invest is whether households are willing to invest or prefer to spend their money on consumption. Most farmers (72%) of the total sample chose not to spend their money on investments in case of windfall profits. Priority is given instead to house improvements and education of children. To the open question how farmers would make long-term investments in case they would be able to make investments, only 31% of the farmers answered that they would start a business or invest in agriculture. In addition to the open questions, several statements were formulated to further investigate the willingness to invest and answers to these question are somehow different. Only 12% agrees with the statements 'I will not make any investment because you never know what will happen' and with 'It's better to enjoy what you have right now'. Here, no differences were recorded in terms of willingness to invest between members of weak and of strong cooperatives.

Regression confirms that the performance of the cooperative and the level of trust do not have a significant direct influence on the choice whether to invest or to consume. There is, however, a significant relation between the variable risk and willingness to invest. This is consistent with theory which states that when future returns are uncertain, risk-averse decision makers will favour projects with shorter payback periods and will be less willing to invest in projects with long-term benefits (Bluffstone and Yesuf, 2008).

---

[48] The chow tests reveal that regressions must be conducted separately for weak and strong cooperatives for both general and institutional trust.

It can be the case that the farmers do acknowledge the importance of making investments in escaping poverty but are actually facing several constraints for doing so. Farmers interviewed argued that many members indeed acknowledge the importance of investments for several reasons: 'to grow/develop', 'to have an income' (7) and 'to stay alive'. As another respondent said: 'Who lacks to invest, lacks food' or 'This country can only develop/grow by working and investing'. Reasons given for not investing in practice were a narrow-mind, ignorance and lack of knowledge, laziness and fear of risks.

The second analysis of investments addresses the preference for individual or collective investments (in the case members are willing to invest). Data show that most farmers give priority to individual investments (e.g. house improvements, education of children), while only 5% gives priority to collective investments (at community and cooperative level). The preference for individual investments is confirmed (93% agrees) in the statement: 'Whatever happens, you should first invest in your family'. There are – contrary to the expectation – no differences in results between weak and strong cooperatives.

Regression analysis shows that just a few variables (notably household size, machinery assets and risk attitude) have a significant influence on willingness to invest collectively (with an adjusted R^2 of 17%). Interestingly, there is no significant relationship between the performance of the cooperative and the willingness to invest collectively. There was also no significant relation detected between trust and the choice to consume or invest. However, regarding the interaction between trust and collective investments, data show a significant and positive relation between trust and collective investments. Interviewees confirmed (10) the influence of trust on their willingness to invest. As quoted by one respondent: 'The refusal of working together is due to lack of trust'. It's not only about trust in each other but also on trust in the investment itself. One needs to trust that the investment in for example a school building will benefit each of them.

Although there is a preference for individual investments, farmers acknowledge the importance of investing in the community, as 90% of the respondents agree with the statement that 'It's worth investing in the community because it will perform better then'. The fact that farmers acknowledge the importance of collective investments also appeared from the open interviews. All mention the importance of investments and the role that community members play. Actual practice of community investments is, however, bounded by low level of education, scarce initiative and lack of finance. It appears that members of weak and strong cooperative have more or less the same (un)willingness to invest.

6.6.3 Engagement with cooperative affairs

Members of the cooperative can be engaged with their cooperative in different ways. Engagement with the cooperative is operationalised through four concepts: (1) loyalty, (2) participation, (3) commitment, and (4) financial investment. Data with regard to engagement is gathered through the survey, interviews and the VCM game. The VCM game confirms the survey results, while interviewees gave some more insights into the underlying behavioural dynamics. It appears that members of strong performing cooperatives are significantly more engaged with their cooperative compared to members of weakly performing cooperatives (Table 6.5).

Regarding loyalty, it appears that 27% of members sells their crop only to the cooperative, while 66% sells to both the cooperative and other parties and that 7% only sells to other parties. Members of strong cooperative sell their coffee significantly more often to their cooperative than members of weak cooperatives. Another question with regard to loyalty refers to the price that members accept to sell their coffee to another party. A percentage of 61% states never to sell to any other party, no matter what price is offered by other buyers. There is a significant difference between members of strong and weak cooperatives; 89% of the strong ones will never sell to other parties compared to only 35% of the weak performing cooperatives. Also the turning point, the amount where a farmer decides to sell to another party, differs significantly per cooperative. Members of a weak cooperative start delivering to another party at a mean price of 4.7 Birr (per kg), where this price rises to 5.7 Birr in the strong cooperatives.

With regard to the statements 'I would sell more of my coffee crop to the cooperative if...' most farmers show their willingness to sell more of their crop under specific conditions as shows the mean value of 4.2 (on a range of 1 to 5) on the index (Table 6.5). Three conditions are considered especially important: most farmers (90%) would sell more of their crop if the Board operated less corruptly, if payments were made immediate, and if there were more dividend payments. There are no significant differences with regard to these statements between members of strong and weak cooperatives. In the

Table 6.5. Engagement with cooperative affairs.

Variables	N		Mean		Standard deviation		Sign.[1]
	Weak	Strong	Weak	Strong	Weak	Strong	
I would never sell to another party (1 = never)	119	113	0.35	0.88	0.48	0.32	***
I would sell to another party (for 4.5-6 Birr)	77	13	4.76	5.73	4.18	3.88	***
Sales to cooperative (2), mixed (1), outside (0)	119	113	0.96	1.47	0.46	0.50	***
Index statements 'I would sell more if' (1-5)	119	112	4.16	4.17	0.53	0.42	
Index statements 'I would participate more if' (1-5)	119	113	3.84	3.96	0.52	0.48	*
Index statements 'Commitment cooperative' (1-5)	119	113	3.63	3.89	0.57	0.49	***
New variable 'Engagement cooperative' (1-5)[2]	119	113	3.85	3.97	0.53	0.48	*

[1] * significant at 10%; *** significant at 1%.
[2] Index of the different variables loyalty, participation, commitment, investment and dividend division.

interviews farmers were also asked about their loyalty to the cooperative and reasons for selling coffee to the cooperative or to other parties. One of the questions was why farmers still sell their coffee to their cooperative when performance is very weak and when there is no dividend payment. Four interviewees said that the cooperative can only grow if members supply their coffee and that they have hope for future dividend payments and better performance. As one farmer said: 'It's not about the money, I want my cooperative to develop'.

Participation in the cooperative can be practiced by attending the General Assembly and by voting for board and committee members. At this moment, 72% of the farmers always attend the General Assembly and 17% are sometimes present. It appears that there are differences in attendance for members of strong cooperatives that attend the Assembly significantly more often. Almost all members participate in voting (86%) and there are no differences between weak and strong cooperatives.

In addition to the previous questions about participation, several statements were presented with regard to participation: 'I would participate if...' (Table 6.5). The mean of the index on these statements is 3.9 for the whole sample. Only 1.3% of members state never to participate more. Particularly important is the statement 'I would participate more in the cooperative if they take my opinion seriously' to which 91% agrees. The results of the index of these statements shows that members of the strong cooperatives exhibit significantly higher scores on their willingness for participation in cooperative affairs.

Most interviewees of both weak and strong cooperatives argue that participation in the cooperative is both important and necessary. People need a strong cooperative and a cooperative needs the participation and commitment of its members to become strong. Development of the cooperative means development of the members. Although members of weak and strong cooperatives agree with this basic principle, there are significant differences in actual participation of members. Members often do not see the possibility to participate more, due to personal constraints (e.g. limited possibilities to cultivate more coffee trees or low understanding of cooperative organisation) or to organisational constraints (e.g. not informed or invited for the general assembly or voting rounds). Several interviewees of Dongora Kabado cooperative, for example, face constraints from the board to participate more. One farmer of Dongora is not willing to participate more 'because it is not possible to bring change on my own opinion'. This statement shows the different atmosphere between weak and strong cooperatives, as one farmer of a strong cooperative expressed: 'This strong cooperative is the result of participation of all members'.

Commitment is another way of engagement with the cooperative. Several statements measure members' commitment. The mean of the index is 3.8 on a 1-5 scale) and 85% of all respondents state to be very committed to their cooperative. Most farmers (97%) intend to continue the relationship with the cooperative and 34% might leave the cooperative when better opportunities would elsewhere appear. Data show significant differences in commitment between members of strong and weak cooperatives. The reasons mentioned most for being committed to the cooperative is ownership and membership of the cooperative. Members are also committed because the cooperative helps them and they consider that the development of the cooperative leads to personal growth. Reasons for low or no commitment are: limited understanding/knowledge of responsibility, no trust in organisation and board, and no real benefits. Differences in commitment between members of weak and strong cooperatives appear from two quotes about leaving the cooperative. One interviewee of a strong cooperative said: 'I won't leave until I die for the cooperative is my home and it benefits me'. Another member of a weak cooperative, stated it this way: 'It doesn't matter to be member or not, it doesn't bring any benefit either to leave the cooperative, so why leaving then'.

6.7 Loyalty, trust and investments

The relationship between cooperative trust, loyalty and the derived willingness to investment in collective action deserves further consideration. We therefore analysed in more detail the underlying factors explaining willingness to invest, and the individual and institutional determinants underlying investment preferences.

6.7.1 Financial investment

Four statements were used to assess the willingness of members to invest in the cooperative (Table 6.6).

Almost all members (96%) of both types cooperative agree with the statement that the cooperative can only develop when all members invest in it. There is, however, a significant difference between members of weak and strong cooperatives in answers

Table 6.6. Motives for investment in cooperatives.

Variables	N		Mean		Standard deviation		Sign.[1]
	Weak	Strong	Weak	Strong	Weak	Strong	
The cooperative can only develop when all members invest in it	119	113	4.25	4.26	0.627	0.609	
I would never invest in the cooperative because it won't benefit me	119	113	2.50	2.00	1.073	0.791	***
Dividend should be divided among the members of the cooperative	119	113	4.28	4.33	0.610	0.589	
Dividend should be re-invested in the cooperative	119	113	4.40	3.99	0.587	0.750	***

[1] *** significant at 1%.

to the statement 'I would never invest in the cooperative because it won't benefit me'. There is also a significant difference in answers to the statement if dividend should be re-invested in the cooperative. Members of weak cooperative more often agree with this statement which seems contradictory to answers on other questions and statements. Interviews revealed that members argue that dividend should be divided among the members to motivate them to supply their coffee and to stimulate them to plant more coffee whenever possible. Other reasons for division of dividend among the members is to increase their trust in the cooperative organisation and in the board members (5), and to increase the feeling of ownership. Reasons for a re-investment of dividend in the cooperative are to strengthen and develop the cooperative (6), to be able to purchase more red cherries (3) and to be able to provide services (like transportation) to the members. Significant differences between members of weak and strong cooperatives could largely be explained in this way. The weak cooperatives need, among others, financial inputs to improve their performance that remains very low and is not satisfactory to its members. One interviewee used the phrase 'One finger cannot wash the single face' to explain that every member must invest in the cooperative by using the dividend for development cooperative. Strong cooperatives operate already fairly well, so there is a less need for additional financial resources derived from re-investment of dividend.

6.7.2 VCM game

Results of the VCM game (Table 6.7) show significant differences in behaviour between members of strong and weak cooperatives. The mean amount sent to the cooperative in weak cooperatives is 2.30 Birr compared to an average amount of 3.30 Birr in strong cooperatives. The VCM game confirms the survey results that register that members of strong cooperatives are more willing to invest in the cooperative and are more engaged to their cooperative compared to members of weak cooperatives.

Summarising the most important findings, it appears that all members acknowledge the importance of engagement with their cooperative. Actual differences in engagement

Table 6.7. Members willingness for collective action (VCM game).

Variable VCM game (Birr)	N		Mean		Standard deviation		Sign.[1]
	Weak	Strong	Weak	Strong	Weak	Strong	
Amount sent to cooperative	64	64	2.30	3.30	1.268	2.068	***
Amount total in cooperative	64	64	36.75	52.75	5.583	16.90	***
Amount individual member	64	64	4.00	5.50	0.000	0.508	***
Total amount game	64	64	11.88	12.78	1.040	1.128	***

[1] ***significant at 1%.

appear, however, as members of strong cooperative are in practice significantly more engaged with their cooperative compared to members of weak cooperatives. Farmer members of strong cooperatives have higher scores on loyalty, participation, commitment and invest financially more in the cooperative.

6.7.3 What determines cooperative engagement?

As appeared from the descriptive analysis, engagement with the cooperative has been operationalised with 10 different variables. Regression analysis is used to analyse the influence of these variable in a model which includes trust, perception of and satisfaction with the cooperative, individual and household characteristics, wealth indicators and assets. The model (Table 6.8) is given for three outcome variables which are regarded as the most important indicators for engagement: (1) loyalty; (2) participation and commitment; and (3) cooperative investments.

T-tests from descriptive statistics already showed significant differences in *loyalty* between members of weak and strong cooperatives (Annex) and the regression analysis performed here confirms the positive relation between performance of the cooperative and loyalty (Table 6.8). If members are positive about the performance of their cooperative, they tend to be more loyal. A strong cooperative offers more benefits (like dividend, premium, fair price) and thus rewards members' loyalty. Results also show that perception, institutional trust and risk are of significant importance for loyalty with the cooperative. Trust is also an important predictor for loyalty. If members have more institutional trust, they tend to be more loyal to their cooperative. It appeared from the interviews that members even sell their coffee to the cooperative without receiving immediate payment (delivery on credit) when there is a high level of trust. Loyalty is also influenced by risk: a more risk-taking attitude positively influences members' loyalty. This means that loyalty to the cooperative has a strong risk-sharing dimension for these farmers. This can be explained with the same example just mentioned. Selling the coffee crop to the cooperative without receiving an immediate payment, implies taking risk: it might be that the cooperative might not be able to pay (the whole amount) for the coffee purchased.

Institutional trust and risk are of importance for participation and commitment and show a positive relation. T-tests already showed significant differences in the level of participation and commitment between members of weak and strong cooperatives. Members of strong cooperatives have significantly higher scores. Something interesting needs to be noted: the regression analysis shows a positive and significant relation between performance and participation and commitment as long as institutional trust is not taken into account. When controlled for institutional trust, the relationship between performance and participation and commitment is not significant anymore This means that institutional trust is of great mediating importance for members' participation and commitment to their cooperative. Trust is thus even more important than cooperative performance!

Table 6.8. Factors explaining loyalty, participation/commitment and investments in cooperatives.

Variables	Loyalty[1]			Participation and commitment[2]			Collective investment[3]		
	Coeff.	SE	Sign.[4]	Coeff.	SE	Sign.[4]	Coeff.	SE	Sign.[4]
Individual and household characteristics									
Gender	0.108	0.103		0.082	0.028	**	2.524	1.238	**
Age head	0.005	0.005		0.001	0.001		-0.054	0.033	
Education head	0.002	0.015		-0.001	0.004		0.088	0.072	
Household size	0.001	0.019		0.011	0.005	**	0.195	0.144	
Household age	0.004	0.009		0.001	0.002		0.110	0.066	
Household employment	-0.180	0.303		-0.181	0.084	**	2.898	2.138	
Assets									
Household	0.070	0.047		0.0005	0.013		0.250	0.264	
Livestock	-0.001	0.019		0.000	0.005		0.313	0.162	*
Machinery	0.026	0.071		-0.011	0.019		-0.666	0.371	*
Wealth									
Total income	0.0006	0.000		-0.0007	0.000		0.000	0.000	
Total land	-0.004	0.043		-0.002	0.012		-0.060	0.023	**
Cooperative									
Perception	0.160	0.041	***	-0.014	0.011		0.165	0.240	
Satisfaction	0.044	0.051		0.033	0.014	**	0.066	0.327	
Trust									
General	0.040	0.110		-0.057	0.030	*	-0.551	0.787	
Social	-0.043	0.048		0.000	0.000		-0.035	0.403	
Institutional	0.153	0.076	**	0.234	0.065	***	0.071	0.469	
Behavioural determinants									
Time horizon	-0.002	0.001		0.000	0.000		0.003	0.007	
Risk attitude	0.130	0.057	**	0.065	0.015	***	-0.131	0.295	
Constant	-1.208	0.479	**	0.666	0.134	**	-3.76	3.440	
Adjusted R^2	0.344			0.306			0.334		
F-test	4.729		***	4.133		***	1.975		*
Durbin-Watson	2.053			2.147			2.316		

[2] Loyalty statement: never selling coffee to other party (1 = agree, 0 = disagree).

[2] Index of both variables.

[3] VCM game: amount out of 10 Birr sent back to the cooperative account.

[4] * significant at 10%; ** significant at 5%; *** significant at 1%; SE = standard error.

In the VCM game, some other factors are of importance as well. Gender, land and assets all have a strong relation with collective investment in the cooperative. Women and members with more livestock contributed significantly more money to the cooperative account. Land and machinery assets are negative related to the amount sent.

Data also reveal that less risk-aversion, a longer time-horizon and a higher income do not necessarily and automatically lead to more engagement with the cooperative (as presumed in the theoretical framework). The only positive and significant relation that was detected is between risk-attitude and engagement. It appears that less risk-averse members are more likely to be fully engaged with their cooperative.

It can be concluded that institutional trust is of importance for loyalty, participation and commitment. Perception of the performance has a strong and positive relation with loyalty, but this relation is not significant anymore when controlled for with institutional trust. Another strong relation exists between risk attitude and engagement as well as with loyalty. Income and time-horizon are not of significant influence. Regressions show that these relations are more or less the same for both the weak and strong cooperatives.

6.8 Conclusions and outlook

Given the importance of cooperatives in rural development and the role that coffee production plays in the economy of Ethiopia, this study focused on the performance of agricultural coffee cooperatives in rural Ethiopia. We aimed (1) to understand the role played by cooperative organisations in influencing behavioural relations with regard to trust and willingness to invest, and (2) to get insight in the horizontal cooperative action mechanisms in the context of weak and strongly performing cooperatives. Conclusions are based on results from a farmers' survey, games and interviews conducted among members of two strong and two weak performing cooperatives of the Sidama Coffee Farmers cooperative Union in Southern Ethiopia.

6.8.1 Main outcomes

We were able to disentangle the positive relations between the performance of the cooperative, members' engagement with the cooperative and the level of mutual trust amongst the members. It is not possible to express full causalities in these relationships given the cross-sectional nature of this research. It can be stated, however, that the performance of the cooperative, members' engagement and trust tend to reinforce each other in a positive way. Further longitudinal research is recommended to reveal which aspects of this relationship are more powerful.

The field research enabled to draw the following partial conclusions:
- Farmer-members from strongly performing cooperatives have higher level of social and institutional trust than farmer members from weaker cooperatives.
- Better performing cooperative exhibit higher levels of trust.

- There is more engagement with the cooperative among members of strong performing cooperatives.
- More trust leads to more engagement with the cooperative and to more collective investments.
- Less risk-aversion leads to more willingness to invest and to more engagement with the cooperative.

A most important finding is the influence of the performance of the cooperative on trust. It appears that members of a better-performing cooperative exhibit more trust. This is an important relationship because trust in turn, has a strong and positive influence on the engagement of members with their cooperative and with members' loyalty. It appears that the relation between trust and engagement is even of greater significance than the relation between performance and engagement. T-tests show significant differences in the level of cooperative engagement between members of weak and strong cooperative: farmer members of strong cooperatives are significant more engaged with cooperative affairs. The regression analysis shows a positive and significant relation between performance and engagement as long as institutional trust is not included as an independent variable. When relations with engagement are controlled for institutional trust, performance and engagement do not show a significant relation anymore. This implies that institutional trust is of great importance for mediating members' engagement with their cooperative.

Another interesting relationship is registered between the level of trust and members' willingness to invest collectively. Collective investments are based on collective action of individuals and our data show a strong and positive relation between trust and willingness for collective investment.[49]

These outcomes confirm theories of for example Six (2007) that state that when individuals are placed in a relational context where trust is involved, trust and collective action mutually reinforce each other. Interpersonal trust-building is a reciprocal process in which both parties are involved in building trust interactively. Six relates trust to collective action which is confirmed in our research, because trust is related to both willingness to invest collectively and to collective engagement with the cooperative. Further research is necessary to find a plausible explanation for the fact that members of strong performing cooperatives do have more levels of trust but do not show more willingness to invest collectively. It can be the argued that if the cooperative successfully invests in the community, individual members of that cooperative are less willing to do so.

---

[49] Theories of Zak and Knack (2001) also confirm that trust is positively associated with investment and growth. Investment sufficient for positive growth is facilitated by trust between economic agents. With their equilibrium growth model it becomes clear that low trust environments reduce the rate of investment. As Arrow (1972: 357) puts it, 'Virtually every commercial transaction has within it some element of trust, [...] It can be plausibly argued that much of the economic backwardness in the world can be explained by the lack of mutual confidence'.

The hypothesis that there is more willingness to invest among farmer members of strongly performing cooperatives must, however, be rejected. This hypothetical relation was based on different theories. Lee (2005) stated for example that institutions, like an agricultural cooperative, do play an important role in reinforcing the willingness to invest of poor farmers. Many smallholder farmers in vulnerable areas continue to face complex challenges in adoption and adaptation of resource management and conservation strategies. Improved market access that raises the returns to land and labour is often the driving force for adoption of new practices in agriculture. Market linkages, access to credit and availability of pro-poor options for environmental conservation, are critical factors for stimulating livelihoods and willingness to invest (Shiferaw *et al.*, 2009). An agricultural cooperative is an organisation which mobilises collective action for reaching a common goal. In a situation of collective action by the community-members, the cooperative may further enhance and supplement individual production and investment possibilities. Benefits from these investments should outweigh the added costs (Lee, 2005). Statements collected from qualitative results seem to confirm this theory. According to the farmers interviewed there is a strong relation between the performance of the cooperative and members' willingness to invest. A strong cooperative can according to them, for example, enable people to make investments through credit services and with training about investments. A strong cooperative reduces uncertainties by offering stable prices, the guarantee of an honest purchaser and by paying dividend. In addition, a strong cooperative provides the example that investments can be rewarding and motivates members to also invest inside and outside the cooperative. There appears, however, a contradiction between stated and actual behaviour, since the relation between a strong performance and willingness to invest is not fully confirmed with the quantitative data of this research. Our findings here are more consistent with those by Holden and Shiferaw (2002) who state that Ethiopian farm households' planning horizons are very short, subjective discount rates are generally high, and consequently their estimated willingness-to-pay for future productivity increases is very low.

Other factors which can influence willingness to invest are, among others, the attitudes towards risk, the time preference and composition and level of income. Research results show the importance of risk for peoples' willingness to invest, confirming several prevailing theories: a risk-taking attitude has a positive relation with cooperative engagement and loyalty and enhances willingness to invest. It appears that farmers which are less risk-averse are more engaged with their cooperative and are more willing to invest. This means that cooperative engagement and loyalty have a risk dimension for members: potential pay-offs from engagement and loyalty are not automatically guaranteed. This can be caused by negative experiences in the past. Cooperatives did not always have success and they were in the past more used as political instruments than as genuine farmer organisations. In addition, cooperatives of the same districts sometimes show very different performance, where one cooperative is very strong and successful while another cooperative in the neighbourhood shows opposite performance. Two additional variables considered in this research – time-horizon and income-composition – do not show significant relations with cooperative engagement or willingness to invest. Apparently, it does not make a difference whether members have a short or long time horizon for their degree of cooperative engagement or for their willingness to invest. Members also do not have significant differences in the composition of their income which may explain that investments are mainly dependent on the agricultural income component.

6.8.2 Implications for policy and practice

This research confirms a substantial part of the literature suggesting that agricultural cooperatives are not always successful business organisations. Results show the importance of a strongly performing cooperative that influences members' engagement, level of trust and their willingness to invest collectively. Trust is of key importance for explaining engagement with the cooperative and for analysing collective investments.

Based on the data and results of this study, a two-track policy which focuses both on the performance of the cooperative and the level of trust is recommended. It is important to strengthen the cooperatives' organisational structure for improving its performance. It appears, however, that several exogenous factors strongly influence the performance of a cooperative. Often, uneducated board and committee members are elected to rule the organisation and there are no exchange experiences and learning processes in place between strong and weak cooperatives. Due to the strongly decentralised structure of cooperatives' organisations in Ethiopia with all kinds of layers and levels, responsibilities are unclear and information is not consistent. Based on these outcomes and information of the interviews, a more central coordination can be suggested with direct communication lines between the Union and the Primary Cooperatives. It appeared in the interviews that members have trust in the Union and they are positive towards a more significant role of the Union in the cooperatives' organisation. The performance of primary cooperatives has a strong relation with members' loyalty to and trust in that cooperative; ingredients which are in turn of significant influence for the existence and success of cooperatives. Six (2007) mentioned already this downward and upward spiralling process of trust and feedbacks. Cooperatives are to be regarded as autonomous and democratically ruled organisations and should not be (as in the past) used as a political instrument. The main challenge is to generate a well-balanced strategy to strengthen the cooperative organisational structure and its economic performance while preserving their autonomous character.

Besides strengthening the organisational structure, attention is also necessary for the significant role of trust in cooperative performance. One indicator of a well-organised cooperative structure is regular and stable information provision to the members which can in turn positively influence the level of trust. Information and transparency are important to increase the level of trust. Members may start distrusting the cooperative board, for example, when the Fair Trade premium was not divided among the members individually (even while according to Fair Trade regulations, the premium should be invested in collective goods for the whole community). Due attention must therefore be paid to the dynamic role of trust of members in their cooperative (board and organisation) and amongst cooperative members, and the instrumental value of cooperative management mechanisms for reinforcing trust.

Finally, our results largely confirm the proposition of Mistzal (1996) that internal coordination and resource allocation in cooperatives are primarily determined by the quality of interpersonal relations between its members. So, improvement of the quality of interpersonal relations is necessary to increase the level of cooperative engagement and collective investments. The better the personal relationship become that members develop with each other and with management, the more flexible and smooth will be the processes of communication, coordination, and collective decision making. This will ultimately lead to stronger organisations and agri-business development for many farmers. Donors and the Ethiopian government rightly consider agricultural cooperatives to be a fundamental pillar of their rural development policy, but need to provide more opportunities for strengthening cooperative governance and trust.

References

Anteneh Woubie, A. (2009). Coffee marketing cooperatives in supply chain: analysis of performance and their impacts on member farmers in Ethiopia. PhD Thesis. Nijmegen, the Netherlands: Radboud University.

Arrow, K. (1972). Gifts and exchanges. *Philosophy and Public Affairs* I: 343-362.

Barrett, C. (2005). Rural poverty dynamics: development policy implications. *Agricultural Economics* 32: 45-60.

Bernard, T. and D.J. Spielman (2008). *Mobilizing Rural institutions for sustainable livelihoods and equitable development: a case study of agricultural marketing and smallholder cooperatives in Ethiopia*. Addis Ababa, Ethiopia: International Food Policy Research Institute.

Binswanger, H.P. (1980). Attitudes towards risk: experimental measurement in rural India. *American Journal of Agricultural Economics* 62 (3): 395-407.

Blokland, K. and C. Gouet (2007). Peer to peer farmer support for economic development. In: G. Ton, G., J. Bijman and J. Oorthuizen (eds.) *Producer organizations and market chains*, Wageningen, the Netherlands: Wageningen Academic Publishers, pp. 71-90.

Bluffstone, R. and M. Yesuf (2008). Wealth and time preference in rural Ethiopia. *Environment for Development* DP 08-16. Available at: http://tinyurl.com/naol8yj.

Borgen, S.O. (2004). Rethinking incentive problems in cooperative organizations. *Journal of Socio-Economics* 33: 383-393.

Cardenas, J.C. and J. Carpenter (2008). Behavioural development economics: lessons from the field labs in the developing world. *Journal of Development Studies* 44(3): 311-338.

Central Intelligence Agency (CIA) 2009. CIA world factbook 2009. Availbale at: https://www.cia.gov/library/publications/the-world-factbook/.

Collier, P., S. Radwan and S. Wangwe (1990). Labour and poverty in rural Tanzania: Ujamaa and rural development in the United Republic of Tanzania. Oxford, UK: Clarendon Press.

Dakhli, M. and D. De Clercq (2004). Human capital, social capital and innovation: a multicountry study. *Entrepreneurship and Regional Development* 16: 107-128.

Federal Democratic Republic of Ethiopia (FDRE) (2005). *Plan for accelerated and sustained development to end poverty*. Addis Ababa, Ethiopia: FDRE.

Federal Democratic Republic of Ethiopia (FDRE) (2012). *Agricultural cooperatives sector development strategy 2012-2016*. Addis Ababa, Ethiopia: FDRE.

Francesconi, G.N. (2008). *Cooperation for competition linking Ethiopian farmers to markets*. Wageningen, the Netherlands: Wageningen Academic Publishers.

Gambetta, D. (2000). 'Can we trust trust?' In: Gambetta, D. (ed.), *Trust: making and breaking cooperative relations*. Oxford, UK: University of Oxford, Department of Sociology, pp. 213-237.

Heras Muñoz, J. (2009). Social capital within coffee cooperatives in Ethiopia. A comparative study on the influence of SC on the governance of coffee cooperatives. MSc. thesis. Nijmegen, the Netherlands: Radboud University.

Hellin, J.M., M. Lundy and M. Meijer (2009). Farmer organization, collective action and market access in Meso-America. *Food Policy* 34: 16-22.

Holden, S.T., B. Shiferaw and M. Wik. (1998). Poverty, credit constraints, and time preferences: Of relevance for environmental policy? *Environment and Development Economics* 3: 105-130.

Holden, S.T. and B. Shiferaw (2002). Poverty and land degradation: peasants' willingness to pay to sustain land productivity. In: Barrett, C.B., F. Place, and A.A. Aboud (eds.) *Natural resources management in African agriculture: understanding and improving current practices*. Wallingford, UK: CABI Publishing, pp. 91-102.

Isaac, R.M., J. Walker, J. and S. Thomas (1984). Divergent evidence on free riding: an experimental examination of possible explanations. *Public Choice* 43: 113-149.

Jahnke, H.E. (1982). *Livestock production systems in livestock development in tropical Africa*. Kiel, Germany: Kieler Wissenschaftsverlag Vauk.

James Jr., H.S. and M.E. Sykuta (2005). Property rights and organizational characteristics of producer-owned firms and organizational trust. *Annals of Public and Cooperative Economics* 76(4): 545-580.

Knack, S. and P. Keefer (1997). Does social capital have an economic payoff? A cross-country investigation. *Quarterly Journal of Economics* 112: 1251-1288.

Lee, D.R. (2005). Agricultural sustainability and technology adoption in developing countries: issues and policies for developing countries. *American Journal of Agricultural Economics* 87: 1325-1334.

Misztal, B. (1996). *Trust in modern societies*. Cambridge, UK: Polity Press.

Murphree, M. (1993). *Communal land wildlife resources and rural district council revenues*. Harare, Zimbabwe: CASS, University of Zimbabwe.

Newton, K. (2001). Trust, social capital, civil society and democracy. *International Political Science Review* 22(2): 201-214.

Novkovic, S. (2008). Defining the co-operative difference. *Journal of Socio-Economics* 37 (6): 2168-2177.

Paldam, M. and G. Tinggaard Svendsen (2000). An essay on social capital: looking for the fire behind the smoke. *European Journal of Political Economy* 16: 339-366.

Plaisier, C. (2010). Blessing of the bean or curse of the cooperative? Willingness to invest, engagement and trust of coffee farmers in the context of good and bad performing coffee cooperatives in Ethiopia. Msc thesis. Nijmegen, the Netherlands: CIDIN.

Platteau, J.P. (1994). Behind the market stage where real societies exist. Part 1: the role of public and private order institutions. *Journal of Development Studies* 30: 533-573.

Putnam, R. (1993). *Making democracies work: civic traditions in modern Italy*. Princeton, NJ, USA: Princeton University Press.

Olson, M. (1971). The logic of collective action. Harvard, MA, USA: Harvard University Press.

Ostrom, E. (2003). How types of goods and property rights jointly affect collective action. *Journal of Theoretical Politics* 15(3): 239-270.

Oxfam (2008). *A consultancy reports on Ethiopian coffee marketing cooperatives*. Addis Ababa, Ethiopia: Oxfam.

Poate, C.D. and P.F. Daplyn (1993). *Data for agrarian development*. Cambridge, UK: Cambridge University Press.

Reardon T, E. Crawford and V. Kelly (1994). Links between nonfarm income and farm investment in African households: adding the capital market perspective. *American Journal of Agricultural Economics* 76(5): 1172-1176.

Ruben, R., R. Fort and G. Zuniga-Arias (2009). Measuring the impact of fair trade on development. *Development in Practice* 19(6): 777-788.

Shiferaw, B.A., E.J. Okello and R.V. Reddy (2009). Adoption and adaptation of natural resource management innovations in smallholder agriculture: reflections on key lessons and best practices. *Environment, Development and Sustainability* 11(3): 601-619.

Six, F.E. (2007). Building interpersonal trust within organizations: a relational signaling perspective. *Manage Governance* 11: 285-309.

Uslaner, E. M. (2002). *The moral foundations of trust*. New York, NY, USA: Cambridge University Press.

Valentinov, V. (2004). Toward a social capital theory of cooperative organisation. *Journal of Cooperative Studies* 37(3): 5-20.

Wolday, A. and E. Gabre-Madhin (2003). An analysis of the structure, conduct, and performance of the Ethiopian grain market. Presented at the Workshop on Harnessing Markets for Agricultural Growth in Ethiopia: Bridging the Opportunities and Challenges, ILRI, Addis Ababa, Ethiopia, 7-8 July 2003.

World Bank (2005). Ethiopia well-being and poverty in Ethiopia the role of agriculture and agency. Washington, DC, USA: World Bank.

World Bank (2007) World development report: agriculture for development. Washington, DC, USA: World Bank.

Zak, P.J. and Knack, S. (2001). Trust and growth. Economic Journal 111: 295-321.

Annex

Table A.1. Descriptive statistics

Variables	Weak cooperative		Strong cooperative		t-test
	Mean	SD	Mean	SD	Sign.[1]
Family size (no)	7.34	2.323	7.96	2.411	**
Family average age (yrs)	23.74	6.686	21.57	7.887	***
Age household head (yrs)	52.45	13.468	46.29	12.88	***
Education household head (yrs)	3.78	3.484	4.34	3.178	
Employment ratio household	0.2542	0.15037	0.2668	0.1572	
Asset index livestock[2]	2.7765	2.5702	2.8023	1.8275	
Asset index machinery/equipment/transport[3]	0.67	0.525	0.82	0.577	*
Assets index household goods[4]	1.0353	0.841	1.6442	0.969	***
Total land owned (ha)	1.0593	0.8564	1.7121	4.6976	
Land for coffee trees (ha)	0.4363	0.9479	0.42032	2.78382	
Total trees (no)	2,638.55	3,865.2	3,083.70	3,464.98	
Total coffee trees (no)	988.70	1,599.5	1,224.16	1,369.98	
Young trees (no)	188.71	506.91	310.43	403.059	**
Fruit bearing trees (no)	712.02	946.37	898.68	1,181.074	
Coffee harvest in 2009 (red cherry)	1,135.57	1,515.860	1,376.73	1,716.422	
Coffee harvest (dry) in 2009 per hec.	0.25	2.750	221.19	1038.059	**
Consumption coffee (red cherry+dry)	86.42	97.309	94.12	124.863	
Coffee sales in 2009 (red cherry kg)	820.08	1,194.470	1,084.07	1,378.540	
Coffee sales in 2009 (dry coffee kg)	222.35	549.034	184.16	903.997	
Household expenditures	413.898	317.59	634.431	547.764	***
Production expenditures	94.801	238.05	113.785	149.279	
Total expenditures	4,382.87	3,649.9	6,773.58	6,007.89	***
Total expenditures/adult[5]	1,678.647	1,366.4	2,589.10	2,717.192	**
Farm income per adult	1,125.45	1,495.43	2,995.12	11,851.91	*
Farm income per hectare	3,002.423	3,004.490	5,640.51	11,319.01	**
Non-farm income per adult	106.02	361.097	484.79	1,356.345	**
Self-employment per adult	188.84	489.841	301.71	944.055	
Assistance per adult	140.11	404.599	120.345	439.628	
Total income per adult	1,570.47	1,611.015	3,920.94	12,189.57	**
Total income per hectare	4,742.113	4,327.545	8131.74	12,643.84	**
Coffee sales to cooperative in 2009	648.76	1,141.406	1,408.68	4,781.341	*
Sales to cooperative (2), mixed (1), outside (0)	0.96	0.460	1.47	0.501	***
Sales cooperative (1), sales outside (0)	0.87	0.335	1.00	0.000	***
Membership cooperative (yrs)	24.78	11.120	24.73	10.802	
Attendance General Assembly	0.81	0.394	0.91	0.285	**
Participation voting board members	0.84	0.368	0.88	0.320	ns
Additional shares from cooperative	0.27	0.445	0.47	0.501	***

[1] * significant at 10%; ** significant at 5%; *** significant at 1%; SD = standard deviation.

[2] Tropical livestock index (Jahnke, 1982): cows 0.7, oxen 1.0, goats 0.15, sheep 0.15, chicken 0.02, donkey 0.5, mule/horse 0.75.

[3] Index: bicycle 1.0, donkey cart 0.6, plough 0.4, wheel barrow 0.3, plough parts 0.1, hoe 0.1, pitch fork 0.02, hammer 0.02, spade 0.02, sickle 0.01.

[4] Index: fridge 1.0, television 0.9, radio 0.7, telephone 0.6, wrestwatch 0.5, bed 0.3.

[5] Index of calorific requirements by age and gender for East Africa (Collier *et al.*, 1990).

Chapter 7

Gender equity within Utz certified coffee cooperatives in Eastern Province, Kenya

Eveline Dijkdrenth
For correspondence: edijkdrenth@me.com

7.1 Introduction

Development agencies are becoming increasingly aware of the importance of a gender approach in their projects. This is also the case for certification programs like Fair Trade, Max Havelaar and Utz certified (Utz). These labels have – in addition to the aim of reducing poverty – the objective to empower women and achieve gender equity. The results in terms of poverty reduction have been studied in several impact studies (Bechetti and Constantino, 2008; Ruben, 2009). However, the objective that certified producers, especially women become empowered, so that we can speak of gender equity, has hardly been assessed in thorough empirical studies.

Broadly speaking, there are two gender approaches within the field of development. First, the Women in Development (WID) approach, which assumes that the benefits of modernisation would eventually trickle down to women. This approach upholds the view of seeing women as victims of poverty and underdevelopment problems. The common believe is that the provision of employment might empower women. This is based upon the assumption that gender relations will change automatically as women become full economic partners in development. Therefore, the WID approach focuses on the public domain and the economy. The concept of gender became visible in the 1970's in development analysis, but it focused mainly on 'women' instead of addressing inequalities between men and women and amongst men and women (Kabeer, 1994; Rathgeber, 1990).

The second gender approach, Gender and Development (GAD) was defined because the WID approach was considered as inadequate. It failed to deal with inequality and it did not address and understand underlying structural problems (Brown, 2007). The GAD approach therefore shifted its focus from women to gender and unequal power relations between and amongst men and women. The concept of social construction of gender is explicitly included into the formulation of GAD policies and programmes (Razavi and Miller, 1995). According to the GAD approach, gendered problems in the society are not fixed, but they are historically created so they can also be changed (Cartier and Rothenberg-Aalami, 1999). It is thus a more holistic approach to gender, looking at gender relations and is focuses on the meaning of masculinity and femininity and the power relations between and amongst men and women. These power relations are not only present in the public domain, but also in the private domain; they cannot be seen as separate domains, since people are part of both domains.

Although, by the beginning of the 1990's, the concept of social construction of gender had become a dominant discourse around the world and non-governmental organisations (NGOs) began to add some elements of the GAD approach into their existing WID programmes, traditional development goals still dominate many development projects, programmes and gender analysis. This is also the case with certification programmes, where the emphasis lies on 'involving women within the economy' through certification. Besides positive effects, improving of self-esteem and status, this approach has also led to negative effects, because gender power relations are not fully addressed. Certification can also lead to heavier workloads and reinforce the unequal division of labour at home (Hutchens, 2010). After studying 18 Fair Trade producer-partners of Oxfam, Hopkins (2000) noted that in all cases gender relations remained largely unaffected. Van Dooren (2005) states that there is often little attention to the woman's responsibility toward the family and their gender role in the Fair Trade rice production. Finally, Mayoux (2001) problematises women's disadvantage position with respect to access to revenues and premiums of Fair Trade. Payments usually go to the man within the household, even though women also participate in the Fair Trade production.

In this article, I look into the gender approach of Utz certification as part of a wider impact study of Utz (see Chapter 2). The main objectives of certification concerns poverty reduction, but for the last few years Utz has been more concerned with gender equity in their certification program. Their gender approach is formulated in the following criteria of the Code of Conduct: 'discrimination based on gender is prohibited; in compliance with the International Labour Organization convention 100, equal work must be remunerated with equal pay; the responsible person for worker health and safety must be able to demonstrate awareness of and access to national regulation concerning maternity leave; health and safety conditions is applicable to permanent as well as temporary workers' (Utz Kapeh, 2010). In 2009, maternity leave, maternal health care and protection against sexual harassment were added (Utz, 2009). Poverty reduction relies on involving women within the economy and giving them equal rights in the workplace. Cooperatives are themselves responsible for implementing the Code of Conduct which they signed.

The gender approach of Utz mainly focuses on the public domain and explicitly on women' work. Taking the GAD discourse into mind, this gender approach leaves some questions: How, for example, are the structural problems of gender relations addressed when it only focuses on women? Why are men not involved in this approach? Why are structural problems of gender asymmetry not addressed, like social norms an perceptions about the division of labour? How is the private domain affected by this gender approach, when the focus is only on the public domain? Finally how can cooperatives themselves implement this gender approach, especially when they are not trained in addressing gender issues? Are they even aware of gender differences and power relations?

All these questions concern the approach of Utz on power relations and its understanding structural problems. If one of the objectives of Utz is gender equity, it is important to understand how gender relations are structured both within the public and the private domain. Therefore, we wanted to know what are the effect of the gender approach of Utz on gender relations within an Utz certified cooperative. In terms of methods, we relied on a comparison of a Utz certified cooperative with another non certified cooperative. We focussed on the following research question: Are there differences in how an Utz certified and an non-certified cooperative try to influence gender equity within the cooperative and does this have influence on the gender relations within the household?

In this study, the gender approach of an Utz certified coffee cooperative was analysed and compared with an non certified coffee cooperative in Kenya. We both focussed on the field of the cooperative (public domain) and that of the household (private domain). Gender relations within both cooperatives and within the farm-households in both cooperatives were compared in order to see if there were any differences, and if gender based programmes within the coffee cooperative led to changes in gender relations within the cooperative and the household.

Field research was conducted in Kenya in the Eastern Province, north of the city of Embu, in cooperation with the East African regional office of the NGO Solidaridad. Rianjagi Cooperative Society Limited (hereafter called: Rianjagi) was chosen as the Utz certified cooperative because women formed a majority of the management committee. The NGO saw this as an interesting development, because in Kenya most management committees of coffee cooperatives consists of a majority of men. Kithungururu Farmers Cooperative Society Limited (hereafter called: Kithungururu) was selected as the non-certified cooperative. Both cooperatives are located on the same geographical location at an altitude of approximately 1,700 m. They are comparable by size and composition of members.

7.2 Gender equity

Defining what is meant with 'gender' in this research is crucial for understanding why the focus in gender approaches needs to be not only on women, but on men too, because both are part of the social construction of gender relations. When talking about gender, we talk about the cultural meaning that is given to someone's sex. Someone's sex is not the only factor that determines gender (Erikson, 2001; Moore, 1994). Gender is more complex. The differences between gender are socially and culturally constructed. For example: embroidering and rugby are two hobby's that do not have anything to do with biology. There will only be a few people who think that embroidering is typically a hobby for men and rugby a typical girls sport. However, what in one society is seen as a typical female-thing, can in other societies be seen as the opposite. For example, in western societies, like Northern America and Europe, nobody would frown upon two girls walking hand in hand. People would probably presume that they are friends or perhaps sisters. While this is 'normal' in western societies, it is different in, for example, Nepal. Here, two girls walking hand in hand is something that is socially not accepted, and it is seen as a sexual expression. However, if two men would walk hand in hand, it would be considered as normal, while this would likely to be the opposite in western societies.

The example above shows that gender is socially created and is also hegemonic in that many of its foundational assumptions and ubiquitous processes are invisible, unquestioned, and un-examined. Davis *et al.* (2006) explain further that 'gender is constructed and maintained by both the dominant and the oppressed, because both ascribe to its values in personality and identify formation and in appropriate masculine and feminine behaviour'. Furthermore gender is about the division of people into two different groups, 'men' and 'women', and the organisation of major aspects of society that comes along this binary division. Davis *et al.* (2006) explain this as follows:

> It overrides individual differences and intertwines with other major socially constructed differences – racial categorisation, ethnic grouping, economic class, age, religion, and sexual orientation – which interact to produce a complex hierarchical system of dominance and sub-ordination (Davis *et al.*, 2006: 2).

Gender division is not only visible in families and friendships, but it also structures relationships in, for example, education, law, medicine, the military, politics, religion and work. Gender is a system of power that privileges some while disadvantaging others. Gender is about power relations, meanings, social relations, perceptions, norms and hierarchy (Chambers, 1996). There are large variations between gender relations in different societies, ranging from almost completely equal, to societies where women's influence over their own destiny seems very limited (Howell, 1989).

7.2.1 Gender equity and empowerment

Gender equity and gender equality are often used to describe the same process. But these concepts are not the same. An important distinction must be made. Equality stresses that people are treated the same. Gender equality indicates that women have the same opportunities in life as men. Progress in women's status is measured against a male norm. Through measures to increase women's participation in public life, policies and legislation try to tackle the problem of inequality. However, when people are treated the same this does not automatically mean that other significant differences are taken into account, which may affect the outcomes of 'equal' treatment. Equality policies assume that once the barriers to participation are removed, everybody can play by the same rules. It does not recognise that women's reality and experience may be different from men (Reeves and Baden, 2000: 10). 'Where conditions do not take the difference in gender into account, 'equal' treatments tends to default to the unequal status quo' (Chambers, 1996).

Gender equity recognises differences in gender and takes this into account in order to prevent the continuation of the inequitable status quo. It emphasis fairness in process and outcome, and it does not presume that people are the same and need the same, as is the case with gender equality (Chambers, 1996). Gender equity thus recognises that women and men have different needs, preferences and interests and that equality of outcomes may require a different treatment of men and women (Reeves and Baden, 2000).

Gender equity can lead to gender equality in certain fields. For example, a woman gets the same amount of salary paid for the same work as a man. We then speak of equality because men and women are treated equally. However, a woman can still be seen as inferior to men, or be discriminated because gender relations are not changed by giving equal payment. Gender equity takes the differences between men and women into account. For example, a pregnant woman cannot do heavy work and when she delivered her baby she needs a period of rest before she can come back to work. In this case, it is important that a woman is treated differently than a man and that her situation is taken into account. However, if the salary payment is not hers but controlled by her husband, we cannot talk of gender equity if he decides how the money is spend and she only gets a small portion. Therefore, to achieve gender equity, there not only need to be equal in certain fields, but the differences between women and men and unequal power relations need to be fully considered, also in the private domains (Chambers, 1996). To achieve gender equity, social power relations need to be changed. Both women and men are part of the social construction of gender relations therefore both need to be included in gender development programmes that fundamentally address gender relations.

Empowerment is therefore often seen as an important factor. Kabeer (1999) understands empowerment in terms of power and social justice. She formulates it as follows:

> the notion of empowerment is that it is inescapably bound up with the condition of disempowerment and refers to the processes by which those who have been denied the ability to make choices acquire such an ability.

Empowerment is a process. People who have a great deal of choices may be powerful, but they are not necessarily empowered, because they were not disempowered in the first place. Empowerment means the change from disempowerment to empowerment, thus from not having the ability to choose towards having the ability to choose. The ability to make a choice is of key importance in the empowerment process and to make this choice someone must first gain power. Kabeer (1999) defines three main dimensions of empowerment and thus for women to be able to make choices (Figure 7.1).

Resources are pre-conditions for the ability to make choice, agency is the process of making choices and achievements are the outcomes of the choices made (Kabeer, 1999). The resources include material and non-material resources. Material resources are for example economic assets, non-material resources are for example someone's social network. As far as empowerment is concerned, possible inequalities in people's capacity to make choices are of particular interest, rather than differences in the choices they make.

Empowerment cannot be given through purely economic means. It is something that can be created if the opportunity is given and taken; these opportunities may be limited by power relations. To understand how this mechanism works, we first need to understand the concept of power.

7.2.2 Power, discourse and habitus

Power is a complicated concept. Power has different faces and is more than only the outcome of conflicts. Power is also about making compromises, negotiating and struggling, it refers to a process in thinking. This does not mean that power cannot be measured by looking at a reaction to or the significance of the effects of a reaction. It is not the case that one can only possess power when the other has none. Power is also not inherent to a position, space or a person, but power can be restricted by those in inferior positions. These restrictions, or the thought on these restrictions, are shaped by the ideology of the dominant class and determines the demands of the subordinates and prevents them from trying to exercising control (Villareal, 1994). Dominant classes are those who have most power to influence discourse – the formalised way of thinking – and shape socially defined boundaries of what can be said about a certain issue, or, as Butler (1999) puts it: 'the limits of acceptable speech'. Such discourses constrain the actions of the power that someone has. In order to exercise power, power must be excepted, or as Villarreal (1994) puts it: 'The wielding of power presupposes the exercise of yielding to it, of recognising the other as powerful'. When

Figure 7.1. Interrelated dimensions of choice (Kabeer, 1999).

we talk about power in the field of development we consider processes that produce or change gender relations, hierarchy, division of labour, perceptions, norms, etc.

So we could say that power relations reproduce power relations and establish systems of domination and social hegemonies. However, this is often taken as an explanation of the patterns that social relations assume. Villarreal (1994) argues that these dominant systems and social hegemonies could also be outcomes of the process of power relations. For opening these black boxes, we need to look at the dominant discourses and at the social processes that produce these discourses. In this research, this means looking at how gender relations work, what the division of labour is, who owns and controls the resources, what the social perceptions and norms are and how these social processes reproduce power relations. Foucault's and Bourdieu's theories will help to better understand in which way social processes reproduces power relations.

For Foucault, power is not localised in institutions or sovereigns, but it is shaped through the use of strategies, tactics and techniques. Discourse influences gender relations in particular ways. Discourses are embedded in social relations and activities and are mostly taken for granted (Foucault, 1980). Villareal summarises Foucault approach to power; it is a 'particular understanding of the way in which the world is organised and should be organised, images of self and other, of people's roles and capacities, and associations with the environment help reproduce and maintain power relations and fix asymmetries' (Villarreal, 1994). Discourse influences gender relations in particular ways; they are embedded in social relations and activities and are mostly taken for granted (Foucault, 1980). Social relations are portrayed as systems and chains where individuals are embedded. In this way, individuals have limited agency.

Bourdieu considers individuals more as 'creative, active subjects with inventive capacity, social agents in their roles as practical operators of the construction of objects' (Bourdieu, 1990). He argues that the actions of agents are structured by their habitus. To put it simple: habitus are those things that we do, that are a habit and that we find ordinary. This originates from an adaptation of certain habits which have been created in the past. In every field (i.e. social context) people unconsciously develop certain habitus, a sustainable way to observe, think and act, that people apply to maintain themselves in a certain field. The position of people on certain issues is not calculated – in a way that all objective regularities and calculated outcomes could be most successful. Rather, the position of people is caused by earlier experiences, acquired in comparable situations, and ethical concepts. An individual thus internalises the reality that presents itself from the outside. At the same time, the individual presents this internalised reality in its own way to the society. This shows that there is a constant (albeit slow) process of incorporations and objectification (Bourdieu, 1977). Habitus is, in other words, a discourse that is taken for granted.

The concept of habitus can be helpful to understand those discourses that are not questioned and seen as natural or as part of the culture. A certain habitus is formed in a certain field, a social context. Fields are areas where meanings and interpretations are debated and defined through habitus, which defines the 'categories of perception and assessment'. They are normative processes, reflected in practices, where the battle around power struggles over economic, social and cultural capital influences social relations. We can consider these fields as a particular setting, for example a school or the household/family. The social world is made up by all kinds of fields, like religion, family relations, labour conditions, markets, education, etc.

7.2.3 Gender analysis of certification

The gender approach of Utz certification concerns both coffee cooperatives and their affiliated farmers. The fields of the cooperative is of special interest, as is the field of the household. As explained before, if we would leave out the field of the household we would not take into account that gender relations are socially constructed in both fields and that these fields interact with each other. Discourse analysis within the field of the cooperative concerns an analysis of the power relations as documented in the policies of the cooperative and a study of social norms and perceptions that exits about men and women within the cooperative. Within the field of the cooperative a limited number of people are active that run and control cooperative affairs. Coffee farmers all have to deal with the cooperative because they sell their coffee through the cooperative; therefore, the policies of the cooperative directly influence livelihoods of farmers. We analysed policy documents and looked at how certain rules affected the participation of men and women and what the perception were about men and women within the cooperative. We made a discourse analysis based on answers given during open interviews with farmers and with staff members. We also looked at practices that were seen as normal or part of their culture, in other words in their habitus.

In the field of the household, all persons were included living under the same roof or working on the same plot (this could be a nuclear household or an extended household). Decisions within a household can be influenced by family members who are not actually living within the household, but co-decide on certain issues. For example, it concerns decision with whom a person will marry, how money is spend, how labour is allocated, etc. This field is concerned with the activities in the homes of the farmers and on the family farm surrounding the home, as most of the households were self-sufficient. This includes activities on the coffee plot, but also the cultivation of other crops, dairy farming and other income-generating activities. The discourse analysis in the field of the household concerns the division of labour, control of assets, decision making power and social norms and perceptions about gender relations. We analysed the answers given to questions during individual and group interviews: what were the respondents saying, how did they express this, what kind of examples and explanations were given especially concerning social and cultural norms, and whether respondents were aware of their own habitus.

7.3 Analytical framework

In this research gender relations in the field of the household and the cooperative are the central focus. Gender relations are influenced by power relations and social norms and perceptions that people have. In return, power relations and social norms and perception also influence each other. A gender policy of the cooperative will try to influence social perceptions and power relations. By trying to change power relations and social perceptions, it tries to achieve better or more gender equity. Since gender relations in both fields are influenced by power relations and social perceptions within the society, certification may contribute to gender equity insofar as it contributes to an alternative discourse and a new habitus.

Based on the theoretical framework, we formulated nine sub-questions. Five sub-questions concern the field of the cooperative and four questions focus on the field of the household. Questions in the field of the cooperative were mainly referring to the type of gender equity approach that was used, while questions in the field of the household mainly concerned with power relations. The first two sub-questions at cooperative level address issues of power relations within the cooperative. In order to appreciate the gender policies of the cooperatives we asked: (1) What are the formal policies in place towards gender within the cooperative? (2) What is the real position of women and men in practice within the cooperative? Hereafter, we further specify the policies of the cooperatives that were especially developed to achieve gender equity, asking: (3) What kind of programmes are in place to achieve gender equity? and (4) How are programmes to achieve gender equity implemented? This will give more insight into how the cooperative interpret gender equity, and how they try to influence gender relations. The gender discourse of the cooperative will become more clear in this way. For analysing the social perceptions in the field of the cooperative that allows people to understand the individuals and groups of their social world (Smith and Mackie 2000) we included sub-question (5): What are the social perceptions about men and women within leadership positions? Social perceptions will give more insight in the habitus of the respondents. Together, these five sub-questions made it possible to get more insight into the gender policies and the existing gender relations within the cooperative.

In order to get more insight in the existing gender relations within the household and to see if gender policies of the cooperatives had any influence on gender relations within the household level, we defined four sub-questions. The first three sub-questions concern power relations within the household and refer to the division of labour, decision making power, and control of assets: (6) How is the division of labour within the household?; (7) Who decides on which issues within the household? and (8) Who owns what and who controls what within the household? By concentrating on these three subjects we could get more insight into the hierarchy within the household. The final sub-questions focuses on social norms and perception about men and women: (9) What are the social norms and perceptions about men and women within the household? This allowed us to get more insight in the habitus of the respondents.

By making the division between the cooperative and the household level we could analyse how gender relations are shaped and materialise within both cooperatives and how cooperative organisation in turn influenced household gender relations through their policies and practice.

7.4 Materials and methods

Field research was conducted in three phases. In the first phase, semi-structured interviews were held with employees of the cooperatives and as many committee members as possible. In the second phase, focus-group discussions were done with a total of 40 farmers (20 per cooperative). In the third and last phase, a total of 63 semi-structured interviews were conducted. Households were visited multiple times. In this way, it was possible to closely observe also the activities of household members. Especially the activities of men differed between what they said in the semi-structured interview and what they actually were doing. We used discourse analysis to analyse the semi-structured interviews. We looked especially at those answers that implied that it is a norm in the local society. In these cases respondent often said that it is 'their culture' or that is 'how they always do it'. For triangulation, as far as this was possible, we depended on own observations and the observation of the enumerator, who spoke the local language.

7.4.1 Case study cooperatives

We started research with Rianjagi cooperative that was supported for certification by Solidaridad. They selected this cooperative because it had a majority of women within the management committee. The cooperative had been established in 1997 after splitting from the coffee cooperative Kapingazi, due to mismanagement. Rianjagi had a total of 1,519 members of which 1,037 were active members in 2011: 673 members were men and 353 were women. The cooperative had one factory and two cherry mills.[50] Rianjagi has been Utz certified since 2008.

It was important that the control cooperative needed to have a similar size of membership and a likewise composition of male and female memberships as Rianjagi, in order to be able compare the both. Based on official data obtained from the district cooperative officer in Embu, Kithungururu cooperative was chosen. This cooperative was located close to the village of Gatoori, into the mainland. The cooperative had been established in 2001 after splitting from the same coffee cooperative where Rianjagi originated from, Kapingazi, also due to mismanagement. Kithungururu had a total of 1,811 members of which 1,262 were active members: 878 were men and 374 were women. Kithungururu currently (2011) has one factory, but in the near future this will become two. The current factory has two cherry mills. The factory manager

---

[50] Cherries are the coffee beans when they are not yet dried. A cherry mill is a tool to rinse of the outer layer of the cherry before it can be dried.

was a man. Kithungururu had no certification, they only received some training from the Melinda and Bill Gates foundation.

Both cooperatives were fairly comparable in terms of the number of members, shared capital, production in kilogram and payments. The fact that both cooperatives are localised in similar agroecological conditions and split from the same Kapingazi Cooperative Society made Kithungururu a suitable cooperative for comparing gender relations with Rianjagi.

Table 7.1 shows the membership from both cooperatives. Active membership refers to the number of members that in the studied harvest year (2009/2010) have delivered their coffee harvest to the factory. Not all members delivered their coffee to the factory; some sold it to another farmer (although this is illegal it happens because farmers need money earlier than the cooperative can pay them) or because their harvest failed. Shared capital (in Kenyan Shillings) is the amount of money the cooperatives had in savings. This money was used to pay staff and for repairing property of the factory, and was sometimes used to give a loan to members. The production in kilogram gives the amount of coffee beans that had been sold in total to the middleman before it went to the auction. The sales (in Kenyan Shilling) presents the amount of money that the cooperative received for the total produced coffee. The Payment in Kenyan Shilling represent the amount of money that was eventually paid to the farmers. For Rianjagi, 75.8% of the amount of money received after selling on the auction was paid to members, while for Kithungururu this was 85.3%. Kithungururu delivered a higher percentage to their farmers, but Rianjagi got a better price per kilo. Therefore, the final payment rate in Rianjagi (50 KSh) is higher than that of Kithungururu (47 KSh).

7.4.2 Selection of farmers

Table 7.2 shows the sample of farmers for both cooperatives. We interviewed 63 farmers, chosen trough snowball sampling. The criteria was that they had to be a member of Rianjagi or Kithungururu. Rianjagi consists of 11 villages and in each village two households were interviewed. A total of 19 households participated and

Table 7.1. Cooperative membership, production and sales (2009/2010).[1]

Cooperative	Active membership			Shared capital (Ksh)	Production (kg)	Sales (KSh)	Payments (KSh)	Paid to members (%)
	male	female	Total					
Rianjagi	673	353	1,036	305,600	857,641	50,324,992.90	38,154,930.70	75.8
Kithungururu	859	360	1,229	326,400	643,637	39,755,102.03	33,911,102.03	85.3

[1] Data provided by the district cooperative officer in Embu.

Table 7.2. Composition of the sample of farmers.

Cooperative	Total households	Total of interviews	Men	Women	Single women	Widow(s)
Rianjagi	19	31	14	17	0	1
Kithungururu	19	32	12	20	3	2
Total	38	63	26	37	3	3

we conducted 31 interviews with 14 men and 17 women. Kithungururu consists of five villages, and in almost every village four households were interviewed for a total number of 20 households. For Kithungururu, 32 interviews with 12 men and 20 women were conducted. It was for several different reasons not always possible to interview both the wife and the husband within the household. Some husbands were employed in another region of Kenya and only came home a few times per year. Others were employed in town and were too busy to make time to be interviewed. Although it was also not always easy to talk to women (mainly because some women were afraid that their husband would find out that they were interviewed), only two women could not been interviewed because they were employed as civil servants in another region of Kenya.

A majority of the households (22) were nuclear households. There were six households with a single woman or widow as head of the household. The remainder (10) were extended households. Extended households often consisted of children and grandchildren or multiple families living on the same plot because the land was not yet divided. While elderly couples often had six or more children, most younger couples had five or less children.

7.5 Gender development at cooperative level

Finding concerning the sub-questions at the level of the cooperative – i.e. policies towards gender within the cooperative, the position of women and men within the cooperative, social norms and perceptions about women within the cooperative and finally gender equity programmes that are implemented – are first discussed.[51] Before we turn to discussing the data of the sub-question in the field of the cooperative the difference between the composition of both cooperatives is discussed.

---

[51] Due to the privacy of the respondents the names of farmers are not used, instead, respondents are referred to as numbers plus letters. A woman gets a number plus a, and a man gets a number plus b. Members of the same family have the same number. For example, a woman and man in one household were interview, the woman is 1a and the man 1b.

7.5.1 Cooperative organisation

Both cooperatives had a similar organisational structure. Shareholders are the ones who own the cooperative. Shareholders elect the management committee members, which all must be shareholders. The elected members decide themselves who gets which position. The management committee works closely with the manager. The manager works together with a bookkeeper and clerk(s). The supervisory committee controls both the management and the management committee and consists of a chairperson, vice-chairperson and secretary. The manager is the superior of the factory manager. The factory manager is in charge of all labourers, which are often casual labourers, and he is responsible for the factory, the maintenance and the machinery. Finally, at the bottom of the structure are the workers that assist during the harvesting seasons, in between with repairs and do all kinds of other chores at the factory. All these functions were the same for Rianjagi and Kithungururu.

The difference between Rianjagi and Kithungururu lies in the composition of the management committee and the functions that women fulfil within the cooperative. The manager of Kithungururu was a woman, while at Rianjagi this was a man. However, in the former it was only a formal title: she had only administrational duties and the management committee did not consult her. However, at Rianjagi the manager had a powerful position and consulted regularly with the chairperson. The most important difference between both cooperatives was the fact that Rianjagi had three women in some influential positions within the management committee, whereas in Kithungururu there were none.

The first woman to enter the management committee of Rianjagi was Sophia Ndwiga in 2007. She was elected after the former vice-chairperson (currently chairperson) started to make shareholders aware of the importance of women within the management committee. He felt it was important to include women within the committee because women were also an important part of the community. He was aware that women were the ones who did most of the work within the household and on the coffee farm. However, women were not respected by men for their work. To empower them he saw it as an important development that women would become part of the management committee. Besides, the Kenyan government aimed at a 30% representation of women within institutions, organisations and parliament. So, the awareness of problems that women face and the wish to favour women, as within the policies of the government, finally resulted in the appointment of three female committee members from 2008 onwards.

Sophia Ndwiga was elected by the shareholders and chosen to be the treasurer. In 2008 Cynthia Njoka and Molly Njeru joined the management committee, after being elected by the shareholders. Cynthia Njoka has since been the secretary, and Molly Njeru the vice-chairperson. While the position of treasurer and secretary is not particularly a position of influence, the position of vice-chairperson is important. The vice-chairperson had the same power and duties as the chairperson in case s/he was absent or had other duties to attend on behalf of the cooperative. A woman in the position of vice-chairperson was not very common at coffee cooperatives, which are mainly dominated by men.

Kithungururu had no women within the management committee. Although the chairperson, James Namu, liked to see women in the board he thought they were too shy to vie for a position during elections. However, female farmers of Kithungururu gave other reasons for the absence of women within the management committee. For example, men were bribed with alcohol by members who wanted to be (re-) elected and the meetings were rather chaotic, and this discouraged women to be present. Women were not taken serious, when they wanted to say something they were booed. Another problem which is noticed is that the latest election (8 March 2011) was announced only a few days before the election, which made it difficult for both male and female shareholders to campaign for getting elected.

7.5.2 The position of women within the cooperative

The position of women within the cooperative societies is influenced by the representation of women within the management committee, but also by the rules concerning participation during general meetings and elections. The rules and requirements for both cooperatives will be discussed, trying to understand how women of both societies feel that they were represented within the cooperatives.

Cooperative societies in Kenya are free to make their own rules concerning requirements to participate during general meetings and to be elected within the management committee (Co-operative Societies Act 1997: article 7:1:g). The rules are made by the management committee, presented to the shareholders during general meetings and if agreed upon by the shareholders documented in the by-law of the cooperative. Rules to participate concern, among other things, the required minimum amount of produced cherries to be allowed to participate during general meetings – where decisions of the management committee are presented and where shareholders can discuss these decisions and present new topics – and the requirements to be able to vote during elections for new management committee members. Rules to be elected within the management committee also concern a required amount of produced cherries – which is often higher than the required amount of cherries to participate during general meetings and elections – and also the ability to write and speak English. English is the official language of Kenya and members of the management committee have to communicate with government officials in this language. Because cooperatives are free to make their own rules, there can be differences between cooperatives, as was the case with Rianjagi and Kithungururu.

Table 7.3 shows the required kilos for participating during general meetings and vote during elections, and the required kilos to be elected for Rianjagi and Kithungururu. Shareholders of Rianjagi needed to produce at least 300 kg of cherries to participate during general meetings and to vote in case new management committee members

Table 7.3. Requirements for participating during meetings and election in the management committee at Rianjagi and Kithungururu (in kg cherries).

Cooperative society	Participation in general meeting	Election within management committee
Rianjagi[1]	300	500
Kithungururu[2]	500	1000

[1] By-laws of Rianjagi Farmers' Cooperative Society Ltd (2008)
[2] By-laws Kithungururi Farmers' Cooperative Society (2005).

needed to be elected, whereas shareholders of Kithungururu needed to produce at least 500 kg of cherries. In case a shareholder would like to nominate him/herself for election to a position within the management committee, s/he would have to produce at least 500 kg of cherries for Rianjagi and 1000 kg of cherries for Kithungururu. Rianjagi thus required significantly less kilos of produced cherries for participating, voting power and possibility to be elected within the management committee, than Kithungururu.

These rules of requirement certainly influenced the percentage of female and male members that could participate or be elected (hereafter called 'active' shareholders). In general women produced less kilos than men, because they often own smaller portions of land, or could only use a small part of the land of their husband. Figure 7.2 gives an overview of the number and percentage of active shareholders in Rianjagi and Kithungururu. Figure 7.2A presents the percentage of male and female shareholders of both cooperatives.[52] Figure 7.2A indicates that the percentage of male and female shareholders of both cooperatives were comparable. In Rianjagi 34.0% of the shareholders are female and in Kithungururu 29.3% of the shareholders are female. However, the percentage of active female shareholders, who could participate during general meetings and vote, differs considerably between both cooperatives (Figure 7.2B). In Rianjagi 37.3% of the active shareholders were female, while in Kithungururu this percentage was significantly lower at 16.6%. This means that in Rianjagi an significantly higher percentage of women could participate during general meetings and vote during elections. In absolute numbers we observe that in Rianjagi 115 women are active shareholders, while at Kithungururu only 41 women are active shareholders. While both cooperatives have in absolute terms an comparable number of women members, significantly more women in Rianjagi had the opportunity to be eligible for the management committee (Figure 7.2C). The rules of requirement of both cooperatives thus clearly influences the degree in which women can be represented within the cooperative. It remains to be seen, however, if this also means that women felt that they were better represented.

---

[52] The category of 'others' includes churches, schools and other organisations who have a share at the cooperative.

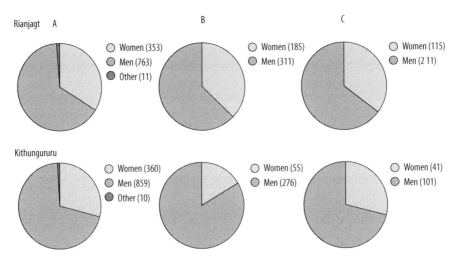

Figure 7.2. Gender composition of (A) shareholders, (B) active at cooperative meetings and voting, and (C) that are eligible at elections for Rianjagi and Kithungururu cooperatives in 2009/2010. Absolute numbers are given in parenthesises.

7.5.3 Perceptions regarding women representation

The fact that women were present or absent in the management committee had a large influence on how women of both cooperative perceived their position within the cooperative society and if they felt they were represented. In general, women were shy and felt uncomfortable to talk to men who were not related to them. For women of both cooperatives it was important that they could talk to a woman in case of problems. However, this was not possible for women in the society of Kithungururu. Since no woman was part of the management committee they did not feel represented. They also did not think that this situation would change, because it was very difficult for women to get elected. During interviews with women of the Kithungururu society they told that, besides that women often did not have a share, the relatively high amount of required kilos of cherries and the hostile climate during general meetings and elections, was considered one of the largest obstacle for women participation. Even if a woman delivered the required amount of kilos, they were discouraged to go to general meetings and to participate in elections. Men were bribed with alcohol during elections and this resulted in chaotic circumstances.

In contrast, women within the society of Rianjagi felt that they were represented, because women were seated within the management committee. They could go to one of these women if they faced problems. These women could bring up their issues during discussions at meetings with the rest of the committee. A female farmer of Rianjagi emphasised that women were familiar with the problems faced at home and therefore were more willing to help women:

It is easier now to get the school checks, because the women know how difficult it is to pay the school fees. Men sometimes forget about the school fees. You will find the men is employed somewhere and he goes to the bank, forgetting that he has children at home that need to go to school. Women are not like that, women are generally concerned.

A female farmer of Rianjagi explained why for her women in the management committee were important and how it benefited women:

They are at least able to fight for women issues. Women are now able to approach them [the management committee] and tell them the problem they are facing. And women are generally kind. If you need pesticide they see you have potential, but not the kilos. If you approach a woman and you can explain, they usually understand and are kinder and they try to get you more pesticide.

Having women within the management committee of Rianjagi had as result that women within the society felt better represented, and in case they needed help they had someone to go to. Nevertheless, the fact that women in the society of Rianjagi felt represented, did not imply that relations were equal between men and women within the cooperative. The cooperative is still dominated by male shareholders. Women were often 'next of kin'[53], but they needed permission from their husband (the shareholder) to do businesses with the cooperative or to be representative at meetings. Even while women were the ones who were most active on the coffee farm, yet they were often not the ones with shares in the cooperative. As a consequence, a large part of women in Rianjagi society had no opportunity to influence the decision-making process. This was the same for a large part of women in the Kithungururu society. Therefore, a lot of women in both societies rarely interacted with the cooperative. However, when women became shareholder at Rianjagi, the opportunity to be actively involved in the decision-making process within the cooperative gave them the opportunity to influence the process. In this way these women had the ability to strengthen their position within the society, which could also benefit other women within the society. In summary, representation of women within the management committee and during general meetings and elections did make a difference in the position that women had within the cooperative society, even while men still dominate cooperative affairs.

7.5.4 Empowerment programmes

The presence of an empowerment programme in Rianjagi has important consequences. Kithungururu did not have any programme in place that had as objective to empower farmers; not for women, neither for men or youth. The only activity of Kithungururu

---

[53] A next of kin is a person that is written down in cooperatives document as the person who would inherit the cooperative share of a certain shareholder when this shareholder would pass away.

was to process cherries and buni[54] that farmers brought to the factory and sold to middlemen. These middlemen then took it to the auction, and paid the farmers once their share was sold at the auction. When farmers wanted, they could also buy new coffee plants at the cooperative. In other words, all activities were only focussed on the coffee production.

The empowerment programmes of Rianjagi were not developed by Utz, but were the result of the commitment of the chairperson and the rest of the committee members. In 2011, Rianjagi started an empowerment programme. According to the chairperson, women do most of the work in the household. 'Yet everything in the home belongs to the man. Because everything belongs to the man, the man tends to think that all the other things from the wife are his, and the wife is an inferior person'. The chairperson wanted to empower women and used the dairy programmes for this purpose. He explained his idea as follows:

> I will show you how we could bring women in some activities. For example, with fish dairying, this is an activity that will be done in that chamber. So, at the end of the day she will have access to some funds and she now will be a member of the society through that activity. So whatever income earned from that activity will be in the possession of that woman. She will start feeling that she owns some things and brings some income to the home, and the man will have to be taught that the activity belongs to the woman and not him. We will use the society for this purpose.

In this program, also women were included that are not shareholders, but are in fact next of kin. In this way, those women who were not officially members of the cooperatives, could eventually become members. By giving women their own way of generating income, the chairperson expected to give women the feeling that they are contributing to the household. However, as he also explained, women already had a lot of work on the plot and in their homes, so this would mean that women could have more work. It was not clear how this would change power relations. The chairperson did understood that the man of the household also needed to be educated on the fact that woman have ownership over this activity and thus control the money that is earned with this activity. For educating men, the chairperson used the general meetings, in which he discussed the position of women within the household.

There are two critical underlying assumptions about gender relations in the empowerment programs of Rianjagi that deserve to be commented. First, the assumption that if a woman gets her own income, she will be respected at home, because she contributes to the household. Women already contributed financially to

---

[54] Buni are those cherries picked after they are fully grown at the very end of every coffee season. Buni does not need to go through the whole process of drying, because they are already dried while hanging on the plant. At the cooperative, the buni is collected and goes into a machine which gets rid of the outer layer of the buni. Buni is of less value, compared with cherry.

the household by cultivating the coffee and often other crops like banana's; the only difference is that women often do not control the income derived from these crops and are not respected for their contribution. The chairperson further assumed that women would get control over the income from these activities. However, he also recognised that in other income-generating activities women did most of the work and yet they were not in control of this money.

Second, the assumption that including women into the economic market will empower women and modify gender relations is debatable. This assumption was also present in the gender discourse of the WID approach. As discussed in Section 7.1, this gender approach does not pay sufficient attention to power relations between men and women, and the social construction of gender. Both men and women have certain perceptions about women that could constrain the empowerment of woman. The chairperson wanted to change the perception of male farmers. However, he did not discuss the perceptions that women themselves had about power relations within the household. He only planned to discuss the position of women within the household with male farmers, and he wanted to empower women by giving them more work and an own income. It is therefore questionable if existing power relations will sufficiently change with the proposed empowerment programs of Rianjagi.

7.5.5 Social perceptions about women in leadership positions

The social perception and norms about women in leadership positions needs to be elaborated. This will provide more insight in the different discourses about the perception on the position of women within leadership positions. By looking into what farmers thought about women in leadership positions, two issues emerged. Both men and women from Rianjagi and Kithunguruu were asked questions whether they considered that women could lead a cooperative society, and if a woman would be part of the management committee which position she was able to hold. First of all, there was a clear difference in how women of Rianjagi perceived the abilities of women to lead a cooperative society. Second, no difference was found in how men (of different age) in both cooperatives think about this issue. Using some examples, we provide in the next paragraphs a more general insight into the social perceptions on women.

After analysing the data of the interviews, four different categories of reasons were found why male and female farmers of Rianjagi and Kithunguruu thought a woman could be in a leadership position. The first category explained that women could be in leadership positions, but only if she met certain qualifications ascribed to persons in leadership positions. In the second category women were seen as less corrupt and more trustworthy than men. In the third category women were seen as developers and therefore should have been in a leadership position. Finally, in the fourth and last category the leadership of women was seen as something positive and was explained by giving examples of successful women within other cooperatives or in politics. Table 7.4 gives an overview of the positive answers given by male and female respondents of both cooperatives.

Table 7.4. Perceptions on women's leadership by male and female respondents (n=24, Rianjagi and n=28, Kithungururu).

Category	Rianjagi		Kithungururu		Total	
	Male	Female	Male	Female	Male	Female
Qualifications	7	0	3	8	10	8
Trustworthy	4	1	4	3	8	4
Women as developers	1	7	1	5	2	12
Female leaders	3	1	3	1	6	2
Total	15	9	11	17	26	26

Regarding female leadership qualifications, seven male and none of the female farmers of Rianjagi and three male and eight female farmers of Kithungururu answered that a woman was well able to lead an cooperative society, but only if she met certain qualifications. These qualifications varied between having the gift of leadership, being intelligent, and having experience. For example. a male farmer of Rianjagi said that not all women could lead 'because not all have the gift to lead, even not all men have that gift, but most men have it'. A male farmer of Rianjagi explained that 'if women were wise, than they could lead'. Even though not all men were wise, according to him most of them could lead. In other words, according to these male farmers most men can lead and also a few women, only if they had certain qualifications. Key leadership skills were defined as having a strong character and being able to stand up against corruption.

With respect to trust, four male and one female farmer of Rianjagi and four male and three female farmers of Kithungururu answered that women were not, or less corrupt than men (or, translated from Swahili: 'more kind') and therefore could lead the society. The description of 'more kind' refers to kindness and honesty that is ascribed to women. Especially when it came to financial issues within the cooperative, women were considered as more trustworthy. All farmers ascribed to women the position of treasurer or secretary.

Most male respondents were rather critical about women in leadership positions in these two categories. Interestingly enough, also few women from Rianjagi expressed belief in these capacities, and from Kithungururu slightly more positive answers were registered.

With respect to the female developer role, seven female farmers but only one male farmer of Rianjagi and five female farmers and only one male farmer of Kithungururu answered that women were more aware of the needs of families and were therefore able to lead the cooperative, taking the needs of farmers into account. A female farmer of Kithungururu said that 'women are able to see the problems that the community has and can bring development'. Another female farmer of Rianjagi explained that 'women were more understanding than men'. A female farmer of Rianjagi said that women in the management committee were 'more concerned with solving problems of women'. A male farmer of Rianjagi explained that most farms were being taken care of by women and most homes were taken care by women of well.

In the category of women leadership, one male and three female farmers of Rianjagi and one male and three female farmers of Kithungururu considered women suitable for leadership positions as a more natural development. These eight farmers saw women in leading positions in other settings, and according to them they did a good job. This made them arrive at the conclusion that they thought women could also be in a leading position within the cooperative. They explained this by giving examples of other situations where women were already in a leadership position. A female farmer of Kithungururu referred to situations she knew in her direct surrounding where women were in leading positions:

> Nowadays women are the ones who go for more meetings and trainings and it are men who become more and more lazy. Women do more and work more. Men drink a lot and do less work. The sub chief is currently a woman and at the school the board has more women than men. The women are 12 and the men are 2.

She was critical about this development, because she did not necessarily believe this to be a positive development, since for her this was a result of men doing less work than before. A female farmer of Kithungururu referred to the women who work at the cooperative. She thought women could do a better job than men, if they were given a chance: 'The ones who weigh the coffee are women and they do good'.

Overall, female farmers of Rianjagi appeared to be more positive about women in leadership positions. The majority of female farmers of Kithungururu and the majority of men of both cooperatives preferred men to lead the cooperative and women to be in control of money belonging to the cooperative. The position of women regarding women in leadership positions within both cooperative differed because of two factors. First, the position of three leading women within the cooperative of Rianjagi ensured that women at Rainjagi felt better represented. Second, the lower amount of required kilos for becoming member at Rianjagi compared to Kithungururu ensured that more female farmers could participate during general meetings and opt for positions within the management committee. The opposite was the case for Kithungururu, where women were discouraged to participate because of the high amount membership requirements and the more hostile environment.

7.6 Gender relations at household level

In order to achieve gender equity or to try to change gender relations, it is important to look at the construction of gender relations in both the public and private domain. The construction of gender relations not only takes place in the public domain, like the domain of the cooperative, but also in the private domain. Therefore, we will turn attention now to the field of the household, and discuss how the gender relations are structured within farm-households.

7.6.1 Social norms and perceptions on gender relations within the household

Throughout the interviews, the social perceptions and norms became apparent. The general perception was that the man was the head of the household, because it was a norm that a man owned the land and most of the assets and therefore he could make most of the decisions. When it concerned decision making within the household, men were in charge. Key decisions concern financial issues (what was bought or sold and who could spend what) and the education of children. It was often up to the male head of the household to make these decisions, sometimes in consultation with the spouse. Only in certain areas, like cleaning the household or cooking, women could decide for herself. It was often explained that the man is the head of the household because that was 'how it is' in their culture or because 'the bible said so'. Not only men thought about the hierarchy in the household this way, female farmers often agued in the same way. A female farmer of Kithungururu explained this through a Swahili saying 'Ngingo ndivitukaga kjongo', translated it means 'the neck cannot pass the head'. This means that there is no single moment that a woman could be in charge or take the lead. It was the head who tells the neck which way to bend. She said, 'If I would make a decision about the cow or the goat it would bring conflict to the home'.

When it came to the norm on who controls assets, like money, land, cattle and other livestock, it was also the man who was in control. Not many people said something about why men owned most of the assets and not women, but those who spoke about it said it was part of their culture. For example, a female farmer of Rianjagi said that:

> In our culture everything with blood and land is owned by men. The cow
> is his, because women do not own cows. Although I milk it, I can never
> own it. Even the sheep and chicken are his.

A male farmer of Rianjagi confirmed this, 'All things that have blood are the property of men'. In general, in all households (except the households with single female farmers or widows) the land belonged to the man. Inheritance law in Kenya was part of the reason why men owned land and women often did not. The inheritance law is discriminatory against women, only enabling the registry of men's right and inhibiting women's registration of rights to land. Furthermore, it is a customary law that women do not inherit land because when they marry they would live on the land of her husband, so she does not need land (Human Right Watch, 2003).

7.6.2 Power structures within households

While in the previous section about the position of women within the cooperative, women were perceived as being an important part of the cooperative, within the household this perception was different. A man was perceived to be the person who needed to have most of the power, because he was the head of the household. Both male and female farmers are imposing this habitus. It becomes apparent that differences in gender relation between both cooperatives not automatically lead to differences in gender relations between farm-households in Rianjagi and Kithunguruuru. We therefore dig somewhat deeper into intra-household power structures.

7.6.3 Decision making power

We can distinguish three kinds of households with respect to decision making power. First, there were households where all decisions were made by the male head of the household. A female farmer of Kithunguruuru explained it is a custom that men took all decisions:

> It is a custom that women do not make decisions. If I need to make a decision I will call my husband to make the decision or wait until he comes home. If I would make the decision my husband would come and chase me away. Even if it is about school fees, I cannot withdraw money without asking, I will have to consult first. If he says no I have to wait until he is back.

She saw it as a norm that women do not make decisions and that she did not have the power to make any decisions. Even when her husband was not around, she could not make decisions. Second, there are households where overall decisions were made by men, but women could make some smaller decisions, like what to cook for dinner. When women had power, it was their husbands who granted them these powers. A male farmer of Kithunguruuru explained in which situation his wife could make decisions: 'She can decide over farm output like arrowroot, beans, potatoes and I decide on cows and coffee'. In the third place, there are also households where the overall decisions are made in consultation with the spouse. A male farmer of Rianjagi explained why he consulted his wife, 'We decide together, because you cannot force someone, so we discuss it equally'. His wife said the same and explained that besides the decisions they made together, she could decide on small things herself: 'If I want to sell the chicken or milk, or what we will eat or if I want to buy something for myself'.[55]

In households where there was a male head, either actually living under one roof or living away from home due to work related activities, women had limited decision-making power. In the first group of households, women had little to no decision

---

[55] The last kind of households where all decisions were made by women are single women or widowers household.

making power and their husband made all the decisions. In the second group, women had some form of decision making power, even though it were decisions about small matters. Only those women who lived without a husband (either he died or they chose to stay separated), had all the decision making power on all matters concerning their household. We can conclude that if there was a male head of the household he had most of the decision-making power and he was in a position to give his wife some power to make her own decisions. The power women had thus depended on the power 'granted to them' by men. The habitus of male and female farmers imposed on men the power to make overall decisions and – even if a woman can take these decisions together with her husband – it is seen as natural that it is the husband who grants her this power and not the other way around. Even the chairman of Rianjagi ascribes to this gender regime, by giving women the opportunity to become included within the economy and trying to give them more power by providing them with work.

7.6.4 Control of assets

Besides decision making power, farmers were also asked about who controlled which assets within the household. We can make a similar division between three different groups. First, there are households where all assets are controlled by men. Women in these households had little or no power to decide about these assets. This is seen in almost all households as a norm, because men owned land and therefore owned everything on it, or because he was the head of the household. Not only did men look at it this way, women did too, except for some female farmer: she tried to send her children to school by using her own money that she got from casual labour. However, in many households women did not own money they earned themselves. Like male farmer said: 'my wife does not own anything, so where would she got the money from?' This meant that even if she would sell bananas which she harvested herself, the revenues could not be hers, because the bananas grew on the land of the man and therefore he also owned whatever profit would come from selling bananas.

In the second group households, women had control over certain categories of assets. Although land was owned by men, women still had a form of power over those assets belonging to the household and situated on the man's land. For example, a female farmer of Kithungururu said: 'My husband is the owner of the land, but the cattle is ours and even the sheep'. Often livestock that was more valuable, like sheep, was controlled by men, and she was aware of this and therefore said that 'even the sheep' was hers. It was her husband who gave her the power to control this asset together. Finally there is also a third group of households, consisting of single women and widows, who controlled all assets.

Overall, men are in control of most or every asset within the household. Men have power to control these assets because they own the land. However, in most households women also gained some control over some assets. Often, these assets are of little value, like chicken, or when it concerns assets of more value they have shared control over these assets. In all cases, it was the man who decided if his wife could have control over assets. Only single women or widows had control over all or almost all their assets. We can again conclude it is the male head of the households who has the power to control assets or to give power to their wife to control certain assets alone or together. Both men and women ascribed to this habitus.

7.6.5 Division of labour

Concerning the division of labour within the household, respondents were asked to register their daily programme: and what they did on the farm, in the house and other forms of activities. Only two categories are made between households. In the first group, women did most of the work in the house and at the farm. In the second group, tasks were divided between household members. The difference between these two groups refers to how tasks are divided on the farm, because in all households without any exception, women were responsible for household tasks. Only in certain circumstances a man would do some household tasks, like in case the wife was sick. Male farmer of Rianjagi says the following about this:

> I think the tasks are divided equally, because everyone has tasks to do. My wife does the subsistence farming, maize and beans. I am in charge of the cash crops. My wife also does the cow that is her responsibility. My work is not a lot, but my wife also does not do a lot, only when she wants. The household, my wife does that, that is the work for women.

He was not aware of the time his wife was spending on housework chores and he thought it was normal that she did take charge of activities. His wife agreed with her husband: 'Even my husband does some work and in the farm we do an equal amount of work'. When asking if this was the same for the household she responded, 'In the household he cannot help, because he cannot cook'.

Household tasks in all households thus depended fully and exclusively on women and whether tasks on the farm were divided between men and women depends on men's decisions. Even though a woman could complain about the division of labour it was not up to her to decide if her husband helped on the farm or in the household. Some women were aware of the amount of work they did when they compared it to what their husband delivers. Others perceived it as normal that household tasks were done by women and that outside the household they had to do at least half of the work. The power to divide labour rests for most part with men, and to a large extent it was decided through social norms regarding who was supposed to do what in the society. It was apparent that the habitus of both male and female farmers imposed women to do most of the work in and around the house. Note that women themselves also maintained this habitus: no woman questioned it. Even though they complained about men not doing enough, they only referred to men not doing enough on the farm.

In some households, women were aware of the existing unequal power relations within their family. However, it was difficult for them to change this because they did not have the power and the dominant discourse perceived men to be in power within the household. This dominant discourse is also reinforced through inheritance law, which favours land ownership men. Not only men, but also women perceive it as a social norm that male heads of the household were the ones who maintain most power. This is almost opposite to what both male and female farmers said about the division of power within the cooperative that could be adjusted in the case Rianjagi.

7.7 Gender interactions between the cooperative field and the household field

In the previous sections we discussed how gender relations were structured within the households of both Rianjagi and Kithungururu farmers. There were no major differences registered, while at the cooperative level there was indeed a substantial difference in gender relations between both cooperatives: Women at Rianjagi were better represented, they felt more represented and they were more positive about women in leadership positions than female farmers in Kithungururu.

The rules of requirements of Rianjagi included a significant larger number of women able to vote and to be elected compared to Kithungururu. Overall, women were more included and had more power in Rianjagi compared to Kithungururu. However, this has not (yet) led to changes in the gender relations within the household of Rianjagi farmers. The position of women within households of Rianjagi remains the same as at Kithungururu. This leaves the question: Why do gender equity programmes or changes in gender relations at the cooperative level not lead to changes in gender relations at the household level? Addressing, this question implies that we have to go back to the definition of gender and power. Understanding these concepts in the context will help to better understand why the gender approach of Rianjagi has not led to a change in gender relation within the household.

The dominant discourse in the household for both Rianjagi and Kithungururu was that the man is the head of the household and therefore he had most of the power. He controlled most assets, decided on the important issues, or – in case the woman had some power – it was granted to her by her husband. The same holds for division of labour. The dominant discourse is one where women do all the household tasks and besides this an equal or sometimes larger share of the tasks outside the household. As long as this discourse is not addressed, it will be difficult that changing power relations in the cooperative will automatically lead to changing gender relations within the household. As long as the dominant discourse is not addressed in both fields, it is difficult to change power relations in all fields.

At Rianjagi, female farmers were given a change to become active member (e.g. including three women within the management committee), but also by allowing them more income-generating activities. This was done with the intention of trying to change the perception of women within the cooperative. To say it bluntly: from being of no use to adding value to the cooperative and becoming respected members of the cooperative. The cooperative management committee and specifically the chair person, tried to influence the dominant discourse that men are more important members of society and that they need to be in control and have most of the power. However, this dominant discourse is not only constructed in the field of the cooperative. What we have seen in this chapter is that in the field of the household, most men and women still ascribe to this discourse. Social norms and perceptions perceive men as head of the household being in charge of decisions and in control of assets. Whenever a woman did not wanted to ascribe to this discourse, she had only limited power to do so. The gender discourse and power of the dominant class restricts her from exercising control.

The gender policy of Rianjagi was in most part focussed on including women within the cooperative, e.g. the public domain of the economy. By giving women their own means of income it was thought she would be seen as a person who contributed to the household. But it became rapidly apparent that women already do a lot of work on the farm and contribute most to coffee production, however, they gain no control over the money they earned, because men controlled this flow. As one farmer said: 'it is my land and my wife did not bring anything to the land when we got married, therefore everything that she brought to his land would automatically become mine'. Inclusion into the economy does only change the position of women in the public domain but not in the private domain, because the dominant gender discourse is not challenged. Most of the lives of farmers take place within their households and families, and gender relations within the household were not challenged. Even though Rianjagi accepted three women in the management committee who held influential positions, this did not change the perception regarding men or women within the households, because these perception were never questioned.

For changing gender relations, it is important to change the dominant discourse. Without questioning the gender discourse women can gain some power in one field through economic inclusion, but in society in general the gender discourse does not change.

7.8 Conclusions

We analysed the gender approach of a Utz certified cooperative and discussed how gender equity was addressed, looking at gender relations in the Utz certified coffee cooperative Rianjagi in Kenya, in comparison with gender relations in an non certified coffee cooperative, Kithungururu. As explained, there are broadly speaking two major gender discourses: the WID and GAD discourse. The WID discourse focuses on women and including them into the economy to empower them and adjust gender relations. The GAD discourse takes a more holistic approach to gender and looks at gender relations in both public and private domains, including the power relations between and amongst men and women. The focus of Utz gender approach can be placed within the WID discourse. It includes women within the economy and giving them equal rights in the workplace. This raises questions concerning the construction of gender relations and especially how the private domain of the household can be influenced when attention is only given to the public domain, i.e. inclusion in the cooperative. This approach does not fundamentally address power relations or understands the social construction of gender.

The focus on including women within the economy in Rianjagi cooperative did result in women becoming more involved in cooperative affairs. Since women generally produce less kilos of coffee, and Rianjagi requested a significantly lower amount of produced coffee as a requirement for active participation, women had more opportunities in this cooperative. The management committee consisted of three women and twice as much women could join general meetings and vote for new committee members. Although the relatively low required amount of produced kilos was not part of the gender approach, it made a huge difference in representation of women within the cooperative. The gender approach of Rianjagi was focussed on bringing women into the management committee and had the intention of creating income-generating activities for women. The fact that women were part of the management committee positively changed the perception that women had about their position within the cooperative. However, the intention of creating income generating activities for women could become problematic. As the chairperson of Rianjagi already explained and became apparent in our field research, women already have a heavy workload: they do a lot of work and creating more work does not address power relations nor would it change power relations. Not addressing power relations and only focussing on creating equal opportunities for women within the public domain was exactly the criticism that the WID approach received. Equity is not creating the same opportunities in life as men; gender equity requires recognising the differences in gender, power relations and needs.

What became apparent is that the dominant discourse perceived men as being the most important person within the household and the habitus of both male and female farmers, imposed most of the power to men in society and especially to men within the household. It is important to explicitly state that both men and women construct these power relations. It is not the case that women are a victim of the discourse; they also construct the discourse. This unequal power balance cannot be addressed by involving women into income-generating activities or by giving some women an position within the management committee. Even while significantly more women were involved within the cooperative of Rianjagi this did not lead to major difference in gender relations within the farm-households. Private gender relations remained the same in Rianjagi compared to farm-households of Kithunguruu.

Our field research confirms that the gender approach promoted by the Utz certified coffee cooperative Rianjagi focuses more on including women within the public domain, and does not lead to changing in gender relations in the private domain of the household. Since gender is socially constructed in all domains of the society – whether it is the economy, law or the family – the dominant discourse about gender determines gender relations across society. Both men and women are part of this discourse. To achieve gender equity, as is one of the stated objective of Utz, the dominant discourse on gender relations needs to be discussed with both male and female farmers. The dominant discourse needs to change before women can be empowered in the public as well as in the private domain, in order to finally achieve gender equity.

References

Bechetti, L. and M. Costantino (2008). The effects of Fair Trade on affiliated producers: an impact analysis on Kenyan farmers. *World Development* 36(5): 823-842.

Bourdieu, P. (1977). *Outline of a theory of practice.* Cambridge, UK: Cambridge University Press.

Bourdieu, P. (1990). The logic of practice. Stanford, CA, USA: Stanford University Press.

Brown, A.M. (2007). WID and GAD in Dar es Salaam, Tanzania: reappraising gender planning approaches in theory and practice. *Journal of Women, Politics & Policy* 28(2): 57-83.

Butler, J. (1999). *Gender trouble: feminism and the subversion of identity.* New York, NY, USA: Routledge.

Kithungururu Farmers Co-operative Society Ltd. (2005). Kithungururu Farmers Co-operative Society Limited by-law C.S. NO.8812.

Rianjagi Farmers Cooperative Society Ltd. (2008). Rianjagi Farmers Cooperative Society Limited by-laws C.S. NO 8491.

Cartier, C. and J. Rothenberg-Aalami (1999). Empowering the 'victim'? Gender, development, and women in China under reform. *Journal of Geography* 98(6): 283-294.

Chambers, A. (1996). *Definition of gender equity.* Available at: http://www2.edc.org/womensequity/edequity96/0371.html.

Davis, K., M. Evans and J. Lorber (2006). *Handbook of Gender and Women's Studies.* London, UK: SAGE Publications Ltd.

Erikson, T.H. (2001). *Small places, large issues an introduction to social and cultural anthropology.* London, UK: Pluto Press.

Foucault, M. (1980). *Power/knowledge.* New York, NY, USA: Pantheon.

Hopkins, R. (2000). *Impact assessment study of Oxfam Fair Trade.* London, UK: Oxfam.

Howell, R.W. (1989). *Commonalities among women superintendents in Texas. PhD thesis.* Denton, TX, USA: University of North Texas.

Human Right Watch (2003). Double Standards: Women's Property Rights Violation in Kenya. *Human Right Watch* 15(5A): 1-51.

Kabeer, N. (1994). *Reversed realities: gender hierarchies in development thought.* London, UK: Verso.

Kabeer, N. (1999). Resources, agency, achievements: reflections on measurement of women's empowerment. *Development and Change* 30(108): 435-464.

Mayoux, L. (2001). *Impact assessment of Fair Trade and ethical enterprise development.* Available at: http://tinyurl.com/nfx8s97.

Moore, H.L. (1994). *A passion for difference.* Bloomington, IN, USA: Indiana University Press.

Rathgeber, E.M. (1990). WID, WAD, GAD: trends in research and practice. *The Journal of Developing Areas* 24(4): 489-502.

Razavi, S. and C. Miller (1995). *From WID to GAD: conceptual shifts in the women and development discourse.* Geneva, Switzerland: UNRISD Occasional Paper.

Reeves, H. and S. Baden (2000). *Gender and development: concepts and definitions*. Brighton, UK: Institute of Development Studies University of Sussex.

Ruben, R. (2009). *The impact of Fair Trade*. Wageningen, the Netherlands: Wageningen Academic Publishers.

Smith, E.R. and D.M. Mackie (2000). *Social Psychology*. London, UK: Psychology Press.

Utz Kapeh (2010). *Utz certified. Good inside code of conduct for coffee*. Amsterdam, the Netherlands: Utz Kapeh Foundation. Available at: http://tinyurl.com/kwda8jk.

Van Dooren, C. (2005). Rice value chain analysis 'Each life starts with a little seed'. Report for IFAT/EFTA/FLO. Available at: http://tinyurl.com/l3lptlz.

Villarreal, A. (1994). *Yielding and wielding: power, subordination and gender identity the context of a Mexican development project, rural development*. Wageningen, the Netherlands: Agricultural University Wageningen.

Chapter 8

Back to the birthplace of the bean: women's bargaining position and trust in Ethiopian coffee cooperatives

Annemarie Groot Kormelinck
For correspondence: annemarie.grootkormelinck@wur.nl

8.1 Introduction

Recent years have witnessed a renewed interest in the role of agriculture in international development. The importance of linking smallholder farmers to agri-food markets, and the need for inclusive value chains in order to overcome poverty and to sustainably feed the world, are now widely acknowledged among international organisations and at the highest policy levels (FAO, 2009; World Bank, 2011). Agricultural cooperatives are increasingly seen as key to the development of smallholder agriculture.[56] Such cooperatives can enable small-scale producers to better take advantage of opportunities offered in the market place and can improve members' bargaining position in decision-making processes. Moreover, agricultural cooperatives can be instrumental in addressing some of the challenges facing these smallholder farmers, such as galvanising collective action to benefit from economies of scale and efficiency gains along value chains. Realising this potential requires that agricultural cooperatives perform well (Bernard and Spielman, 2008; World Bank 2007).

Critical for well-performing cooperative institutions, such as agricultural cooperatives, are social capital dimensions, such as institutional trust, cooperation and reciprocity. These can function as bonding elements to reduce transaction costs and enhance coordination, thus contributing to the performance of cooperatives (James and Sykuta, 2005; Valentinov, 2004). Above all, institutional trust is important for successful cooperation and effectiveness in organisations: it conveys real economic advantages

---

[56] For example, the Food and Agriculture Organization of the United Nations, the International Fund for Agricultural Development and the World Food Programme have joined forces to promote rural organisations, including agricultural cooperatives, to ensure that they remain high on the international development agenda.

Ruerd Ruben and Paul Hoebink (eds.) **Coffee certification in East Africa**
DOI 10.3920/978-90-8686-805-6_8, © Wageningen Academic Publishers 2015

to cooperatives and is crucial for the development of long-term cooperative behaviour (Bhuyan, 2007; Lewicki, 2006; Pruitt and Kimmel, 1977).

Cooperatives can also be a powerful mechanism for supporting marginalised groups, such as women. In many regions of the developing world, women represent the majority of farmers (FAO, 2009; World Bank, 2011), and, especially in rural areas, they are among the poorest and most vulnerable people (IFAD, 2012a; Prakash 2003). Nonetheless, most research on (rural) cooperatives neglects the gender perspective, despite the fact that studies have shown that gender equality and women's empowerment are essential for economic growth. Furthermore, excluding women can worsen power relationships, eventually leading to a further disempowerment of women. This necessitates recognition of the key role that women, along with men, play in agriculture (Agarwal, 2001; IFAD, 2012a; Mayoux and Mackie, 2007).

This chapter offers an elaborated theoretical framework and an empirical assessment of the role of gender relations, bargaining power and trust within Ethiopian coffee cooperatives. Through a survey, three behavioural experiments, and semi-structured interviews, data is collected from male and female member households of two high- and two low-performing Ethiopian coffee cooperatives.[57]

8.2 Conceptual framework

The conceptual framework used in this study is based on the key concepts of intra- and extra-household bargaining power and institutional trust (in the cooperative), that are considered of fundamental importance to understand the role and potential of female participation for enhancing cooperative performance and household welfare.

8.2.1 Bargaining positions

Our study of gender perspective focuses on the bargaining positions of men and women. Bargaining positions influence a person's ability to change rules, norms, perceptions and endowments (Agarwal, 1994, 1997; Quisumbing, 2003; World Bank, 2007). In addition, understanding differences in preferences and resource allocation within household bargaining is critical if policymakers are to improve livelihoods (Agarwal, 1994; Frankenberg and Thomas, 2001).

Bargaining positions are addressed here using a collective bargaining model of the household. Such a model takes as starting point the possibility that different

---

[57] This chapter has initially been published for the tenth anniversary of the Prince Claus Chair (Foeken *et al.*, 2014). It is based on Ms Groot Kormelinck's Master thesis (Groot Kormelinck, 2010), which was written for the Radboud University Nijmegen. Annemarie Groot Kormelinck's thesis received the thesis prize of the Gerrit Huizer Foundation and was awarded the runner-up prize of the Cheetah Challenge thesis competition. Ms Groot Kormelinck currently works as researcher and advisor on farmers organisations and value chain development for the Centre for Development Innovation (CDI) and Management Studies group, both part of Wageningen University and Research Centre.

household members have different preference orderings, thereby challenging the more traditional unitary models that treat the household as a 'black box' (Adam *et al.*, 2011; Agarwal, 1997; Kabeer, 1995). If preferences differ between husbands and wives, the final allocation of resources and the production mix will reflect the distribution of bargaining power (Agarwal, 1994, 1997; De la Brière *et al.*, 2000; Kabeer, 1995; Lim *et al,*. 2007).

Investigating gender bargaining relations should go beyond focusing on intra-household bargaining only; it should also look at extra-household bargaining. Quisumbing (2003) reports that membership in organisations can improve bargaining positions by, for example, influencing a person's power to affect household decisions. Research by Holvoet (2005) showed that women with certain positions outside the home – in this case micro-finance institutions – had stronger decision-making power within the household. Similar evidence has been reported by Agarwal (1994, 1997) and Kabeer (1995).[58]

The study, therefore, focuses on both the intra- and extra-household bargaining domains, zooming in on three levels in particular: the household level, the (agricultural) production level and the (coffee) cooperative level. This is measured using four main indicators: (1) a person's 'threat point', which consists of the range of options a person has when a cooperation breaks down (Agarwal, 1997; Kabeer, 1995); (2) ownership of income and assets; (3) decision-making processes; and (4) the task division between spouses. The choice of these four indicators is based on the relevance to the research topic, as well as their prevalence in existing research.[59]

8.2.2 Institutional trust

Institutional trust refers to the trust people have in institutions or organisations (Dakhli and De Clercq, 2004) and is described by James and Sykuta (2005) as 'trust among an organisation's members existing within or impacted by the organisational setting'. Research results from the USA indicate that norms of equality and homogeneity are key correlates of institutional trust in agricultural cooperatives and show that an open membership policy is positively correlated with perceived trust among all members (James and Sykuta, 2005).

From an economic viewpoint, institutional trust has the ability to facilitate inter- and intra-organisational exchanges at relatively low cost (Dakhli and de Clercq, 2004). For instance, trust lowers market transecting and bureaucratic costs, thus facilitating cooperation and coordination within organisations. In addition, organisations

---

[58] According to Sen (1987), women's participation in external gainful employment improves their bargaining position within the household, associated with greater gender equality in the distribution of household resources (see also Kabeer, 1995).

[59] See for instance Agarwal (1997), Bernard and Spielman (2008), Lim *et al.* (2007) and Quisumbing and Maluccio (2003).

exhibiting greater levels of trust among members are likely to operate more efficiently than organisations with lower levels of trust, other things being equal (James and Sykuta, 2005). Given that cooperatives are members-owned and members-controlled and operate for their members' benefit, institutional trust in a cooperative refers to members' trust in both the cooperative and their fellow members.

The measurement of institutional trust in this study is based on the specific layers and characteristics that exist in the agricultural cooperatives concerned. The selected Sidama coffee cooperatives operate with a board and various committees and organise a bi-annual General Assembly. As a result, institutional trust is operationalised as trust in (1) board members, (2) committee members, (3) the General Assembly, and (4) fellow members. Since institutional trust not only concerns persons, trust is also measured in terms of (5) rules of the cooperative, (6) information and (7) services provided by the cooperative.

8.3 Ethiopian context

Fieldwork was conducted in the period January-April 2010 in rural Ethiopia, a context highly relevant for investigating gender bargaining relations and institutional trust in agricultural cooperatives. Agriculture is the backbone of the Ethiopian economy, and the country is characterised by its great potential for agricultural development (see e.g. CSA, 2005; Petit, 2007; World Bank, 2007). With an agricultural growth rate of 10%, the agricultural sector has contributed considerably to the strong economic progress that Ethiopia has made since 2007 (IFAD, 2012b). Hence, agriculture is earmarked to play an important role in achieving sustainable economic growth. The Ethiopian government has allocated 10% of its national budget to rural development, and it has placed emphasis on agricultural growth in its Growth and transformation plan for 2010-2015 (FDRE, 2012; IFAD, 2012b).[60] Furthermore, the Ethiopian government has developed its Agricultural cooperatives sector development strategy 2012-2016 (FDRE, 2012), in which agricultural cooperatives are assigned a key role as facilitators of rural socio-economic development.

Nonetheless, Ethiopia's agricultural cooperatives are currently not living up to their potential. According to Bernard *et al.* (2007) and Francesconi (2008), Ethiopian cooperatives are characterised by exclusion of the poor, low membership, lack of trust and difficulties in obtaining bargaining power. Although the regulations governing Ethiopian cooperatives have no means to exclude particular groups, Frank (1999) and Bernard and Spielman (2008) report that female membership in Ethiopian cooperatives is low and that women face various constraints related to their bargaining position at the cooperative level.

---

[60] In this strategic plan, the Ethiopian government has seven strategic objectives, among which are the following: sustaining equitable economic growth, maintaining growth focused on agriculture and rural areas, and promoting empowerment of women and young people (IFAD, 2012b).

The present study focuses on coffee cooperatives. Ethiopia is the birthplace of the coffee bean, and the country is the largest coffee producer and exporter in Africa (Francesconi, 2008; Petit 2007; World Bank, 2007). In addition, coffee is the most important crop in Ethiopian agriculture – while at the same time, Ethiopian coffee cooperatives are characterised by varied and mixed performance results (Oxfam, 2008).

The coffee cooperatives selected for this paper are located in the Sidama region in southern Ethiopia (Figure 8.1), one of the poorest yet most important coffee-producing regions. Coffee is one of the main cash crops in Sidama, and the area is known for its ideal soil type and climatic conditions for the production of Arabica coffee. In addition, almost every household in the region produces coffee and over half of the total population in Sidama directly or indirectly depends on coffee for their livelihoods (CSA, 2005).

At the time of the fieldwork, the Sidama region had 46 coffee cooperatives. These were characterised by a two-tier structure: the cooperatives receive red coffee cherries from their members, process these cherries, and sell them to the Sidamic Coffee Farmers Cooperative Union (SCFCU) as dried coffee. SCFCU is the umbrella organisation of the Sidama coffee cooperatives and is the second largest coffee-producing union in Ethiopia.

8.4 Research methods

Since institutional trust is assumed to be related to the performance of cooperative organisations, the two strongest and two weakest performing Sidama coffee

Figure 8.1. Location of cooperatives in Sidama region, Ethiopia.

cooperatives were selected.[61] This selection was based on different economic and non-economic indicators[62] collected during interviews with officials and board members at cooperative, district and regional levels.

Between 50 and 60 member households per cooperative were selected using random stratified sampling (i.e. both male and female members were randomly selected from the members' lists of the four cooperatives), with an aggregated number of 232 member households. Considering the importance of measuring gender bargaining relations in this research, both male and female member households were part of the sample. Male member households are households in which the male is the primary member of the cooperative, accompanied by the man's spouse.[63] In female member households, the woman is the primary cooperative member. This group consists of female-headed households (widows) and male-headed households in which the man works for the government or cooperative (and therefore cannot be the primary cooperative member).

Looking at the characteristics of the member households of the two high-performing and the two low-performing cooperatives, there were statistically significant differences in the socio-economic conditions of the member households (Groot Kormelinck, 2010). More specifically, member households of the two high-performing cooperatives had significantly more assets (machinery and household goods) and a higher farm and non-farm income (whether calculated per adult, per hectare or per household member) than member households of the low-performing cooperatives.

Three different research methods were employed. First, a survey was undertaken among the 232 member households. Data were collected on individual and household characteristics, on income and (coffee) production variables, on intra- and extra-household bargaining, and on variables measuring levels of trust, participation, commitment and satisfaction with the cooperative. Second, three different 'one-off' economic experiments were conducted to investigate mechanisms of trust and cooperative behaviour of individual cooperative members: the Trust Game, the Dictator Game and the Voluntary Contribution Mechanism (VCM) Game (see Annex A.1) These were executed among 64 randomly selected male and female members who took part in the survey. Third, 16 semi-structured interviews were held with key informants, i.e. male members and their spouses, and female members. These key informant interviews served to obtain more qualitative and in-depth knowledge about

---

[61] These are denoted below as high-performing and low-performing cooperatives, respectively.

[62] Economic indicators were total sales, net profit and dividends of the cooperative for 2009 and 2010. Non-economic indicators were quantity and quality of coffee delivered, quality of internal governance, and services that cooperatives offer, all of which were annually measured and ranked by the Sidamic Coffee Farmers Cooperative Union.

[63] Officially, households, not individuals, are members of the cooperatives. In practice, in male-headed households, only the male heads are approached by the cooperatives and asked to participate. Only when the male head works for the cooperative or for the government, can the female spouse take his place.

Table 8.1. Overview of respondents by cooperative and by gender.

Method	Total	Low-performing cooperatives				High-performing cooperatives			
		Cooperative 1		Cooperative 2		Cooperative 3		Cooperative 4	
		Male[1]	Female	Male	Female	Male	Female	Male	Female
Survey	232	42+36	18	43+41	16	43+26	13	35+29	22
Games	64	8	8	8	8	8	8	8	8
Interviews	16	2+2	2	2+2	2	2+2	2	2+2	2

[1] The second number in the male members' columns refer to the female spouses in male member households that were included in the survey and the interviews.

concepts and relations between bargaining positions and trust. Table 8.1 presents an overview of the number of respondents for each method.[64]

8.5 Results

This part presents results from the field survey and the experiments for male and female participants and discusses the implications for differences in cooperative performance.

8.5.1 Women's bargaining positions

This section zooms in on the gender equity perspective by examining women's bargaining positions in the household, in agricultural production and in the coffee cooperative. Table 8.2 contains the results on the four bargaining position variables. The table shows indexes as constructed for the four indicators, which are composed of different variables.[65] Considering the bargaining scoring system (1=male, 2=female, 3=jointly),[66] a higher score in the table indicates a stronger position of women in the household bargaining process *vis-à-vis* their husbands.

Concerning women's threat point, when controlled for the situation of female-headed households, not much difference can be seen between (married) female members and spouses of male members. Both groups of women brought no land and almost equally few livestock into marriage. Assets upon divorce are equally divided because

---

[64] For a more detailed account of the research design and methodology, see Groot Kormelinck (2010).

[65] See Annex A.2 for an overview of the indexes.

[66] These are re-grouped categories. Combinations of answers indicating that tasks or decisions were made by spouses with others, for example men with children or women with daughters, were recorded to respectively 1 or 2. This results in mean scores, whereby a higher score represents a stronger bargaining position for women.

Table 8.2. Descriptive statistics on bargaining relations in the household.[1]

	Husband and spouse in male member households[2]	Female member households		
		Total	Married	Widow
	(a)	(b)	(c)	(d)
1. Threat point				
Assets into marriage				
Tropical livestock index	0.21	0.10	0.18 [cd]	0.05 [cd]
Assets upon divorce (1=husband, 2=wife, 3=jointly)				
Assets upon divorce	2.90 [ab]	2.77 [ab]	2.89 [cd]	2.68 [cd]
Assets upon death (0=head's relatives, 1= surviving spouse)				
Index assets death	1.00 [ab]	0.94 [ab]	1.00 [cd]	0.90 [cd]
2. Ownership assets and finances (1=husband, 2=wife, 3=jointly)				
Index ownership assets	2.94 [ac ab]	2.39 [ab]	3.00 [ac cd]	2.00 [cd]
Index ownership finances	1.52 [ac ab]	1.97 [ab]	1.94 [ac]	2.00
3. Task division in household (1=husband, 2=wife, 3=jointly)				
Index task household	2.00	1.98	1.96	1.99
Index task production	1.36 [ac ab]	1.95 [ab]	1.90 [ac]	2.00
Index task cooperative	1.15 [ac ab]	2.01 [ab]	2.02 [ac]	2.00
4. Decision-making in household (1=husband, 2=wife, 3=jointly)				
Index household decisions	1.70 [ac ab]	1.97 [ab]	1.91 [ac]	2.00
Index production decisions	1.36 [ac ab]	1.85 [ab]	1.64 [ac cd]	2.00 [cd]
Index cooperative decisions	1.40 [ac ab]	2.04 [ab]	2.11 [ac]	2.00

[1] Superscripts refer to significant pairwise differences in T-tests (two-sided). Significant differences in bargaining position between spouses in male member households (column (a)) and married female members (column (c)) are referred to as *ac*. Widowed female members have no spouse to bargain with and hence score 2.00 on all variables.

[2] The figures in column (a) are the bargaining outcomes between the male-head and his wife (i.e. according to both spouses' perceptions). The higher the score, the stronger the bargaining position for the female spouse.

of legal entitlements, while cultural norms determine that assets upon death will go to the surviving partner, as confirmed by interviews and literature sources.[67] This outcome is not surprising, given that an increased bargaining position gained through female cooperative membership and participation cannot reinforce the assets already brought into marriage, or the settlements for divorce and death, which are mainly culturally determined.

The findings regarding asset and finance disposition show a different pattern. Regarding all variables measured for this indicator – and especially for financial

---

[67] See for example Frank (1999) and Quisumbing and Maluccio (2003).

resources – female members have a significantly stronger bargaining position than spouses of male members. This means that these female members have more ownership and better access and control over assets and financial resources within the marriage compared with spouses of male members.

The task division between partners in the household shows only minor differences in the household domain, indicating that women perform all tasks in all household categories. Interviews revealed that women's role in household tasks is culturally determined, as can also be found in existing literature.[68] This role is different from women's involvement in production and cooperative tasks: the indexes for production and cooperative tasks show that female members reported a (strongly significant) higher involvement in the execution of coffee (and other crops') production and in tasks related to the cooperative domain when compared with spouses of male members.

The findings regarding decision-making processes between spouses coincide with task division patterns. Female members have a significantly stronger participation in household, production and cooperative decisions than their peers in male member households. The difference is strongest for decision-making in the cooperatives, indicating that female membership in the cooperatives increases their involvement in the decision-making process related to production and cooperative affairs.

From the viewpoint of male members' bargaining position (column (a)), the low scores indicate that male members have a stronger bargaining position than their spouses and female members. Interviews, survey statements and regression analyses on factors impacting bargaining positions demonstrate that bargaining aspects are influenced by cultural aspects, such as religious and social norms, in which men in this rural Ethiopian setting are the dominant sex.[69]

Interview results also revealed that most women – especially female members – felt constrained in their bargaining position in relation to their husbands. Some women, for instance, indicated that they would like to have a stronger voice in decisions about production and the cooperative and that they aspired to more equal ownership of finances and assets. According to one of them, '[i]t is usually the man who takes decisions, so we have less power. If I can make more production and cooperative decisions, it will contribute to the development of our household.'

Yet, not all women advocated a stronger bargaining position *vis-à-vis* their husbands. Some of the spouses of male members stated that it is normal for them to have a weaker position compared with their husband, thereby seemingly accepting their

---

[68] See for example Frank (1999) and Bernard and Spielman (2008).

[69] For instance, regression results show that ethnicity is a determining factor for finance disposition in marriage and that religion is related to women's involvement in production and cooperative tasks. See Groot Kormelinck (2010) for more detailed information. Similar results have been reported by studies of Sen (1987), Agarwal (1994, 1997), Frankenberg and Thomas (2001) and Quisumbing and Maluccio (2003).

situation.[70] Contrary to many spouses of male members, female members (from male-headed households) clearly indicated that they increasingly dared to advocate for a stronger bargaining position. They claimed that – with a higher involvement in the production and cooperative domain – they knew better what was going on and, as a result, dared to advocate for a stronger position.

8.5.2 Trust in Ethiopian coffee cooperatives

This section concentrates on the (agricultural) development part of the study by elaborating on trust results of the cooperatives' member households. Considering that institutional trust is important for the functioning of agricultural cooperatives, it can be assumed that member households of the high-performing cooperatives in this research exhibit higher levels of institutional trust than their peers in the low-performing cooperatives. Table 8.3 presents the results of indicators related to institutional trust, as measured through the survey and the games.

The three columns under performance in Table 8.3 show trust results compared for the low- and high-performing cooperatives. These results indicate that members of high-performing cooperatives indeed have (strongly significantly) more stated trust in their cooperative – as measured in the survey (index institutional trust). Results of the Trust Game and VCM Game reveal that members of high-performing cooperatives also exhibit higher levels of trust and reciprocal and cooperative/investing behaviour than their peers in low-performing cooperatives.[71] Nevertheless, a causal relationship between high levels of institutional trust and a good cooperative performance cannot be made.[72]

In addition to the examination of trust differences between high- and low-performing cooperatives, it is interesting to make assumptions on optional gender differences in trust in cooperatives. A relation between bargaining relations and institutional trust remains largely unexplored in the literature, although research by Brewer (1981) and Tyler and Lind (1992) provides some insights by stating that membership in organisations can provide an important basis for trust. Given the low overall membership of female members in the Sidama cooperatives and the anticipated lower bargaining position of female members and spouses in these cooperatives, it can be expected that male members have the highest levels of institutional trust, followed by respectively female members and spouses of male members.

---

[70] Similar results were found by Frank (1999), Prakash (2003) and Lim *et al.* (2007).

[71] This is in line with findings in earlier studies, e.g. Dakhli and De Clercq (2004) and James and Sykuta (2005).

[72] It can be argued that either higher levels of institutional trust have led to a high performance of these cooperatives or the other way around. In addition, given that members of the high-performing cooperatives reported better socio-economic conditions, higher performance and trust levels can also be related to better socio-economic circumstances in which the cooperative members operate. This was not the focus of the study but would be an interesting topic for future research.

Table 8.3. Descriptive statistics of the survey and experiments.

Variables	Male member households			Female member households	
Stated trust (survey)	Male (a)	Spouse (b)	Total	Married (d)	Widow (e)
Institutional trust[1] (Index) (1-5)	3.48[ad]	3.46[bd]	3.47	3.91[de ad bd]	3.19[de]

	Performance			Gender		
	Low	High	Sig.[2,3]	Male	Female	Sig.[2,4]
Stated trust (survey) (n)	119	113		163	69	
Institutional trust (Index) (1-5)	3.06	3.86	***	See above		
Cooperativeness (VCM) (n)[5]	64	64		96	32	
Sent to cooperative (1-10 ETB)[6]	2.26	3.30	***	2.43	4.15	***
Average amount gained per participant	12.23	13.22	***	13.46	11.99	***
Trust behaviour (trust game)[7] (n)	32	32		32	32	
Sent (1-10 ETB)	1.78	2.45	**	1.95	2.28	
Sent to male (1-10 ETB)	1.78	2.56	**	2.00	2.34	
Sent to female (1-10 ETB)	1.78	2.34	**	1.91	2.22	
Reciprocity (trust game)[8] (n)	32	32		32	32	
Return ratio (1-10 ETB)	0.29	0.37	**	0.29	0.36	*
Return ratio to male (1-10 ETB)	0.26	0.41	**	0.30	0.37	
Return ratio to female (1-10 ETB)	0.31	0.33		0.28	0.35	
Altruism (dictator game)[7] (n)	32	32		32	32	
Sent (1-10 ETB)	0.91	3.02	***	1.83	2.09	
Sent to male (1-10 ETB)	0.94	2.97	***	2.06	1.84	
Sent to female (1-10 ETB)	0.88	3.06	***	1.59	2.34	*

[1] Superscripts refer to significant pairwise differences in T-tests (two-sided).

[2] * significant at 10%; ** significant at 5%; *** significant at 1%.

[3] Sig. tests significant differences between low and high performance.

[4] Sig. tests significant differences between male and female gender.

[5] The number of respondents (n) is higher for the VCM Game than for other games. Results were coupled with Voluntary Contribution Mechanism Game results (n=64) of my co-researcher. These 64 constitute 8 male players per cooperative. See also Annex A.1 for an explanation of the games.

[6] ETB = Ethiopian Birr.

[7] Player *A* behaviour.

[8] Player *B* behaviour.

Survey and game results on gender differences are shown Table 8.3 (under *Gender)*. First, looking at levels of stated trust as measured in the survey (index Institutional trust), female members from male-headed households have significantly more trust than male members, spouses and widowed female members. Second, relating trust to bargaining positions, it is interesting to see that female members exhibit higher levels of trust in the cooperative than spouses of male members. Many interviewees related this to the higher participation of female members in cooperatives. As one female member said:

> I can come here to the cooperative and talk and discuss with other members about the cooperative's affairs. I am involved in this cooperative myself, while spouses only hear information through their husbands. That is why they have a lack of knowledge and information about what is going on.

Comparing male and female member behaviour in the economic experiments, both groups of female members (from male- and female-headed households) were more trusting and reciprocal – although not always significantly (Trust Game) – and invested (strongly significantly) more in the cooperative (VCM Game) than male members. This is in line with some studies looking into gender differences in Trust Game and VCM Game behaviour, but contradicts other studies.[73]

In short, it can be stated that female members (from male-headed households) have higher levels of stated trust than all other groups and that both groups of female members exhibit higher trusting and cooperative behaviour in the experimental situations than male members. For the comparison of female members *vis-à-vis* spouses, these results are in line with Brewer (1981) and Tyler and Lind (1992).

8.6 Discussion

The research findings have implications for the internal organisation of the coffee cooperatives and point to potential welfare effects forthcoming from gender empowerment.

8.6.1 Gender orientation of Ethiopian coffee cooperatives

The results on bargaining positions and institutional trust require a closer examination of the orientation that these cooperatives have towards female inclusion. The four cooperatives had an average female membership of only 2.6%. Although official national and regional cooperative proclamations in Ethiopia make no distinction regarding the gender of cooperative membership (FDRE, 2005), membership is often

---

[73] A considerable quantity of data exists on gender differences in economic experiments, with highly mixed results. The fact that women are more cooperative accords with, for example, Nowell and Tinkler (1994), Sequino *et al.* (1996) and Cadsby and Maynes (1998), but contradicts research of Brown-Kruse and Hummels (1993). The trust results are in line with Eckel and Grossman (1998), Ortmann and Tichy (1999) and Gneezy *et al.* (2003), but partly contradict Chaudhuri and Gangadharan (2002). Based on these mixed results, it seems fair to suggest that gender differences are highly context-specific, as is also concluded in a number of these studies.

related to land ownership and property rights, which in southern Ethiopia are almost always exclusively men's domain.

Male and female members of all four cooperatives indicated that it is always the head of the household – the man – who gets invited to join the cooperative: '[I]t is just because that is how it goes in this area. The husband used to be a member; it has always been that way' (female member). In addition, spouses in male member households are not registered since many cooperative and district officers indicated that 'it makes no sense to also register the spouses' (cooperative board member).

Interviewed members also stated that the four cooperatives had no special regulations to include (more) women, although some interviewees indicated that the Ethiopian government, some cooperatives and higher-level institutions[74] were starting to become more gender-sensitive. For instance, members of the two high-performing cooperatives indicated that their cooperative actively advocated more participation of women:

> [I]n general, we try to include women in the committees, but women often refuse, because of a lack of confidence and because they are not used to it. We try to give them some responsibilities or some small jobs to motivate them' (board member of a high-performing cooperative).

In this context it is also interesting to examine whether high-performing cooperatives are more in favour of strengthening women's bargaining position – in this manner suggesting a potential link between performance and the inclusion of women in cooperatives. Survey results, as summarised in Annex A.3, revealed that bargaining gaps between male and female member households in low-performing cooperatives were (often significantly) greater on all four bargaining position variables than in high-performing cooperatives. In addition, interviews – with district officers, cooperative board members and member households – and personal observations pointed towards more gender-favoured conditions in the high-performing cooperatives. Although this suggests a positive relation between the cooperative's performance and women's bargaining position, the data cannot show a causal relationship between the two variables. Besides, from a gender equity viewpoint, these results should not be received with too much enthusiasm, given the low levels of female membership, and given that many female members indicated that they faced a variety of constraints in their cooperative – as discussed in the following section.

8.6.2 Women's constraints in Ethiopian coffee cooperatives

The results on bargaining positions and institutional trust demand an elaboration on women's participation in the four coffee cooperatives. Interview results showed that female members – despite their higher levels of trusting and cooperative behaviour

---

[74] Coffee-related institutions at district, zonal and regional levels.

compared with male members – were not only restricted in their membership access, but also in their participation in the cooperative. Interviews confirmed that social and cultural norms impact the rural Ethiopian cooperative setting in the sense that the cooperative is regarded as a 'man's domain', influencing attitudes of and towards female members: '[I]t is normal that men are members of the cooperative; women are not supposed to participate here' (male member).

Other constraints that were mentioned in relation to women's participation in the coffee cooperatives were women's lower education, their illiteracy and their lack of knowledge of coffee production and cooperative affairs. For instance, some interviewed members related male membership to better education and opportunities in the past: '[U]sually, women are not educated and they don't participate in these kinds of cooperative activities' (male member); and: 'I did not get a chance to finish my education; I had to get married and work in the household. Therefore, I don't know enough about production and the cooperative – and because of household tasks, I don't have time for it either' (spouse of male member).

In addition, two female members pointed out that they were not regularly informed about the meetings; and if they were, they could often not attend these owing to their household tasks and the children they needed to take care of:

'[W]omen have to perform all household tasks. That keeps them so busy that they usually come too late in the assembly. Then they cannot vote, since they don't know what has been discussed. It is a constraint that men don't face' (male member).

This was confirmed by the survey results, which showed that female members participated significantly less in general assemblies and in voting than male members. Furthermore, multiple interviewees indicated that if women participated in cooperative meetings, they rarely dared to speak and express their opinion, since they formed a small minority and were not used to doing so. Box 8.1 illustrates the constraints that female members face, as outlined by Zem zem, a typical female member.

8.7 Conclusions

This study had two main outcomes. First, female cooperative members appeared to have a stronger bargaining position than spouses of male members. This applied especially to the financial asset disposition and the involvement in tasks and decisions related to cooperative and production affairs. This confirms the conclusion in other studies that women's options outside the household have the potential of improving their bargaining position both within and outside the household.

Second, female members (from male-headed households) appeared to have higher levels of institutional trust than male members and their spouses; and both groups of female members (from male- and female-headed households) showed more

Box 8.1. Zem zem: a typical female member.

Zem zem is a female member of one of the low-performing cooperatives. In addition, she is the female representative of cooperatives in the union in Addis Ababa.

'My dream is to become the first female board member in this cooperative. This is very difficult, because I am a woman. Men are not used to electing a woman. It is not that they don't want to, but more because there has never been a female board member, and because female members are low in number and don't attend assemblies. It is also culture: men don't want their wives to be chosen. However, the situation is changing now. It would change even more if a woman could be elected to show that it works, and that it is possible to choose a woman. Women are also constrained because of their lack of education, so they have few opportunities to do things outside the household or to participate in, for instance, cooperatives.

It is also because of the general attitude here, that it is normal for men to participate and for women to stay at home. I am really trying to change this (…) I have the chance to go out and make myself strong. That way, I can be an example for both male and female members.'

cooperative and trusting behaviour in economic experiments than their male counterparts. This applied in particular to cooperative behaviour as measured in the VCM Game. The higher trust levels of female members *vis-à-vis* spouses of male members was in line with earlier studies, which stated that membership and participation are important conditions for trust.

In conclusion, the findings on bargaining positions seem to work in two ways. First, bargaining results imply that increasing women's outside options – such as in agricultural cooperatives – leads to a stronger bargaining position for these women in their household situation; or put differently: it increases equity in the household. This calls for increased attention to men's and women's preferences and positions in the household in designing future policies and interventions aimed at rural development.

At the same time, the findings on trust indicate that improving women's bargaining positions in the cooperative domain by active membership and participation also contributes to higher levels of trust and cooperation in the cooperative. In this way, this study may stimulate the thinking on how agricultural cooperatives can be improved. Placing women in more equal and participatory cooperative membership processes and positions can ensure an active role in the cooperative rather than being merely spouses of male members. In addition, female inclusion in cooperatives can contribute to an improvement in processes of trust building and, possibly, to improved overall functioning of cooperatives.

References

Adam, C., J. Hoddinott and E. Ligon (2011). *Dynamic intra-household bargaining, matrimonial property law, and suicide in Canada.* CUDARE Working Papers, vol. 1113. Berkeley, CA, USA: University of California.

Agarwal, B. (1994). *A field of one's own, gender and land rights in South Asia.* Cambridge, UK: Cambridge University Press.

Agarwal, B. (1997). *'Bargaining' and gender relations: within and beyond the household.* Washington, DC, USA: International Food Policy Research Institute.

Agarwal, B. (2001). Participatory exclusions, community forestry, and gender: an analysis for South Asia and a conceptual framework. *World Development* 29(10): 1623-1648.

Banerjee, A. and E. Duflo (2009). The experimental approach to development economics. *Annual Review of Economics* 1(1): 151-178.

Berg, J., J. Dickhaut and K. McCabe (1995). Trust, reciprocity and social history. *Games and Economic Behavior* 10: 122-142.

Bernard, T. and D.J. Spielman (2008). *Mobilizing rural institutions for sustainable livelihoods and equitable development. A case study of agricultural marketing and smallholder cooperatives in Ethiopia.* Addis Ababa, Ethiopia: IFPRI (International Food Policy Research Institute).

Bernard, T., E.Z. Gabre-Madhin and A.S. Taffesse (2007). *Smallholders' commercialization through cooperatives: a diagnostic for Ethiopia.* IFPRI Discussion Paper no. 00722, Washington, DC, USA: IFPRI (International Food Policy Research Institute).

Bhuyan, S. (2007). The 'people' factor in cooperatives: an analysis of members' attitudes and behavior. *Canadian Journal of Agricultural Economics* 55(3): 275-298.

Brewer, M.B. (1981). Ethnocentrism and its role in interpersonal trust. In: M.B. Brewer and B.E. Collins (eds.) *Scientific Inquiry and the Social Sciences.* New York, NY, USA: Jossey-Bass, pp. 345-359.

Brown-Kruse, J. and D. Hummels (1993). Gender effects in laboratory public goods contribution: do individuals put their money where their mouth is? *Journal of Economic Behavior and Organization* 22: 255-267.

Cadsby, C.B. and E. Maynes (1998). Gender and free riding in a threshold public goods game: experimental evidence. *Journal of Economic Behavior and Organization* 34(4): 603-620.

Carpenter, J.P. (2002). Measuring social capital: adding field experimental methods to the analytical toolbox. In: J. Isham, T. Kelly and S. Ramaswamy (eds.) *Social capital and economic development: well-being in developing countries.* Cheltenham, UK: Edgar Elgar, pp. 119-138.

Carpenter, J.P., A. Daniere and L. Takahashi (2004). Social capital and trust in South-East Asian cities. *Urban studies* 41(4): 853-874.

Chaudhuri, A. and L. Gangadharan (2002). *Gender differences in trust and reciprocity.* Pullman, WA, USA: Washington State University.

Cox, J.C. (2004). How to identify trust and reciprocity. *Games and Economic Behavior* 46(2): 260-281.

Central Statistical Agency (CSA) (2005). Annual sample survey. Addis Ababa, Ethiopia: Central Statistical Agency of Ethiopia.

Dakhli, M. and D. de Clercq (2004). Human capital, social capital and innovation: a multi-country study. *Entrepreneurship and Regional Development* 16: 107-128.

De la Briere, B., K. Hallman and A.R. Quisumbing (2000). Resource allocation and empowerment of women in rural Bangladesh. In: A.R. Quisumbing (ed.) *Household decisions, gender, and development. A synthesis of recent research.*. Washington, DC, USA: International Food Policy Research Institute, pp. 85-94.

Eckel, C. and P.J. Grossman (1998). Are women less selfish than men? *Economic Journal* 108(448): 726-735.

Federal Democratic Republic of Ethiopia (FDRE) (2005). *Plan for accelerated and sustained development to end poverty.* Addis Ababa, Ethiopia: Federal Democratic Republic of Ethiopia.

Federal Democratic Republic of Ethiopia (FDRE) (2012). *Agricultural Cooperatives Sector Development Strategy 2012-2016.* Addis Ababa, Ethiopia: Federal Democratic Republic of Ethiopia, Ministry of Agriculture, Ethiopian Agricultural Transformation Agency (ATA), FDRE Cooperative Agency.

Foeken, D., T. Dietz, L. De Haan and L. Johnson (eds.) (2014). *Development and equity. an interdisciplinary exploration by ten scholars from Africa, Asia, and Latin America.* Leiden, the Netherlands: Brill Publishers.

Food and Agriculture Organization (FAO) (2009). *How to feed the world in 2050?* Rome, Italy: FAO.

Forsythe, R., J. Horowitz, N. Savin and M. Sefton (1994). Fairness in simple bargaining experiments. *Games and Economic Behavior* 6: 347-369.

Francesconi, G.N. (2008). *Cooperation for competition. Linking Ethiopian farmers to markets.* Wageningen, the Netherlands: University of Wageningen.

Frank, E. (1999). *Gender, agricultural development and food security in Amhara, Ethiopia: the contested identity of women farmers in Ethiopia.* Addis Ababa, Ethiopia: USAID Ethiopia.

Frankenberg, E. and D. Thomas (2001). Measuring power. In: A.R. Quisumbing (ed.) *Household decisions, gender, and development. A synthesis of recent research.* Washington, DC, USA: International Food Policy Research Institute, pp. 29-36.

Glaeser, E., D. Laibson, J. Scheinkman and C. Soutter (2000). Measuring trust. *Quarterly Journal of Economics* 115(3): 811-846.

Gneezy, U., M. Niederle and A. Rustichini (2003). Performance in competitive environments: gender differences. *Quarterly Journal of Economics* 118: 1049-1074.

Groot Kormelinck, A. (2010). *Back to the birthplace of the bean. Women's bargaining position and trust in Ethiopian coffee cooperatives.* Nijmegen, the Netherlands: Radboud University Nijmegen.

Holvoet, N. (2005). The impact of microfinance on decision-making agency: evidence from South India. *Development and Change* 36(1): 75-102.

International Fund for Agricultural Development (IFAD) (2012a). *Gender equality and women's empowerment.* Rome, Italy: IFAD.

International Fund for Agricultural Development (IFAD) (2012b). *Enabling poor rural people to overcome poverty in Ethiopia.* Rome, Italy: IFAD.

Isaac, M., J. Walker and S. Thomas (1984). Divergent evidence on free-riding: an experimental examination of possible explanations. *Public Choice* 43: 113-149.

James, H.S. and M.E. Sykuta (2005). Property right and organizational characteristics of producer-owned firms and organizational trust. *Annals of Public and Cooperative Economics* 76(4): 545-580.

Kabeer, N. (1995). *Reversed realities: gender hierarchies in development thought.* London, UK: Verso.

Lewicki, R.J. (2006). Trust, trust development and trust repair. In: M. Deutsch, E.L. Thorndike and
P.T. Coleman (eds.) *The handbook of conflict resolution: theory and practice*. San Francisco, CA,
USA: Jossey-Bass, pp. 92-119.

Lim, S.S., A. Winter-Nelson and M. Arends-Kuenning (2007). Household bargaining power and
agricultural supply response: evidence from Ethiopian coffee growers. *World Development*
35(7): 1204-1220.

Mayoux, L. and G. Mackie (2007). *Making the strongest links. A practical guide to mainstreaming
gender analysis in value chain development*. Geneva, Switzerland: International Labour
Organization (ILO).

Nowell, C. and S. Tinkler (1994). The influence of gender in the provision of a public good. *Journal
of Economic Behavior and Organization* 25: 25-36.

Ortmann, A. and L.K. Tichy (1999). Gender differences in laboratory: evidence from prisoner's
dilemma games. *Journal of Economic Behavior and Organization* 39: 327-339.

Oxfam (2008). *A consultancy report on Ethiopian coffee marketing cooperatives*. Addis Ababa,
Ethiopia: Oxfam.

Petit, N. (2007). Ethiopia's coffee sector: a bitter or better future? *Journal of Agrarian Change* 7(2):
225-263.

Prakash, D. (2003). *Rural women, food security and agricultural cooperatives*. Theme paper at the
4th Asian-African International Conference on Women in Agricultural Cooperatives in Asia
and Africa.

Pruitt, D.G. and M.J. Kimmel (1977). Twenty years of experimental gaming: critique, synthesis and
suggestions for the future. *Annual Review of Psychology* 28: 363-392.

Quisumbing, A.R. (2003). *Household decisions, gender, and development. A synthesis of recent
research*. Washington, DC, USA: International Food Policy Research Institute (IFPRI).

Quisumbing, A.R. and J.A. Maluccio (2003). Resources at marriage and intrahousehold allocation:
evidence from Bangladesh, Ethiopia, Indonesia, and South Africa. *Oxford Bulletin of Economics
and Statistics* 65(3): 283-328.

Schechter, L. (2007). Traditional trust measurement and the risk confound. *Journal of Economic
Behavior and Organization* 62: 272-292.

Sen, A.K. (1987). *Gender and cooperative conflicts*. Wider working papers. Helsinki, Finland: Wider.

Sequino, S.T., M. Stevens and A. Lutz (1996). Gender and cooperative behavior: economic man
rides alone. *Feminist Economics* 2(1): 1-21.

Tyler, T.R. and E.A. Lind (1992). A relational model of authority in groups. *Advances in Experimental
Social Psychology* 25: 115-191.

Valentinov, V. (2004). Toward a social capital theory of cooperative organization. *Journal of
Cooperative Studies* 37(3): 5-20.

World Bank (2007). *World Development Report 2008: agriculture for development*. Washington, DC,
USA: World Bank.

World Bank (2011). *World Development Report 2012: gender equality and development*. Washington,
DC, USA: World Bank.

Annex

A.1. Outline of the behavioural experiments

The rationale of economic experiments

The number of experimental studies is on the rise, reflecting a general trend towards a growing interest in experimental approaches in development economics (Banerjee and Duflo, 2009). In addition, economic experiments are increasingly used in combination with surveys to measure socio-economic correlates of difficult-to-measure individual attributes (Carpenter 2002; Carpenter *et al.*, 2004; Glaeser *et al.*, 2000). In this study, three experiments (or 'games') were executed.

The Trust Game and Dictator Game

In the Trust Game (Berg *et al.*, 1995), the A-player is endowed with a start endowment X (10 Ethiopian Birr, ETB), and the B-player receives no initial endowment. The first-mover (player A) is given the chance to send any share of the endowment $x \leq X$ to an anonymous second-mover as he/she wishes. The amount x sent to the B-player is multiplied by a constant $c=3$. The B-player therefore receives $3x$. The B-player can return a certain amount, $y \leq 3x$ to the A-player. The game's gain of A-player is calculated by $X-x$, whereas the gain for B-players is $3x-y$. A-player's behaviour is assumed to reveal trust, while B-player's behaviour is supposed to indicate trustworthiness and reciprocity. However, interpreting the outputs of the game may not be straightforward, since A-player's behaviour might be influenced by altruism as well as by the attitude towards risk (Schechter, 2007).

The combination of the Trust Game with the Dictator Game (Forsythe *et al.*, 1994) allows for controlling for altruism (Cox 2004). In the Dictator Game, there is also a first-mover (player A) with a start endowment of X (10 ETB), who can make a transfer to a B-player ($x \leq X$). However, x is not tripled and the B-player is not able to reciprocate. The gain of the A-player is therefore $X-x$, whereas the gain of B-player is x. Thus, there is no self-interested reason to transfer to the second-mover.

Ample attention was paid to an explanation of all games (visually and verbally) to the players, so they would fully understand the games and their mechanisms. The Trust and Dictator games were played in a mixed-gender setting, with two male and two female members simultaneously. This means that one male and one female A-player (respectively $A1$ and $A2$) were coupled to one male and one female B-player ($B1$ and $B2$). Out of the endowment, A-players had the option to send two amounts, i.e. to male and female B-players ($B1$ and $B2$).

The Voluntary Contribution Mechanism Game

The third game that was conducted is the VCM Game (Isaac *et al.*, 1984). This game is the most commonly used experimental situation for measuring cooperative behaviour around a public good (Carpenter 2002). Participants receive an endowment X (10 ETB), of which some part $(x \leq X)$ can be transferred to a common pool (Y). Amount x is doubled by a constant $c=2$. The common pool is therefore constructed as $Y = 2xN$, N being the number of participants. Subsequently, Y is divided among all participants, who receive as final gain $y+X-x$ (the amount they kept for themselves plus the gains from the common pool).

Hence, the VCM Game creates incentives for both free-riding and cooperation. The gains from individuals will depend on the performance of the group as a whole, resembling very much the situation of agricultural cooperatives and other collective action dilemmas around the management of common pool resources. The VCM Game was conducted in groups of 32 participants. All members received two envelopes, one containing the endowment (10 ETB), and the second one empty. Members could decide how much to put in the empty envelope, which was allocated to the common pool.

A.2. Operationalisation of indexes

Indexes related to bargaining position

- Threat point
  - Tropical Livestock Index (ratio)
    Indicators: cow; ox; goat; sheep; chicken; donkey; mule/horse (ratio calculated to TLI formula)
  - Ownership in/upon marriage/divorce/death (5)
    Indicators: land; livestock; house; household goods; money[75]
- Assets and finances in marriage (4)
  Indicators: own income; access to cash; keeping money; keeping money from cooperative[76]
- Task division
  - Task household (5)
    Indicators: cleaning; children; washing; cooking; water[77]
  - Task production (6)
    Indicators: manual weeding; ploughing; disease control; harvesting; drying coffee; transport[78]
  - Task cooperative (3)
    Indicators: going to meetings; delivering coffee; receiving extensional advisors[79]
- Decision-making
  - Household decisions (expenditures on) (8)
    Indicators: food; consumption; child; education; clothes; health expenditures; house investments; house-building materials[80]
  - Production decisions (expenditures on) (6)
    Indicators: input; coffee trees; renting land; buying livestock; buying machines; hiring labour[81]
  - Cooperative decisions (3)
    Indicators: how much coffee to sell to the cooperative; how much coffee to sell to the market; going to cooperatives meetings[82]

---

[75] Cronbach's α ownership in marriage = members 0.986, spouses 0.926; Cronbach's α ownership upon divorce = members 0.977, spouses 0.971; Cronbach's α ownership upon death = members 0.927, spouse: n.a. (no variation in answers); Cronbach's α ownership of assets = (marriage+divorce+death): members 0.858, spouses 0.819.

[76] Cronbach's α finances in marriage = members 0.761, spouses 0.760.

[77] Cronbach's α household tasks = members 0.836, spouses 0.901.

[78] Cronbach's α production tasks = members 0.756, spouses 0.732.

[79] Cronbach's α cooperative tasks = members 0.805, spouses 0.700.

[80] Cronbach's α household decisions = members 0.957, spouses 0.915.

[81] Cronbach's α production decisions = members 0.954, spouses 0.926.

[82] Cronbach's α cooperative decisions = members 0.909, spouses 0.876.

Index related to institutional trust

- Index institutional trust (8). Trust in:
  Indicators: board members; committee members; cooperative members; general assembly; rules; information; services; statement: 'the cooperative is trustworthy'; statement: 'the cooperative I work for is characterised by corruption'.[83]

---

[83] Direction of the last statement is changed from negative to positive in index. Cronbach's α = members 0.905, spouses 0.863.

A.3. Tables

Table A.1. Descriptive statistics: comparing gender bargaining gaps within and between low- and high-performing cooperatives.

	Low-performing cooperatives		High-performing cooperatives	
	Male[1]	Female[1]	Male	Female
	(a)	(b)	(c)	(d)
1. Threat point				
Assets into marriage				
Tropical livestock index	0.17[ac]	0.00	0.27[ac]	0.21
Assets upon divorce (1=husband, 2=wife, 3=jointly)				
Assets upon divorce	2.87[ab]	2.74	2.86[ab]	2.73
Assets upon death (0=head's relatives, 1= surviving spouse)				
Index assets death	1.00	0.94	1.00	0.94
2. Ownership assets and finances (1=husband, 2=wife, 3=jointly)				
Index ownership assets	2.95[ab]	2.12[ab ac]	2.91[cd ac]	2.68[cd ac]
Index ownership finances	1.47[ab]	1.97[ab]	1.56[cd]	1.98[cd]
3. Task division in household (1=husband, 2=wife, 3=jointly)				
Index task household	2.01	2.00	1.99	1.96
Index task production	1.19[ab]	1.92[ab]	1.21[cd]	2.01[cd]
Index task cooperative	1.06[ab ac]	2.00[ab]	1.22[cd ac]	2.01[cd]
4. Decision-making in household (1=husband, 2=wife, 3=jointly)				
Index household decisions	1.61[ab]	2.00[ab]	1.76	1.93
Index production decisions	1.40[ab]	1.94[ab]	1.33[cd]	1.78[cd]
Index cooperative decisions	1.38[ab]	1.98[ab]	1.47[cd]	2.10[cd]

[1] Male = male member households; female = female member households.
[2] Superscripts refer to significant pairwise differences in T-tests (two-sided).

About the authors

Fred Bagamba is a lecturer in the Department of Agribusiness and Resource Economics, School of Agricultural Sciences, Makerere University, Uganda. He has worked before as a research assistant at the Faculty of Agriculture on a Rockefeller-funded Banana Cropping Systems Research Project. He graduated with MSc degree in January 1995, after which he joined the Coffee Research Programme of National Agricultural Research Organization (NARO). He implemented a number of research projects with funding from Rockefeller Foundation, DFID and IDRC. He obtained his PhD at Wageningen University, the Netherlands with a study on Market Access, Agricultural Productivity and Allocative Efficiency in the Banana Sector of Uganda. His research interests concern labour use and resource allocation in agricultural production systems.

Willem Elbers is lecturer and coordinator of the Advanced Master in Development (AMID) at the Centre for International Development Issues (CIDIN) at Radboud University Nijmegen, the Netherlands. He has published about North-South partnerships, development NGOs and managerialism. In 2012, he defended his PhD-dissertation entitled 'The Partnership Paradox: Principles and Practices in North-South NGO Relations' which was based on fieldwork in India, Ghana and Nicaragua.

Eveline Dijkdrenth is teacher and researcher at the school of Social Work at the University of Applied Sciences Saxion, Enschede, the Netherlands. She holds a master degree in Anthropology from the Radboud University Nijmegen and a master degree in Teaching Social Sciences from the University of Twente.

Annemarie Groot Kormelinck holds a Bsc and Msc in international development studies. Her Msc thesis has focused on the relationship between gender bargaining positions and institutional trust in agricultural cooperatives in Ethiopia. Annemarie currently works as advisor rural economic development for the Centre for Development Innovation, and as researcher for the Management studies group – both part of Wageningen University and Research Centre, Wageneningen, the Netherlands. Her main interest lies in strategies for linking farmers to markets, contract farming, famers organisations, inclusive agri-business, and commodity value chains.

Paul Hoebink is extraordinary professor in development cooperation and director of the Center for International Development Issues (CIDIN) of the Radboud University Nijmegen, the Netherlands. He has a long experience with research in the field of development and has done consulting for a number of private development organisations in the Netherlands, as well as the Ministry of Foreign Affairs and the European Commission. He has written several books and numerous articles and reports on issues like aid effectiveness, policy coherence for development, and Dutch and European development cooperation.

Roldan Muradian holds a PhD in ecological economics from the Autonomous University of Barcelona (Spain), and has worked at Tilburg University and Radboud University Nijmegen (the Netherlands). Currently he is visiting professor at the Department of Economics of the Universidade Federal Fluminense, Brazil. His current research interests are in the fields of rural economic development, collective action and environmental governance.

Mzeeh Hamisi Ngutu with **Urbanus N. Mutwiwa** and **Samuel Njuguna** are CEO and field staff of Noble Consultants Company Ltd. in Nairobi, Kenya with extensive experience in the fields of agricultural extension, project management, agricultural credit to smallholders and processing and marketing of agricultural commodities in Kenya. Mr. Ngutu worked as an extension officer with the Ministry of Agriculture in Nyanza and Central Provinces, rising to the position of National Coordinator of the Smallholder Coffee Improvement Projects. He gained considerable experience in the management of Inter-ministerial Projects, involving the Ministries of Agriculture, Cooperative Development, Finance and the institutions of Cooperative Bank of Kenya, the World Bank and the Commonwealth Development. Hereafter, Mr. Ngutu joined the Coffee Board of Kenya first as a Field Services Manager and subsequently as deputy general manager (1990-1999).

Luuk van Kempen is an economist with a specialisation in development and international economics. He obtained his PhD in 2005 from Tilburg University, the Netherlands on consumer behaviour in developing countries and currently works as a researcher at the Centre for International Development Issues (CIDIN) at Radboud University Nijmegen, the Netherlands. He is coordinating the research project on Participatory Impact Assessment (PIA), concerning several mixed-method impact evaluations of NGO interventions in Ghana, Peru and India. His current research is focussed on behavioural economics research on trust and aspirations and collective action in natural resource management.

Christine Plaisier works as a researcher at the Centre for International Development Issues (CIDIN) at Radboud University Nijmegen, the Netherlands. She has a master degree in Development Studies at the same University with a thematic focus on Agricultural Cooperatives in Ethiopia. She also works at Agriterra, an agri-agency based in Arnhem, as a Monitoring & Evaluation officer focussed on strenghtening the M&E capacity of farmer organisations and cooperatives.

Ruerd Ruben holds a PhD in development economics from Free University Amsterdam, the Netherlands. He lived and worked for 14 years in several Central American countries en was engaged in programs of land reform, cooperative development and smallholder agriculture. In 1992 he was appointed at Wageningen University to coordinate multidisciplinary research on food security and sustainable land use in sub-Saharan Africa. Hereafter, he started an innovative program on the prospects for smallholder incorporation into tropical food value chains. In 2006 he obtained the chair in development studies at Radboud University Nijmegen, the Netherlands, to conduct research on voluntary organisations and the development impact of fair trade value chains. Since 2010 he is the director of the independent Policy and Operations Evaluation Department (IOB) at the Netherlands Ministry of Foreign Affairs. IOB conducts robust impact studies on development policies (education, health care, water and sanitation, energy, private sector, food security, etc.) and analyses policy effectiveness of Dutch foreign relations (diplomacy, human rights, European relations). Recently, he joined the Agricultural Economics Institute (LEI) at Wageningen University, the Netherlands, as coordinator of international research programs on food security, sustainable value chains and impact analysis.

Bart van Rijsbergen graduated cum laude from the Research Master Social and Cultural Sciences at Radboud University Nijmegen (2011). He worked at the Centre for International Development Issues (CIDIN) since his graduation. He is involved in several research projects regarding the impact of coffee and tea marketing channels in East Africa, the impact of reproductive health services on socio-economic development in Sub-Saharan Africa, the potential poverty impact of investments in marriage delays in Bangladesh, and Participatory Impact Assessment (of NGO interventions in Ghana, Peru and India. Bart is currently employed as research assistant with the Policy and Operations Evaluation department at the Dutch ministry of Foreign Affairs.

Mirjam Schoonhoven-Speijer is a PhD Candidate at Wageningen University, the Netherlands, at the Knowledge, Technology and Innovation chairgroup. Her research focuses on cooperation between farmers and other market actors in the oilseed sector in Uganda, such as traders and processors. It adresses questions of through which processes collective action between farmers and other actors comes about, is maintained, and is mediated through institutions. She is a Research Master graduate at the Radboud University Nijmegen in Social and Cultural Sciences. Before starting her PhD she has, among others, at the Royal Tropical Institute in Amsterdam as a junior advisor at the Sustainable Economic Development department.

Amsaya Anteneh Woubie is a PhD student in Development Studies at Radboud University Nijmegen, the Netherlands. He submitted his PhD thesis on the role of Coffee Cooperatives on the Livelihoods of Smallholder Coffee Farmers in Ethiopia. Currently he is Economic Advisor to the Regional President of Amhara Region of Ethiopia. He has a large experience in External Development Cooperation where he worked for more than 10 years. He has also served as an instructor for two years in the University of Bahir Dar, Ethiopia. Furthermore he also worked in various organisations such as Ministry of Agriculture, Ministry of Natural Resources and Environmental Protection, and the Ministry of Finance and Economic Development.

Printed in the United States
by Baker & Taylor Publisher Services